A ROMANOV DIARY

The Autobiography of
H.I. & R.H. Grand Duchess George

Copyright 1988

By

Nancy Leeds Wynkoop
David Chavchavadze

ATLANTIC INTERNATIONAL PUBLICATIONS

ISBN 0-938311-09-3
Library of Congress #88-071906

Editor - G. Nicholas Tantzos
Associate Editor - Marlene A. Eilers

For Information:

Atlantic International Publications
260 W. 35th Street, Suite 702
New York, New York 10001
Tel. (212) 714-5505

Published in the United States of America

PUBLISHER'S NOTES

Other than minor technical editing, the text of *A Romanov Diary* is as written by H.I. & R.H. Grand Duchess George of Russia in Rome between 1926 and 1934. A few words, and some historical data, have been added for clarity, which are enclosed in "[ ]", and spellings have been conformed. Genealogical data contained in footnotes has been added by the editors.

Her Highness used British spellings which may be unfamiliar to some Americans, e.g., humour, rumour, judgement, etc. We have left these spellings as were. Place names have, in some instances, changed since this book was written, and even during the period of its time, e.g., St. Petersburg to Petrograd to Leningrad. We have conformed these spellings, except in the case of letters from Grand Duke George wherein he used the spelling "Petrograd".

The genealogical chart was prepared by Serge Oriol for the Publisher.

Prior to 1917, the Imperial Family of Russia did not use the name *Romanoff*. The second name of a Grand Duke, for example, became a form of his father's first name: Grand Duke Michael *Alexandrovitch*, son of Emperor Alexander III.

Use of the title *Tsar* and *Emperor* may be somewhat confusing. The official title was Tsar prior to Peter the Great, who changed it to Emperor. The two were used interchangeable, e.g., ...*The Emperor and Empress arrived,* . . . but . . . .*the people loved their Tsar.* . . .

All photographs contained herein were provided by the grandchildren of Grand Duchess Marie, from her family albums unless otherwise noted.

We wish to express our sincere thanks to Nancy Leeds Wynkoop and H. S. H. Prince David Chavchavadze, for making their grandmother's manuscript available to us for publication, and for their indispensable assistance in proofing, conforming spellings of Russian names, consulting, photograph identification and general cooperation in this project.

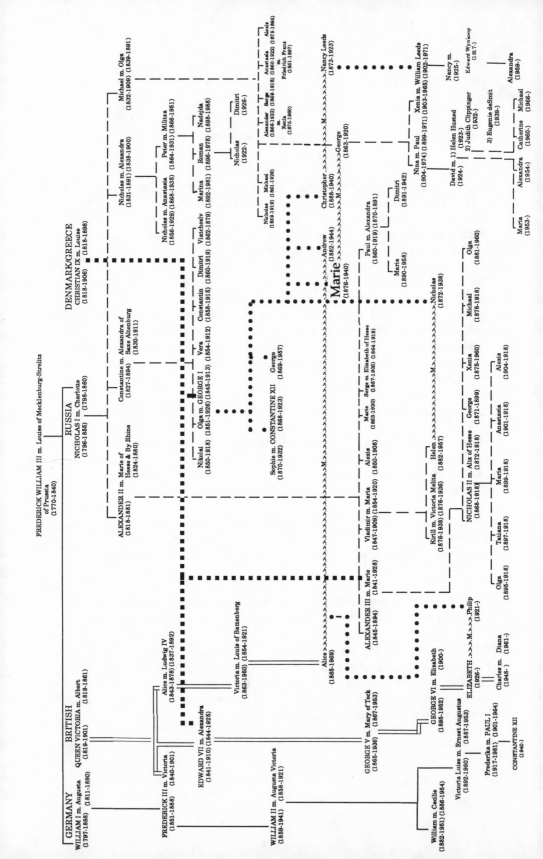

FORWARD

My cousin Nancy Leeds Wynkoop and I had only one opportunity to know our maternal grandmother, the author of these memoirs, to whom I will refer as "Amama," according to the Danish custom observed in the Greek Royal Family, and among some of the Romanovs. One summer in the 1930s, Amama came to the United States and stayed in Syosset, Long Island, close to where her younger daughter Xenia (Nancy's mother) lived.

We both remember her as being extremely humorous, a fact which surprised me at the time since, from my mother's stories, I had been expecting a strait-laced tyrant. Once, when I called her a "dumb Greek," and was rightfully kicked out of the room, she burst into laughter, probably delighted that I thought of her as a Greek. Her love for Greece and her erudition about her native land was probably the single most important emotion in her life.

She was a very adept needleworker and copied many of the old peasant designs, which were somewhat like crewel embroidery. She went on to study Greek religious garments in the old churches, and copied them all in watercolors, as she was afraid of the art becoming lost. All her notebooks were given by Nancy to the Cooper Hewitt Museum, as they were an incredible historical record, and were beautifully painted, and showed how the costumes were created.

Nancy had much more exposure to Amama than I did, since my mother spent most of the summer on Cape Cod. And perhaps this is why Nancy received a great deal of affection from Amama. I don't remember much affection, but she was very good company. Both of us corresponded with her after she returned to Rome. None of her letters to us have survived, but I have the impression that Amama's opinion of the United States was a New York full of gangsters, with cowboy country starting just beyond city limits. In any case, what Nancy and I know of our grandmother comes almost entirely from our mothers and various relatives.

Amama's marriage to our grandfather, Grand Duke George of Russia (Apapa), was not a happy one. It was a love match as far as he was concerned, and a marriage of convenience on her part. Perhaps inconvenience would be a better word, for she had no desire to leave Greece, and it is rumored that she was in love with a member of her father's court, marriage with whom would have been out of the question.

Grand Duke George was Amama's second cousin, being a first cousin of her mother, Queen Olga, born a Russian Grand Duchess. He was the third son of Grand Duke Michael, the youngest son of Emperor Nicholas I, and brother of Alexander II. Apapa was born in Tiflis in 1863, where his father was living as Viceroy of the Caucasus; his mother was born Princess Cécile of Baden. Upon her marriage she became Olga Feodorovna. It was a typical Romanov family: six boys and a girl. Nicholas II's family of four girls and one boy was unique in the dynasty.

Grand Duke George's great interest was numismatics. His books on coins are still considered authoritative and he had a magnificent collection, including almost all the coins ever used on Russian territory, back to ancient times. Part of this collection now reposes in the Smithsonian Institution in Washington. The rest was pilfered.

The marriage resulted in the birth of two girls, my mother Nina in 1901, and Nancy's mother, Xenia, in 1903. Both spoke Russian to their father, English to their mother, while their parents conversed in French. The Crimea was their main residence, after they built a house there to which Amama gave the Greek name of Harax. It was close to Nicholas II's Livadia, and the girls grew up playing with his children and numerous other cousins, notably the children of Apapa's younger brother, Grand Duke Alexander, who was married to Nicholas II's sister, Xenia. But Amama never liked living in Russia.

Both girls felt very close to their father and were resentful when Amama took them to England for a long visit in 1914. While allegedly for Xenia's health, this was probably meant to be a separation. It turned out to be a separation forever. The outbreak of world War I a month later prevented Amama and the two girls from returning to Russia, and they never saw their father again. He was shot by the Bolsheviks in January 1919.

Nina and Xenia thus went through all their teens in England, as nationalistically Russian as their mother was Greek, and, when the revolution came to Russia, they blamed their mother for causing their father to leave the Crimea, where he would have been safe. This was probably unfair, since there was a war on, and their father returned to the army, and probably would have done so in any case.

My mother, Nina, remembers her mother as a Victorian martinet, always forcing the girls to wear black mourning clothes for somebody or other, and insisting on the closest chaperonage at all times. When my mother married at the age of 21, she had no idea of the facts of life: only that husband and wife slept in the same bed.

Xenia was the first to marry. Because she grew close to Amama in later years, I assumed that she did not share my mother's feelings, but Nancy tells me that her 18-year-old mother married her 19-year-old father, William B. Leeds, mainly to get away from Amama, and because she also did not like her new stepfather-to-be. These were also factors in my mother's 1922 marriage to Prince Paul Chavchavadze, but these two were really in love and stayed together until my father's death in 1971. Xenia and William Leeds were divorced in 1930.

A great day in Amama's life was the restoration of her brother, King Constantine I, to the Greek throne in 1920. This is well described in her book. What is not mentioned is her boast that she would marry the first

Greek she met. This turned out to be the commander of the Greek destroyer on which Amama, Nina, Xenia and some of Amama's brothers returned to Greece. Her second husband, later an admiral, was Pericles Ioannides.

In the family he was known as "Perks," because Nancy's other grandmother, the widowed Mrs. William B. Leeds (who had become Princess Anastasia of Greece by marrying Amama's brother, Prince Christopher), had trouble remembering Pericles. She confused it with Hercules, so that it came out "Percules". Nobody liked Perks very much, although the Greek Royal Family went out of their way to be nice to him.

After the death of Amama's aunt, the dowager Queen Alexandra of Great Britain, Amama and Perks settled in Rome where they lived all through the 1930s. Eventually, they found a house on the via Antonio Bertoloni to which the name "Villa Attica" was aptly given. Here the book was written, in English. Amama had a little money, and they lived simply. On one occasion she supplemented her income by writing an article or two for some American fashion magazine on the wedding of the young Duke of Kent and Princess Marina of Greece. She and Perks attended these festivities, staying at Buckingham Palace.

We know little about this second marriage save that they lived in a house in Rome, he loved his little garden, and she marvelled in her letters at his flowers. They went off in the summers on small jaunts, he at the wheel, after they could no longer afford a chauffeur. She relied on him for everything and was very upset at the end when Mussolini would not let him return to their home, and, sick as she was, she had to oversee packing up all their belongings herself. The Greek Ambassador helped her as much as possible.

It was probably not a very happy marriage, and certainly no romantic idyll. Perks was something of a philanderer, and some of his girl friends were rewarded with little Fabergé goodies taken from Amama. But he did see that the household ran smoothly and took care of the little they had.

In Rome, Amama became a whizz at backgammon, so addicted to it that she would go out to play in evening clothes during the afternoon, so that she would not have to break off playing to go home and change! In Syosset, she taught little Nancy to play so that Nancy could fill in for her mother while the latter changed her clothes for dinner.

All her life Amama had been a very outspoken person, never disguising her views or opinions. This got her into trouble with Mussolini, whom she despised and openly said so. A chain smoker, Amama suffered from lung problems, and was taken to a German spa by her niece, Helen (Queen Mother of Roumania), who also lived in Italy. After two weeks, Amama found she was barred from re-entering Italy. Queen Helen telephoned Elena, the Queen of Italy, who sent the royal railroad car to the border to fetch them, but Perks was not allowed to re-enter. Mussolini, who generally tried not to offend the Italian King and Queen, did not interfere, but decreed that Amama must leave Italy for good within three months.

A very sick woman, she returned to her beloved Greece in time for the Greeks' splendid defense against Mussolini's invasion. The Italians had to be bailed out by their German allies, which had a possibly fatal effect on them by postponing the time-table for their invasion of the USSR. The Greeks fought bravely, but could not hold up the Wehrmacht for long.

Just at this time, Amama lay dying in the house of her nephew, Prince Paul of Greece (later King) and his wife, Frederika. The Royal Family was preparing to flee the country, and Amama could not be moved. She was in real danger of being captured by the Germans. But at that point she died, on December 14, 1940. Queen Frederika later said that they barely had time to inter her in the family cemetery at Tatoi, before being evacuated themselves. So ended the life, at age 64, of this Princess of Greece, who as a girl had cried when she was told she had no Greek blood.

H.S.H. Prince David
Chavchavadze

Nancy Leeds Wynkoop

I DEDICATE THIS BOOK TO THE MEMORY OF MY

BELOVED PARENTS.

MARIE

GRAND DUCHESS MARIE

Chapter I

I was born in Athens on March 3, 1876. In all that has happened to me since—in Russia, Denmark, England or elsewhere in Europe—and throughout the misfortunes which have pursued my family, I have always looked upon Athens as my home: looked back as a true daughter of Greece on those happy years spent in the shadow of the Acropolis.

My father was King George I of the Hellenes; he was the second son of King Christian IX[1] and Queen Louise of Denmark[2]; my mother was Queen Olga, the eldest daughter of the Grand Duke and Grand Duchess Constantine Nicolaievitch of Russia, and granddaughter of Tsar Nicholas I. My father, as Prince William of Denmark, accepted the throne of Greece when it was offered him by the Greek National Assembly in 1863, and assumed the name of George I, King of the Hellenes.

At that time King Frederick VII was still reigning in Denmark, and my father's father was heir presumptive to the throne. My grandparents did not like the idea of their young son going to such a faraway, little-known country as Greece then was, and they expressed their unwillingness to see him accept the offered throne. King Frederick, on the contrary, was very anxious that my father should accept and told my grandfather that if he protested he would have him arrested. This rather effectually overcame my grandfather's objections! He [Christian] did not become King of Denmark until after his son was made King of the Hellenes.

In 1867, my father went to Russia to visit his younger sister, the Empress Marie Feodorovna[3], then Tsarevna. There he met my mother, who was just sixteen years old. They fell in love at first sight, and my mother often said to me, "I fell in love with the man and not the King."

---

1. King Christian (1818-1906) was not recognized as heir to the throne of Denmark until 1852, to which he succeeded in 1863, after his second son, William, had become King of the Greeks as George I.

2. Queen Louise (1817-1898), born a princess of Hesse-Cassel, was the heir presumptive to the Danish throne after the childless King Frederick VII, but she ceded her rights to her husband, Christian.

3. In Denmark she had been known as 'Dagmar'. She took the name Marie Feodorovna on her marriage to the Tsarevich, and was known as 'Minny,' particularly by her Greek nephews and nieces.

After the marriage, which was a grand affair as all ceremonies used to be in St. Petersburg in those days, they travelled back to Greece. The reception at the Piraeus and their drive up to Athens in a carriage *à la Daumont*, with four horses, was triumphal. The people had gathered from all parts of the country to see the lovely bride, their Queen. She captivated the Greek people on that day with her fresh young beauty, and they never ceased to love her to the end of her life, even though she died in exile.

I remember my mother reading to us a few of the letters she had written to her own mother, describing her arrival and the warm reception given her. She was too young in those days to be much impressed by the architectural treasures of Athens; the Acropolis and the superb archaelogical museums of our capital did not figure in her letters. Her mother,[4] with true German seriousness, scolded the young Queen in one of her answers to those letters, and advised a stronger interest in the Athens of the past.

My mother had brought with her an old Russian lady-in-waiting of her own mother's, Countess Coucheleff, to instruct the Greek ladies called to the court in their new duties. One day my mother had to give an audience; the old Countess came to say that the ladies had assembled, but to her dismay she found the Queen nowhere. Embarrassed and distressed, the Countess went to my father, who was himself giving an audience at the time; he had to leave his reception and look for his young wife. They found her hiding in a dark recess under the staircase, hugging her favorite Russian stuffed bear, and weeping bitterly. To her these tedious receptions of strange ladies were a nightmare. After much coaxing she was finally persuaded to go and receive the ladies, which she did—but with red and swollen eyes.

In July 1868 my parents' first child was born to them, just a month before my mother's seventeenth birthday. The news of the birth of a Crown Prince caused unbounded enthusiasm and rejoicing throughout Greece. The Prime Minister, Voulgaris, announced the birth from the palace balcony to the thousands of people who had assembled to hear the good news. The Premier fully intended telling them the name which my parents had chosen for their son, but before he had time to do this, the whole crowd roared: "Constantine!" I suppose there may have been rumours that my parents had already chosen this name; but in any case its enormous popularity was due to the tradition—very old and fully believed—that when a Constantine was born again to rule in Greece, the Byzantine Empire would be restored, and all the Hellenes re-united in freedom from the Turkish yoke.

My father was an extremely busy man from the time of his arrival in Athens. He had much more to do than some of his fellow sovereigns in Europe on account of the political passions of the country which had chosen him as its monarch. He loved the country and the Greek people passionately, and never permitted the slightest disparagement of either in his presence. He always drilled into us, his children, that we were Greek and nothing else. I remember being astonished and even shocked when, during

---

4.   Born Princess Alexandra of Saxe-Altenburg (1830-1911)

one of my first visits abroad, I was told that I was a Dane and not a Greek. I was so deeply hurt at this unexpected revelation that I actually shed a few tears.

In our babyhood, thanks to our English nurses, we [children] all began by speaking English to each other. This did not last long. One day my father put his foot down, and ordered us to converse in Greek in the future. Although I was a Grand Duchess of Russia for twenty-two years, and lived for long periods of time in England, all my private papers and personal diaries have been written entirely in Greek[5]. Surely my father's system of education succeeded in its aim in making Greeks of us, and no amount of republican legislation can really take our nationality away.

There was, nevertheless, a rather amusing mixture of languages in our household. We spoke Greek to each other, but English with our parents. My father and mother talked to each other in German, because when he first went to Russia he was not very fluent in French. My mother at first spoke her own mother's language, German, better than she did English.

We were all kept in the nursery up to the age of seven, with our dear old English Nana, whom we all loved. She remained in the house long after we were grown up, and looked after the linen room. My youngest brother, Christopher, had to have another nurse, as Nana was too tired and old, after having reared six children. (A seventh child, my little sister Olga, died when she was less than a year old.)

I am sorry to say we led poor Nana an awful life, as we were all full of spirits and always rather wild. I remember leaving the nursery, when I was seven, and going to live with my sister Alexandra, who was then thirteen. I was rather proud of this at first, thinking that at last I was growing up. But alas! Falling into the hands of a stiff and severe German governess, Countess Groben, after our dear old Nana, dashed all my illusions to the ground. We all detested the Countess. She was tall and thin, with a sharply pointed nose and chin, and when she took us out for walks, she held her umbrella exactly as if she were prepared to beat us at any moment. This irritated me a good deal, as can be imagined. Luckily she did not stay long. During her time as head governess, we had several young ones, mostly Swiss, whom we liked, but as they did not meet with the Countess' approval they had to go. The last one was English, a Miss Boyd, and we particularly loved her; she remained after the countess left.

A year or two later a French governess came, because my parents wished us to learn French properly. Her name was Mademoiselle Constance Hinal, and she had successfully brought up two German princesses before she came to us. She was very devoted to us, and remained for more than ten years; but I do not remember ever fighting with anybody as frequently as I did with her!

My father took the greatest possible care of our education. He insisted upon strict discipline and conscientious work. We had to study

---

5.   This autobiography was, however, typed by the Grand Duchess in English.

languages and literature in Greek, English, French and German, as well as arithmetic, music and drawing, and, of course, religion. This programme was varied by gymnastics and riding lessons. We had to be in the schoolroom at 7:30 in the morning, after a cup of coffee, and read until 9:30 when we met in our mother's drawing room for a family breakfast. Here my father always made the coffee himself, and most delicious stuff it was! At 10 o'clock sharp we had all to be back at our lessons, which continued until twelve. From then until one o'clock we either had gymnastics or ran wild in our beautiful big garden, which we children loved. It was usually my sister and my brother Nicholas and myself, who played together, as my two elder brothers were more seriously occupied.

Alexandra and Nicholas had a passion for taking off their shoes and stockings to paddle in the small brooks in the garden. They never allowed me to paddle too, though I begged hard, because they said I was sure to catch cold and they would be found out. I was made to button my sister's boots afterwards, as no doubt younger sisters have been made to do before.

At one o'clock, the family met for lunch, and at two o'clock we had to be back in the schoolroom again. We read until four, and then went for a walk or had a riding lesson in the manège at the stables. This lesson was bliss to me, as I have always been passionately fond of riding. There were lessons to prepare from five until seven, and then a kind of high tea or supper in my father's rooms. We always had to go to bed at 8:30.

Nevertheless, during our parents' dinner, my brother Nicholas and I used to hide in the next room and waylay the dear old butler, who was married to Nana, and eat all the food off the dishes which were carried back to the kitchen. This was, of course, strictly against orders, and the butler warned us that if we behaved so badly he would be forced to complain against us. But he loved us too much to do this, as we well knew, and our bad habit continued.

On Sundays, after the church service which was at ten o'clock in our private chapel in the palace, we all played in the garden with our friends. These were girls and boys of the society of Athens, usually relations of the people at court. The garden was a mass of orange and palm trees. One of our games consisted in spearing the oranges with sharpened poles, which then became excellent weapons. We would fling the fruit at each other with varying results, depending upon the aim; but I can testify that when one got hit, it was extremely painful and ruinous to one's clothes.

My father had a small estate at the entrance of the port of Piraeus, called *Themistocles* after the victor of Salamis, whose tomb was supposed to be there. We used to go to *Themistocles* on Sundays, and lunched in a small pavilion. Father was very fond of the place because it was so near the sea; he had begun life in the navy, and he never lost his adoration for the sea. He loved to watch the ships entering and leaving the Piraeus. Later, when we were grown up, we had small dances at *Themistocles* on the last Sunday in carnival, and invited all our friends.

4

In 1882, the two sons[6] of the Prince and Princess of Wales,[7] who were midshipmen in the British navy, came in their training ship, the *H.M.S. Bachante*. Although they were older than we, we were great friends, and were very happy to see them. I remember how we all went to the photographer to have a group [picture] taken with our two cousins. After the group photograph, my sister Alexandra was photographed with the Duke of Clarence, but as he was my favorite, I was frightfully offended, and even cried. To comfort me, Prince George at once offered to pose with me—hence my offended expression in the photograph.

My father's youngest brother, Prince Waldemar of Denmark, also came sometimes on the Danish ships, as he was serving in the Navy, as did our cousin Charles.[8] With the Russian fleet came my godfather, the Grand Duke Alexis[9] of Russia. He was a very handsome man, and all the ladies invariably lost their hearts to him. My mother's brother, the Grand Duke Constantine, who was a poet of no small repute, also served in the Navy in those early days, although he later left it for the army. When any of these relations came, they always spent a few days with us at the palace. On such occasions there was a general mix-up of languages. Besides Greek, English and German, the ordinary languages of our household, Russian, Danish and French were added. My mother spoke Russian to her brother, and my father Danish to his; while the brothers-in-law spoke French!

Our summers were spent at a lovely summer place in the mountains called Tatoi, about fourteen kilometers from Athens. My father bought Tatoi in 1871 from a family called Soutso. Tatoi was an old fortress of the Spartans called Dekelia. One could still see bits of the wall of the ancient citadel. At first my parents lived in the original house, which was extremely primitive, like a peasant's house. There were already four children at that time, and how they could all have fitted into that small abode is hard to imagine.

My father loved roughing it, and never allowed us any luxuries. In fact, he used to say, "Who knows if some day we shall not be in need, or in exile? You must get accustomed to being satisfied with little." We never dreamed, in those happy days, how true his words were. For my part, I am more than grateful for his advice.

My father had to set about building a bigger house at Tatoi to make room for our growing family. Papa, like all of us, loved that place more than anything else in the world. We were free to do what we liked there, and run completely wild in the woods. My mother had a small chapel built in the

---

6. Prince Albert Victor, Duke of Clarence (1864-1892) and Prince George (1865-1936).

7. The Princess of Wales was King George I's elder sister, Alexandra (1844-1925) who married the future Edward VII in 1863. She was called *Alix* in the family.

8. Second son of King Frederick VIII of Denmark, older brother of King George I. Prince Charles (1872-1957) was elected King of Norway in 1905 and took the name Haakon VII.

9. Grand Duke Alexis (1850-1908) was the son of Emperor Alexander II and brother of Alexander III, died unmarried.

pine forest, about ten minutes walk from the house, where we were taken every Sunday and on fete days. On our birthdays or name days the military band used to come up from Athens and wake us up by marching three times around the house, playing an old Bavarian march. It gave us a lovely festive feeling, and we would all rush to the windows to see them go by. When we came down for breakfast on such mornings, our parents had their gifts ready for us, and a cake with as many candles as we had years. Then we went to church for a *Te Deum*, after which we all gathered on the terrace in front of the house. The suites and some of our friends, especially invited for the occasion, would be with us to listen to the band and drink chocolate.

We usually had breakfast in the garden at Tatoi, on a platform built over a pond, with creepers, roses and ivy growing up on the bars like an arbour. A flight of steps led down from the chapel to a playground under the pine trees with swings, merry-go-rounds and giant strides, where we enjoyed ourselves between lessons and during the holidays. We all used to ride over the estate[10] with our father, so what with that and our long walks over mountains and ravine, we came to know every path and corner of the place.

We [also] had a big farm at Tatoi, with beautiful Swiss cows, my father's pride. Our parents had given my three oldest brothers and my sister small donkey carts, and we drove all over the place in them, risking our lives at every turn. As I had no donkey cart of my own and refused to be cheated out of any fun that was going on, I would sit with one of the boys. I remember one summer, during the vintage, we were told to go and help cut the grapes in the vineyards. The fruit was put into huge deep baskets. When we got bored with working, we carried off empty grape baskets and put them onto the carts. This suggested a most exciting game: we would sit on top of these inverted baskets and drive at full speed around a sharp corner in the park. Centrifugal force hurled us, with the baskets, off the cart, and we landed almost anywhere. My sister Alix thought she would go one better and sit on top of the opening of the basket. When she was hurled into space she was sucked into the cavity, and landed like that in a field. We had the greatest trouble getting her out. Another useful idea with those donkeys was to ride them up and down the very steep steps which led to the chapel.

We usually remained at Tatoi until the middle of October. In September our professors came up three times a week to give us lessons. They had to come by carriage, which took two hours. This tiring trip had, luckily, no bad results on their tempers; as far as I can recollect, they were always good-humoured. On October 1, my older brothers returned to Athens for their studies.

Besides Tatoi, my father had a lovely place with a villa on the island of Corfu. He called it *Mon Repos* because he said it was the one place where he could really rest. We also had a palace in the town of Corfu, but it was only used for official purposes, such as receptions and dinners. That palace

---

10.　　Tatoi had about 50,000 acres.

had been the residence of the British High Commissioners when the Ionian Islands belonged to Great Britain[11]. One of my father's conditions in accepting the throne of Greece was that the Ionian Islands be ceded to him, and Great Britain agreed.

Mon Repos is situated just above the sea. During the British occupation the English officers used to spend their summers there. The house was typically English and very comfortable, with terraces and balconies. The park was really beautiful, with a lot of very old cypresses, shady trees, and a variety of flowers. There was also a lovely little old chapel at the end of the garden. Both my brother George and my sister Alexandra were born at *Mon Repos*. We usually went there in the spring, when the whole island of Corfu looks like a garden; it seemed like a kind of paradise to us. We used to bathe, go about in boats, and play on the rocks, as there was no beach. We also took long drives in the country, which is very lovely with many private villas [among] the orange groves.

About eleven kilometers from *Mon Repos*, the Empress Elizabeth of Austria had bought herself an estate on a high hill overlooking the sea. There she built a huge house surrounded by terraces. Unfortunately, it looked more like a resort hotel than a villa. She named it *Achilleion*, after a very big and beautiful marble statue of the dying Achilles, which she placed on the principal terrace. The inside of the house was in Pompeian style and rather painful to behold. In the entrance hall there was a flat square marble slab, with the head of a drowned woman in relief. On this object the Empress invariably threw a small bouquet of violets when she left Corfu.

Empress Elizabeth always had a Greek gentleman attached to her, who gave her lessons in modern Greek; and she came to speak the language perfectly. Her one passion in those days (after she had given up riding) was walking; and walk she did for hours at a time, exhausting all those who were obliged to accompany her. She often walked all the way from the town of Corfu up to the *Achilleion*, a distance of nineteen kilometers. She carried an enormous black fan—one of the hugest fans I have ever seen—and when people bowed to her, she instantly flopped it open to hide herself. During these walks the Empress would frequently feel overheated, what with the exercise and the warm climate of Corfu. When this happened, she would remove a petticoat or two behind a tree and give them to her gentleman to carry.

After this unfortunate lady's assassination[12], *Achilleion* was bought by Kaiser William II. The first thing he did was to remove the statue of Heinrich Heine, of whom he did not approve, and replace it with a statue of

---

11.   The actual name was, The United States of the Ionian Islands, and were a protectorate of Great Britain.

12.   Empress Elizabeth, wife of Emperor Francis Joseph, was assassinated by a young Italian, Luigi Luccheni, in Geneva, Switzerland on September 10, 1898 (1837-1898). She was a younger daughter of Duke Max of Bavaria, and a niece of Francis Joseph's mother, Empress Sophie.

the Empress Elizabeth. Then he moved the Empress's fine marble Achilles on to another terrace, and erected in its place a colossal bronze statue of the same hero holding a very long spear, the point of which, illuminated at certain moments by the bright Ionian sun, could be seen shining from the sea.

Our winters were spent at Athens in the palace which was built by the Bavarians for King Otto and Queen Amelia, the first sovereigns of modern Greece, who were exiled in 1862. Nauplia was the first capital of Greece, but when King Otto came from Bavaria it was decided that Athens should again be the capital. The palace was a great white square building, rather like a barrack, except that on the garden side it was embellished by a colonnade, on top of which was a balcony in front of my mother's rooms.[13] All the living rooms were enormous, as were the passages; but this failed to impress us in our youth, and we only recognized it later in comparing it with other houses and palaces.

My father had his study and reception rooms on the ground floor, where he received his ministers and gave audiences. These rooms communicated with my mother's rooms by a big staircase, and also by a narrow iron winding stairway, which we used more frequently. There was no passage in my father's apartment, as one room opened into the next in a series of eight altogether.

One morning he came out of his study and saw a naval officer standing in one of the rooms, in uniform, with a cap on and holding a huge carriage whip. In the middle of the narrow room stood a kind of round sofa, called a *pouffa*, with palm trees in the centre of it. My father inquired what the officer wanted, but the man was silent; he realized at once that the man was very odd, and tried to get at the bell to ring for help. The bell happened to be on the opposite side, and each time my father tried to get round the sofa to it, the man faced him with the whip. At last, in desperation, papa (who was very agile) leapt over the side of the sofa, rang the bell, and jumped back and waited. The servant's came and got the man out with great trouble. They had allowed him to enter the King's rooms because he was in uniform, and they supposed him to be authorized.

Every Monday morning from ten until one o'clock my father received anybody who wished to come and see him. Every kind of person would turn up, including women. My father was very democratic, and loved talking to all these people; and of course this made him very popular. The people felt that they could come and tell him all their troubles, complain of all their grievances, and be sure of sympathetic ears.

My father spoke and wrote Greek perfectly, and could talk and joke with anybody who came. He was extremely witty, and had a lively sense of humour, and although he was very severe with his children, we all worshipped him.

As for me, I never had a better friend. My father and I were much

---

13.   This palace is now the Greek Parliament.

together, as I was always the one, after my sister Alix's marriage, to walk, ride or drive with him. He missed her terribly when she went away, and when she died in 1891 he never got over it. My father was not very tall, but he had a wonderful figure and held himself with great dignity; he was certainly respected, and loved as well as feared, by every one. He was very fair and greatly resembled his beautiful sister Alexandra, whose immense charm he shared. He and his sister were great friends, sincerely devoted to each other, and he was always very happy when she came to [visit].

My mother occupied all of her time in charity and good works. Soon after her arrival in Greece, although she was so very young, she started reorganizing hospitals and every kind of charitable and philanthropic institution. With the help of a very wealthy man called Syngros, she built a huge hospital that was considered the best in the whole of the Near East. She would go there practically every day to visit the sick and see that everything worked properly. When she discovered that women prisoners and young boys were all shut up together in the same prison, she at once started collecting money to build separate prisons. On her silver wedding anniversary, she received a large present in money from a Greek called Averoff, she used it to build a prison for the women and another for the boys. These reformatories were organized on the American system, and their inmates were taught to do useful work which might help them to get a new start in life on their release. My mother also had another hospital at the Piraeus[14] which took up a good deal of her time.

Besides all this philanthropic work, she naturally [as Queen] had many inevitable social duties, such as receiving people in audience and giving dinners and balls.

On the first of January the whole royal family drove officially to the Cathedral in open carriages, *à la Daumont*, with four horses to each. The streets were lined with troops, behind which stood cheering crowds, and we were preceded by an escort of cavalry. After the *Te Deum* we returned to the palace, and my mother and I and all the ladies had to put on a kind of Greek costume which my mother had instituted as a court dress. We then proceeded to the throne room, where my father and brothers, in full dress uniform, awaited us. My parents stood on a low dais in front of the throne, with the Princes on the right of them and Princesses on the left. All the ladies of the society passed one by one before my parents, curtsied, and kissed my mother's hand. Besides the ladies, the ministers and their staff passed us, as well as army and naval officers stationed in the capital. It was great fun to watch them all go by, and if any of our more intimate acquaintances came along we used to make remarks in a low voice to tease them.

There was also a *Cercle Diplomatique* on that day. All the foreign diplomats stood in a row and we had to talk a little while to each of them. This was hard work, I can testify with feeling, and we thoroughly disliked it.

---

14.   Known as the "Russian Hospital".

The Belgian Minister, Baron Guillaume, who was at Athens a long time, was a particular friend of mine, and I remember that when I got to him I would ask him to do all the talking, as I had exhausted everything I had to say on the others.

On the day after the New Year there was a court ball. As children we used to look on at the scene from a window, but we were not allowed to remain longer than midnight. The next morning we would run down to the ballroom, very early, and look for lost jewelry. We actually found things sometimes. One of my brothers once found a large pearl surrounded by diamonds. This remained for years in my father's possession, waiting for its owner, who never appeared to claim it.

I was about seventeen when I was allowed to go for the first time to the ball on the day after the New Year, and I amused myself enormously. As a child I had been to children's balls given for my brothers and sister, and always chose the tallest men to dance with. This court ball was an official affair, and the King's daughters had to choose their own partners; the only exception was during the cotillion, when anybody could come up and ask us to dance. My brothers never much liked state balls, because they had to wear full dress uniform, which was not comfortable for dancing. At midnight we had supper with the diplomats, after which we went back to the ballroom for the cotillion—the best part of the evening. We usually danced until four or five o'clock in the morning.

Two or three times a week my parents gave dinners for all the legations in turn and for the Greek authorities. On Christmas Day we had the Holy Synod, consisting of the Metropolitan, head of the Church, and several bishops. My parents sat opposite each other and I was always on my father's right. I had the bad habit of taking off my shoes under the table, which annoyed my father, so one day he gave me a neat lesson. He rose from the table much earlier than I expected, while my shoes were still off, and I could only get hold of one of them. To my horror I had to hobble out with only one shoe on—which caused my father great joy. To this day I suspect him of having kicked the lost shoe out of my reach. It was brought to me after, in the drawing room, by our old butler, who scolded me.

This kindly old soul—of whom I have spoken before—was a Greek, but, being married to our old Nana, he could speak a little English. He had an English nickname for every member of the family: mine was "Pussy." We used to treat him abominably, I am afraid, and tease him without mercy. One of my tricks was to pinch his calves when he served wine during the official dinners. He scolded us a lot, but we never paid the slightest attention.

In our stable at Athens we had a rink for roller skating. When we were children my parents used to give parties there and invite a few diplomats to skate with us. My father was an expert in this sport and taught us all. Those who were learning usually pushed a chair on wheels in front of them. The late Madame Bakhmetieff, the wife of the last Imperial Russian Ambassador to the United States, always came to these parties. Her husband was then a secretary at the Russian Legation in Athens. Madame Bakhmetieff was an American and a favourite of ours; we had great fun teaching her to skate. Our dear old Master of the Horse, Count Chernowitz, who had served in the Court of Napoleon III, used always to offer us all a vermouth and my mother would put a few drops of it in a glass of water for me. I much enjoyed it after the strenuous exercise. Whenever I taste vermouth now, it brings back all that merry time we had at the skating rink years ago.

At carnival time my brothers and I dressed up in various costumes and came down to our supper in my father's rooms in masquerade. Naturally, since I had so many brothers, my one wish was to be a boy myself, and I invariably tried to get hold of some sort of manly garb to wear on these occasions. I remember putting on one of the boys' tailcoats one evening. My father was much amused by the sight, and so, early one Sunday morning my brother Nicholas made me dress up in this suit, took me downstairs to the courtyard and photographed me as a surprise for my father. The results justified my brother's wisdom and foresight: he bided his time until he wanted to put my father in a good humour—he wanted to go to some party or other, and was afraid Papa would not give him permission. On the day of the party he presented the photograph of me in the tailcoat to my father, who was so pleased that he immediately granted my brother's wish.

The carnival processions of masqueraders on Sunday was a charming spectacle. We were sometimes taken to see them from the windows of one of the Ministries, giving on the principal street, the Stadium Street. We were given bags full of confetti and flowers and threw them about with gusto. We had regular battles with the happy carnival crowds, who always seemed greatly amused by our eagerness and high spirits. Those Carnival scenes are amongst the pleasant memories of many happy years in Athens.

During the late winter or spring—I do not remember precisely—of 1881, Archduke Rudolf[15] arrived at Athens with his young wife, Stephanie, on their honeymoon. As I was only five years old, I am unable to give a detailed description of their short stay, but I very clearly remember that they came to dinner at the palace with my parents, and I was struck by the fact that they always stood hand-in-hand and never seemed to wish to be separated. This happened when all the family met in my mother's rooms, before they went in to dinner and I was sent to bed.

---

15.   The Crown Prince of Austria, only son of Emperor Franz Joseph and Empress Elizabeth. Married May 10, 1881, Princess Stephanie of Belgium.

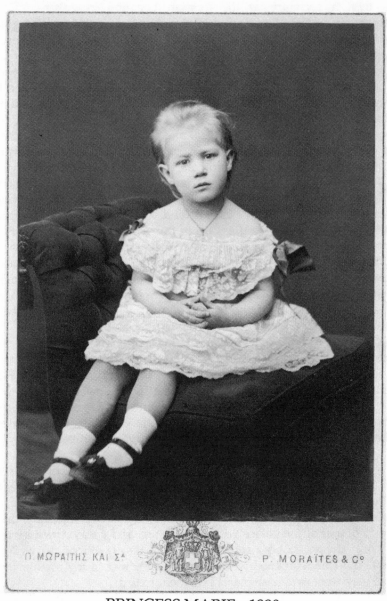

Π. ΜΩΡΑΪΤΗΣ ΚΑΙ Σ^Α   P. MORAÏTES & C°

PRINCESS MARIE - 1880

PRINCE GEORGE and PRINCESS MARIE - 1882
(Later King George V)

KING GEORGE I

QUEEN OLGA

PRINCESS MARIE - 1882

FREDENSBORG CASTLE

Emperor Alexander III is seated to the right of the center piece with Queen Alexandra on his left; King George I is to the left of the center piece with Empress Marie to his right.

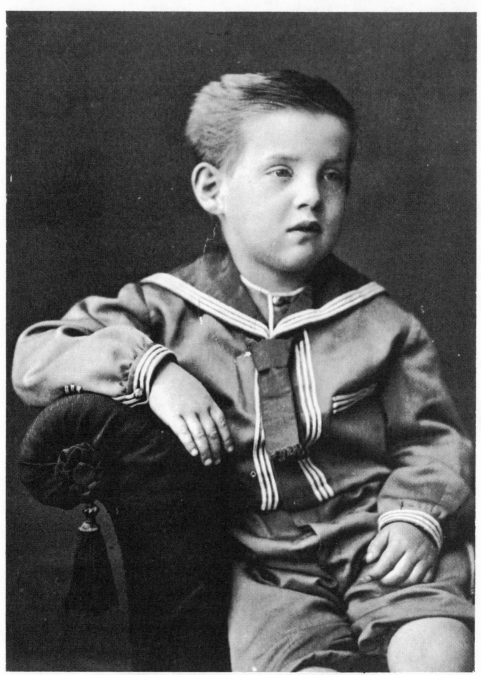

PRINCE CHRISTOPHER of GREECE

Chapter II

My first journey abroad was to Denmark, but I can scarcely be said to remember it, since I was only six months old at the time. I have been told that I very nearly died of whooping cough before returning to Greece.

In the year 1882 my second visit took place when we all went to Wiesbaden to meet my grandparents, the King and Queen of Denmark, who were taking a cure there. Their eldest daughter, the Princess of Wales, came with her five children. They were Albert Victor, Duke of Clarence, George[1], Louise[2], Victoria, and Maud[3]. We made a very gay and noisy party, with so many children. We lived at the Park Hotel where the entire family wrote their names with a diamond ring on one of the window panes; many years afterwards, I was told that an American wished to buy this window pane for a great sum of money, but had to give up the idea for fear of the glass breaking when it was moved.

Years after this gathering at Wiesbaden, I met an American gentleman at Cannes. His name was Mr. Brantingham, and he told me that he had happened to be at Wiesbaden at the same time as ourselves. He gave me the following extract from his diary, which I preserved as a curiosity in my own:

"Queen of Denmark and the King and Queen of the Hellenes and their children have been here since Friday. One meets them everywhere. This morning they went off somewhere in the train we took to Mayence. The car they were in bore a royal crown on top of the Danish arms on the panels. The Prince and Princess of Wales arrived here three days ago. He has since gone to Homburg, but the Princess remains. She and the Danish and Greek royalties pass much time in the open air, promenading the streets and looking into shop windows, and, when the music plays, walking in the Kurgarten. The Princess is charming and looks very young to be the mother of her eldest son Albert Victor. The two

---

1. Prince George, second son of Edward VII and Alexandra, became heir to the throne on the death of his brother, Albert Victor, in 1892, and King as George V in 1910.

2. Created Princess Royal in 1905.

3. Future Queen of Norway.

little Greek Princesses are very pretty children."

I was the youngest of all these children, but insisted upon being always with them and taking part in all their fun. I have since been told that I was much in their way. We all had dancing lessons together. A very stout German lady came to instruct us, and had a hard time keeping order in such a noisy crowd of girls and boys. We made friends with the staff of this hotel in Wiesbaden, especially with our landlady, who seemed to take a fancy to us and was always very kind and friendly.

There were two coachmen belonging to the hotel who used to change their horses in the yard beneath our windows. One of them we liked; the other we detested because he was grumpy and usually in a bad humour. My brother Nicholas got hold of a kind of pipe, from which one blew a small sharp pin attached to some feathers. It never went very far, but one day he blew it out of the window at the disagreeable coachman—and to our horror and dismay it stuck in his cheek, close to the eye. He set up an awful row, and we all ducked, but alas! he had seen us before we disappeared. He hurled German curses at our heads and said he would complain and make us pay for this. The elder cousins at once ran to our kind landlady and begged for her intervention. She succeeded in calming her irate coachman so well that no more was heard of the incident just then.

That same afternoon we all went for a drive to take tea somewhere in the country. When we got out of the carriage I deliberately pointed my finger at the coachman, announcing in a loud voice: "Look, that man has a scratch on his face where he was shot." This unfortunate remark gave the whole show away and caused my brother to get a severe reprimand, and his beloved pipe was taken away from him. Of course I got a beating [from Nicholas], which was well deserved.

One day the old Emperor William I of Germany, the grandfather of William II, came to call on my grandparents. We children were all presented to him, and he took me (as the youngest) on his knee. I am told that I started twisting the buttons of his tunic at once, and the accusation—just or unjust—is that I twisted one right off.

What I loved best during our stay in Wiesbaden was when my grandmother took me with her to the sweet shop and bought delicious cherry pies for tea. I distinctly remember the taste of those cherry pies even now.

Sometimes we made an excursion to a place in the Taunus called Königstein, which belonged to Duke Adolph of Nassau, the grandfather of the present Grand Duchess of Luxembourg[4]. His wife, Adelaide[5], was my father's first cousin. Königstein was a delightful little castle on the top of a

4.   Grand Duchess Charlotte (1896-1985), abdicated in 1964 in favor of her son, Grand Duke Jean.

5.   Born a Princess of Anhalt. Her mother, Marie, was a sister of Queen Louise of Denmark.

hill. The Duke would meet us at the station in a kind of *char-à-banc* with four beautiful horses which he drove himself.

He had a daughter called Hilda[6] who had been brought up by our own French governess, Mademoiselle Hinal. She was about the same age as our English cousins, and added one more to our lively family party when we went to Königstein. We would lunch and dine there, returning to Wiesbaden at night. Once when we spent the night there, all the girls had to sleep in one room, and all the boys in another, as there was not enough room for so many children. I was told that being the baby I could not sleep with the big girls, who went to bed much later. I instantly protested, and complained to my grandmother Louise. She said that I might sleep with the big girls on one condition, which was that I should be in bed and asleep before they all went down to dinner. I was put to bed, and before going down, my grandmother came to see if I was asleep. I distinctly remember that I was not, but kept my eyes tightly closed and breathed regularly for fear of being turned out. When the girls came to bed I was, of course, wide awake and we had a lovely romp. All in all we loved Königstein because it had a charming garden and—what is most important for children—excellent things to eat!

My first recollection of Denmark dates from 1883, the year after our visit to Wiesbaden, when we all went to stay with our grandparents at a beautiful place called Fredensborg. The children and grandchildren of the Danish King and Queen used to meet there every two years. It was a very large old castle with a lovely garden, an immense park and a lake. The whole family assembled there: the Prince and Princess of Wales, the Emperor Alexander III and Empress Marie, the Duke and Duchess of Cumberland, and all the children. Besides these and, of course, our family from Athens, there were the Crown Prince and Princess of Denmark, Prince Waldemar and his wife Princess Marie of Orléans.

It was in that year that I met for the first time my cousin Xenia, eldest daughter of Emperor Alexander III, and we became life-long friends. Much later we also became sisters-in-law by marrying brothers, the Grand Dukes George and Alexander [Mikhailovitch]. We met in the great entrance hall of the castle, in the centre of which stood a big wooden table which in those day's was higher than myself. I remember making Xenia's acquaintance for the first time underneath that table! These meetings in Denmark were a great joy to us, for we were an extremely united family.

We all had breakfast together at 9:30. Besides tea and coffee, we had a Danish national dish called *Ologbród*, a thick soup made of black beer and black bread. At the bottom of the plate you put crushed Demerera sugar, then the soup, and on top of all, thick fresh cream. The only trouble was that it made one gain weight alarmingly.

After breakfast we youngsters all went out for a walk in the park, invariably led by the Emperor Alexander III, who was the heart and soul of our merry band. We loved him because he allowed us to treat him like a pal.

---

6.   Married Grand Duke Friedrich II of Baden in 1885.

In fact, we led him rather an awful life, teasing and worrying him; but he never minded, and was always kind and good to us. He was very tall, and rather stout, so we nicknamed him "Uncle Fatty."

At one o'clock the family gathered again for lunch. There were no servants handling the food around: everything was laid on the table and on the sideboard, and we helped ourselves and each chose his particular chum to sit by. The older generation occupied the top of the table, and all the rest of us sat at the bottom.

When lunch was over we adjourned to the huge drawing room next door, where there were two pianos. My grandmother and her three daughters [Alexandra, Marie and Thyra] at once went to play music for eight hands. They were all extremely musical. The Queen played with her youngest daughter on one piano, the two eldest sisters on the other. Sometimes they would play waltzes for us and we danced. After this music we either drove in the *char-à-bancs* or went for endless walks with the Tsar. Returning home, we had tea in my grandmother's sitting room.

Dinner was a grand affair in the huge marble hall with a balcony running round the top. The table was always beautifully decorated with flowers in great silver bowls. We ate off silver plates, and a band played during the meal. All the suites, Danish, English, Greek and Russian were present. The placing was arranged by the Master of the Household and every night we changed neighbors. The meal was at 6:30 and afterwards everyone in the family talked to the ladies and gentlemen of the suites. Then we young ones ran up to our English cousins' rooms and amused ourselves until 9 o'clock when we had to go down again for tea. The adults often spent the evenings playing a card game called Loo. When we were not considered old enough to sit amongst the 'grown-ups' we were all seated together at one end of the table. [Although] we all enjoyed it and had a lovely time, we behaved outrageously, throwing bread pellets at people and sometimes blowing pepper across the table, when no one was looking, to make someone sneeze! My grandfather would start throwing paper arrows at us and we immediately retaliated. Our parents, I am afraid, often found that our grandfather—Apapa as we called him—gave us too much liberty. He loved romping with us, and we were not a bit afraid of him.

Next to the big drawing room at Fredensborg there was a smaller one in the middle of which stood a kind of low flat sofa. On this object we used to turn somersaults, and sometimes, to our great joy, the older generation joined us in this undignified pastime. First went my grandfather, then my father, and sometimes even our aunts. The Princess of Wales was the best at it, because she somehow managed to turn over without her head touching the sofa. It must be remembered that this had to be done in smart evening *décolleté* dresses with jewelled ornaments or flowers in the coiffure, and when our aunts accomplished it, they aroused our unbounded admiration.

The whole family was certainly very agile. I remember my grandfather saying that if some day we were all in need or turned out of our countries, he would start a circus with his own family. Each one of us was given a role in the circus, but my mother and the Crown Princess of Denmark, who were not so acrobatically gifted either on or off a horse, were told that they would have to be programme sellers!

During one of our stays at Fredensborg an amusing incident took place—a real ghost story. It was on a warm night, and all of us cousins went out in the garden and sat on a great long bench which just fitted us. It was dark, and we were quietly talking and enjoying the calm and beautiful night, when we saw something white through the trees. As it approached it seemed to be getting taller and thinner. We sat spellbound and as the castle was supposed to be haunted, we shook in our shoes. When the thing was about twenty paces from us we got up like one man and fled shrieking into the house. Only one of the boys stuck it out courageously: this was Grand Duke George,[7] the second son of Alexander III.

He got up on the bench and waited. When what he thought was the ghost came quite close to him he gave one leap and landed on it. The spectre collapsed, and my cousin started hitting and pounding away with all his might. He only stopped when he heard faint cries of: "It's I, Apapa!"

Poor George's amazement and horror can well be imagined. Our grandfather had draped himself in a sheet, which he held over his head with a long broomstick: hence the impression that the ghost was getting taller and thinner in its stealthy approach. The King complimented his grandson on his courage, and the rest of us were all dubbed cowards.

After the wonderfully good times we had at Fredensborg it was always rather a strain when we got home to Greece again and back to our lessons. My great despair was that all our masters, in every language we studied, assigned me the same task: to write out all our doings and impressions during the holidays. This bored me to such an extent that I cried over it. In the end I devised a way of not having to write the same thing in so many different language. I divided the story of the holidays into chapters and did one chapter in each language. I was rather pleased with this invention, which was immensely labor-saving.

We usually returned home by way of Vienna, where we spent a week or ten days at the Hotel Imperial. We loved Vienna. Walking about in the streets of such a big town and looking at the lovely shops was an unaccustomed treat to us. My father always bought Christmas presents there, and lovely things he found for us too. From Vienna we went to Venice or Trieste where our yacht, the *Amphitrite*, waited for us. It was now already October, so we had to settle down at once to our studies.

Our next trip abroad, I remember, was in 1886. My mother took my sister, myself and my small brother Andrew, who was only four years old, to Russia. We were greatly excited as we had never been there before, though our mother went every year. I was only ten years old; my sister Alexandra was sixteen. We went by ship through the beautiful Dardanelles and the

---

7. Died in 1899 at the age of 28 from consumption.

Black Sea, landing at Odessa. We stopped a few hours at Constantinople but remained on board.

There the Sultan Abdul Hamid, hearing of my mother's passage, sent us quantities of strange and wonderful Turkish sweets in big cypress wood boxes, and at the same time some beautiful black and white hens. My mother knew that my father would be delighted to have these hens on the farm at Tatoi, and gave orders to have them taken back to Greece in our yacht. All the hens proved to have diphtheria, and not only did they die, but they caused the death of our own hens. This was a disaster at Tatoi, and my father was considerably annoyed with the Sultan's wonderful gift.

At Odessa we were met by the Russian Imperial train, sent by the Tsar to take us to Pavlovsk, where my mother's parents resided. The Imperial train was a revelation to us: we had never set eyes on anything to equal it. It was just like a yacht, with a drawing room, bedrooms, and a dining room. One car communicated with the next—a convenience which did not exist in those days on European trains. I especially remember my mother's sleeping compartment which impressed me most. It was all pale blue brocade, and in lieu of a bed hung a great net of blue silk cord, suspended from the ceiling like a hammock. There was a beautiful soft mattress on this hammock which swung gently with the motion of the train and obliterated all bumps and jerks.

It took us two nights and three days to get to Pavlovsk. The one thing I can never forget was the light nights. At eight thirty o'clock I was told to go to bed, but I protested that I was being cheated and that it was really only five o'clock because the sun was still visible. When they told me it would never get any darker, I was obliged, a little incredulously, to obey.

My grandmother, the Grand Duchess Constantine, was at the station of Pavlovsk to meet us. It was the first time I ever saw her, and her beauty and stateliness made a great impression on me. She was extremely tall, with a magnificent figure and was always exquisitely dressed. She had such wonderful feet that she had the shape of the sole of her shoe made in ivory and gave these away to her friends as paper knives. I was rather awed at first, but the sensation quickly passed, as she was so extremely kind and made us laugh, so that we were devoted to her ever after. We always spoke German with her.

The Grand Duchess Constantine was famous throughout Europe for the marvelous jewels she possessed, and on official occasions she was literally plastered with them. At that time it did not much impress me, but later when I grew up, the spectacle amazed me. She had one string of pearls which were each as big as a hazelnut. All these priceless jewels disappeared along with everything else during the Bolshevik revolution.

Pavlovsk was a magnificent palace in the country, not far from Tsarkskoe-Selo. It had been built by Emperor Paul I[8] and his wife, the Empress Marie, who was a Princess of Württemberg. The palace was built in

---

8. (1754-1801).

the shape of a crescent around a huge court, in the centre of which stood a bronze life-size statue of the Emperor Paul. It contained priceless treasures, pictures, china, silver, etc. My grandmother's rooms were beautiful, because she had collected most of the best things around her. The floors were all parquet, with inlaid designs of different coloured woods.

My grandmother had a passion for clocks and watches, and I remember during my first visit how it fascinated me to sit quietly in her rooms and listen to them all. I imagined that they were having a conversation, as some ticked slowly, others gently and some loudly and others fast—they seemed to be talking busily to each other, amusing themselves. Little did I know then that for one of these clocks or watches many a museum would have gladly paid a ransom. I have inherited the love of clocks and watches, but have never been able to collect so many as my grandmother, nor such beautiful ones.

Everything in Russia was quite new to us. We were overawed by all the luxury and riches which surrounded us, and I must confess to having enjoyed it thoroughly. After we had been for some time in Pavlovsk, the Emperor and Empress asked us to come and stay with them at their summer residence, Peterhof, by the Baltic Sea. They were living in a small villa, built in Gothic style, in the Park of Alexandria. It was called *The Cottage*, and was just big enough to fit the Emperor and Empress and their five children. There was, of course, a big palace at Peterhof, but it was used only for receptions and on official occasions. We were lodged close to the sea in a small Italian villa which had just been built. We were the first occupants and my Uncle, who was very fond of my sister Alix, gave it the name by which he used to call her—which was *Baboon*. Much later, when my cousin, Emperor Nicholas II, married, he lived in this *Villa Baboon* with his family, but he had to build on to it because it was too small.

When my mother returned to Pavlovsk with my sister and brother Andrew, I was invited by my cousin Xenia to stay with her. We lived in the same rooms, like sisters. That visit has remained like a lovely dream to me. It was the very first time in my existence that I was on my own, and I enjoyed every minute of it. My uncle, aunt and cousins spoiled me terribly. They showered presents on me, and the Empress even gave me hats and dresses like her own daughter's, so that we should be dressed exactly alike. I ate sweets to my heart's content, a thing which was strictly prohibited at home by my father, who never allowed us to touch anything between meals.

My uncle was highly amused at the way in which I enjoyed all these new liberties and luxuries, and he rather encouraged me in them. He always came to say goodnight to Xenia and me when we were in bed, and we had great romps, flinging pillows at him and being chased around the room.

During that same summer the Emperor and Empress asked me to go with them and Xenia to Krasnoe-Selo, the military camp of the Petersburg troops. It was a delightful place, everyone living in small wooden villas or cottages. The end of the military manoeuvres usually took place there in the presence of the Tsar. On the first day there was a kind of tattoo. The Tsar on horseback followed by all his staff and the commander-in-chief—then his brother the Grand Duke Vladimir— made the round of the whole camp. The Empress followed in an open carriage driven by four horses and postilions. Each regiment—and there were many of them—stood all along the route and cheered at Their Majesties' passage, and the military bands played the Imperial Russian national hymn, which undoubtedly was the most beautiful of all national hymns.

A few days later there was an enormous parade of all the troops to mark the end of the manoeuvres. This took place in a huge field prepared for the purpose. In this field, which was as flat as a board, there was one small high hill on which a big tent had been erected. This hill communicated with the parade ground by steps cut out in the sod on the four sides. Outside the tent stood the Empress and the Grand Duchesses to look at the Parade. The Tsar, below on horseback, all his staff at his back, took the salute. All the regiments of the guard, in their gorgeous uniforms, Cossacks and regiments of the line, filed past him.

This parade ended in a huge field where an enormous tent stood for Their Majesties, their guests and suites. In front of this tent all the military bands of the entire camp were massed. The Lord's Prayer was recited by a drummer and then all the bands played together an evening prayer or hymn. It was one of the most imposing spectacles I have ever seen.

This march past lasted a couple of hours, and it was a stupendous and glorious sight never to be forgotten. All this was followed by a huge lunch in the tent, after which the Tsar promoted to the rank of officer all the young gentlemen of the *Corps des Pages*.

During that year, 1886, the Duchess of Edinburgh,[9] the Emperor's only sister, was also staying at the camp with her son and two eldest daughters. It was then that I made the acquaintance of the future Queen of Roumania[10], Marie, and her sister Ducky[11]. My cousin Xenia, Missy, Ducky and myself were about the same age—ten and eleven—and we three latter ones took a violent dislike to each other. Xenia, who was always sweet-tempered, got on better with them. What I especially resented at that age, was that they were what the French call *maniérés* and thought too much of their looks and clothes. I, who had grown up among a lot of brothers who treated me like a boy, did not care much what I looked like or how much I romped. We used to meet and play in the garden and I confess that I did my

---

9.   Born Grand Duchess Marie Alexandrovna of Russia, daughter of Emperor Alexander II. Married in 1874 to Prince Alfred, Duke of Edinburgh, second son of Queen Victoria.

10.   Princess Marie of Edinburgh married King Ferdinand I of Roumania in 1893. She was known in the family as *Missy*.

11.   Princess Victoria Melita of Edinburgh was known in the family as *Ducky*. Her first marriage to her first cousin, Grand Duke Ernst Ludwig of Hesse and By Rhine, ended in divorce. Her second marriage was also to a first cousin, Grand Duke Kirill Vladimirovitch of Russia.

best to irritate them in every way. I disliked anything which was not absolutely natural.

In later life, when we were grown up, we became quite friendly and when much later I often visited my niece Helen[12] in Roumania, Missy was most kind to me and we got on beautifully. We often talked and laughed over the animosity of our early youth.

Soon after this visit to Peterhof, my sister and brother and I went to Denmark to meet my father. The Emperor actually gave us a man-of-war to take us to Copenhagen. The battleship was called the *Asia*, but I remember very little about it; I know that I had a fight with my governess on the journey, and that the sea was not very smooth.

In Denmark we stayed with our father and his parents at Bernstorff, their delightful little country place near Copenhagen. The house was much smaller than the castle at Fredensborg. My grandmother was particularly fond of Bernstorff because she loved flowers and gardening; here she had a big rose garden. Inside it was a small bungalow where the boys lived when there was no place for them in the big house. The Queen was very proud of her roses, and I was always delighted when she gave me a basket and scissors and allowed me to pick them for her, instructing me exactly how to cut them. Near the wooden railings around the rose garden grew some gooseberry bushes, which my sister and I soon discovered. We ate this new and strange fruit with relish, gooseberries being unknown in Greece.

Not far from Bernstorff was the summer residence, Charlottenlund, of our Uncle Freddy[13], the Crown Prince of Denmark, where he lived with his wife and eight children. We used to meet quite often, especially for meals. We sometimes went to Copenhagen and were allowed to go shopping. This was always exciting to us, as we were never permitted to walk in the streets or go shopping in Athens.

On our way home from Denmark we sometimes went to pay a visit to my father's youngest sister [Thyra], the Duchess of Cumberland, at Gmunden. The Cumberlands then lived in a small villa in the centre of a garden. Later, they built a very big house on a hill. As their house was not big enough to put us all up, we children stayed at an hotel in the town. Every day at mealtimes a landau came to take us to the villa. My three eldest brothers and my sister, as I was told, behaved so badly during some of these drives, climbing all over the carriage and opening and closing the doors, that the coachman complained to the Master of the Household, saying that if we were not made to behave ourselves he could not be responsible for our safety. The coachman was then ordered to pull up his horses and stop short each time any of us started any of our tricks. This method had good results, but none the less, the rumour spread among the inhabitants that the young Greek princes were desperate characters, and that one of them even dressed

---

12.   Eldest daughter of King Constantine XII of the Hellenes. Married to King Carol II of Roumania, eldest son of Queen Marie and King Ferdinand of Roumania.

13.   King Frederick VIII, elder brother of King George I.

up as a girl!

One year the Duchess of Teck[14] was there with her four children, Adolphus, Francis, Alexander and Mary[15]. One day when we were all playing together in the garden of the villa, I had a bad fall and broke my collarbone. I was very sorry for myself, because I was of course obliged to keep to my room for some time, and missed all the fun. But the cousins came and sat with me, bringing me presents, usually various china animals.

The old Dowager Queen Marie of Hanover, who was the sister of my Russian grandmother, also lived at Gmunden in a charming little villa with her daughter Princess Mary. Marie was the mother of the Duke of Cumberland, and was a delightful, sweet old lady, with snow-white hair under a widow's cap. She was particularly kind to us and often asked us to lunch or dinner. In those days very few ladies smoked, but Queen Marie did. She always smoked two very thin cigarettes at once, and to our great amusement she puffed out the smoke in rings.

She had, I remember, a dessert service which I much admired, with different kinds of flowers painted on each plate. One day I loudly admired my plate, which had wild roses on it, and the Queen immediately presented it to me. I kept this plate as one of my most treasured possessions for years, until it was lost with all the rest of my belongings during the Bolshevik revolution.

When we left Gmunden we returned by way of Vienna. The Emperor Francis Joseph always came and called on my parents at the Hotel Imperial, where we stayed. He appeared in a uniform consisting of a white tunic, red trousers, and a cocked hat with green plumes on it. He was not particularly tall, but he made an imposing and stately figure with his white whiskers. He never remained very long and did not talk much.

Once during one of our stays in Vienna, the Maharajah of Kapurthala happened to be staying at the Hotel Imperial; I believe it was his first visit to Europe. My brother Andrew and I were very excited at meeting his Indian servants in their brightly coloured turbans, which we greatly envied. One day we discovered that the Rani was having dancing lessons, so we two stood in front of the door of her sitting room hoping to have a glimpse of the performance. The door opened for a moment and we just had time to see that the carpet had been neatly rolled away, and the Rani was dancing with her Viennese dancing master, who was holding her hands and dancing in front of her. I also remember that when the Maharajah called on my father he asked permission to present my brother with a turban. My father of course consented, whereupon the Maharajah sent for one of his attendants, who draped a pale green cotton turban with gold edging around my brother's head, whose pride knew no bounds.

In 1888 my parents went to Russia and we remained at Tatoi with

---

14.   Born Princess Mary Adelaide of Cambridge. Married in 1866 to Duke Franz of Teck.

15.   Married 1893 to Prince George, Duke of York, second son of Edward VII and Queen Alexandra, who became King George V in 1910.

28

our governesses and tutors. That July, as I was returning to the house, a servant handed me a telegram to take up to my sister. When I came into the room I found her sitting together with my brother Nicholas. I showed them the telegram, which they tried to grab, and as I saw they were so excited about it, to tease them I refused to give it up. An awful rumpus ensued when they tore it out of my hands. My amazement was great when they announced that the wire was from our father telling us that a new little brother had been born, and was to be called Christopher.

That same year in October, my parents' silver wedding [anniversary] took place. Quite a number of our various relations came to Athens for the festivities. Among them were the Grand Duke Serge [Alexandrovitch] and his wife, Grand Duchess Elizabeth[16], who later, after her husband's murder, became a nun and was herself killed by the Bolsheviks in Siberia in 1918. With them came the Grand Duke Paul, the youngest brother of the Emperor Alexander III. The latter had spent several winters with us at Athens: he had weak lungs and was ordered to winter in the south. He was my mother's first cousin, their fathers being brothers. We were extremely fond of him, as he was full of fun, a good sort and not very much older than my elder brothers. It was then that he proposed to my sister Alexandra, and was accepted. We were highly delighted, although we dreaded the moment of losing her from our family circle, for she was indeed everybody's favorite.

I have no very clear recollection of the silver wedding festivities, but I do remember being taken for the first time to the Opera, which happened to be *Carmen*. This treat I owed to the Grand Duchess Elizabeth, who had begged my parents to take me. Music was a great joy to me, so I was deeply impressed and sat silent and awed in a corner of the box listening intently. The Grand Duchess pointed out the best parts to me—I have never forgotten the feeling of utter joy at hearing that first opera.

After that I developed a passion for the theatre, and actors and actresses. We did not have a regular operatic company at Athens, but had to rely on passing Italian or French companies. Some were fairly good, others painfully bad to say the least. Later on, especially when my father built a new theatre, with the help of rich Greeks abroad, to encourage the Greek stage, a lot of famous foreign actors came during the winter season. Among these were the great Coquelin, Mounet-Sully, Sarah Bernhardt, Suzanne Meunthe, Yvette Guilbert and others. We were always present at their performances. I remember, too, the wonderful Eleonora Duse coming with D'Annunzio. They were received at the Palace by my father and he allowed me to be present. What an extraordinarily fascinating woman she was! She had the most melodious voice imaginable.

In early spring, during April, we always made a tour in the Greek provinces, choosing a different part of the country every year. The chief reason for this was that April 23, St. George's Day, was my father's saint's

---

16.   Born Princess Elisabeth of Hesse and By Rhine, Elder sister of Empress Alexandra, wife of Emperor Nicholas II. She was known in the family as *Ella*.

day and he wished to spend it with his people. Birthdays are not much observed in Greece, but name days are of great importance. These provincial tours were interesting and entertaining. [As there were few roads] we usually drove in horse carriages, by train where there was a train, [or] by yacht when the visit was to an island.

One year, on our way to Sparta over the mountains, we stopped at a small place where the mayor, in national costume, with his peasant wife standing next to him, awaited my parents with a paper in his hand. The paper warned us that he would make a speech. My father shook hands with them, and then the old man proceeded to put on his spectacles, gave his cap to his wife to hold, and started reading his words of welcome. He got slightly mixed-up, and my father told him it was all right about the speech, he need worry no more.

"Not so," said the old man, "I wish you to know exactly how we are all faring in this place." He started discussing his speech with my father, to everybody's intense amusement. All the villagers collected round, and quite a patriarchal scene it was!

After Sparta we went to rejoin our yacht at a place called Gythiuon, which is renowned for its fine pigs. All these poor beasts had been safely locked up for our arrival. We went straight to the church as usual on these visits, where a *Te Deum* was sung. All the officers of our yacht were there to meet us. When we came out of church and walked to the port through a terrible crush of wildly cheering and excited people, a pig got loose, came squealing down the street, and passed right between the legs of the Commander of our yacht. The pig threw him to the ground and continued its mad career. The poor Commander was very nearly reduced to pulp, but was fortunately saved by a policeman.

Another time, when passing Patras on our yacht, we stopped for a few hours and all the authorities were asked on board for lunch. The prefect sat next to my mother and to her horror he ate with his knife. She was so afraid he would cut himself that she told him to be careful. He casually answered her that it was all right; that he was accustomed to eating like that. My mother said no more, but when a second time he was asked on board, he started his old trick again and cut his lip right through. My mother said, "I told you so," to which he answered, "But you see your knives are so sharp!"

The people were always so friendly and so warm in their reception that we all loved coming into close contact with them. The country people were as sincere and natural in expressing their feelings towards us as children. My father and mother talked and joked with them, and they used to tell my parents all their troubles like friends and equals. This touring in the country usually lasted from a fortnight to three weeks, and we were always very sorry when it was over. We also visited places of archaeological interest, such as Delphi, Mycenae and Olympia, where stands the world-famous Hermes of Praxiteles, which, with the Victory of Samothrace in the Louvre, are the summit of ancient Greek art.

GRAND DUCHESS ALEXANDRA

Constantine, King George I, Prince George of York, Queen Olga, Prince George, Duke of Clarence, Marie, Nicholas, Alexandra - Athens 1882

**GRAND DUKE PAUL and
GRAND DUCHESS ALEXANDRA c. 1895**

EMPRESS MARIE
QUEEN ALEXANDRA

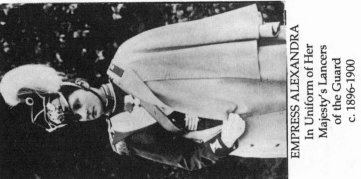
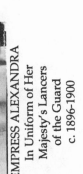

EMPRESS ALEXANDRA
In Uniform of Her
Majesty's Lancers
of the Guard
c. 1896–1900

GREEK and RUSSIAN ROYAL FAMILIES

King George, Alexandra, Nicholas, Queen Olga, Empress Marie, Crown Prince Constantine, Xenia, Marie, Olga, Emperor Alexander III, Michael

- Peterhoff c. 1890

KING EDWARD VII

Eilers collection

PRINCESS VICTORIA
Eilers collection

QUEEN ALEXANDRA
PRINCESS VICTORIA
Eilers collection

FREDENSBORG CASTLE

Chapter III

People in Athenian society vied with each other to give my sister a good time during her last winter at home. She had a very jolly character and enjoyed everything to the full. The officers arranged paper hunts for her, as fox hunting did not exist. She loved this more than any other amusement as she was a very good horsewoman, absolutely fearless. I was not allowed to ride, but drove to these hunts, with my mother in a carriage. My father was a wonderful rider too, and my sister and I inherited from him our great love for riding and horses.

In the winter of 1888 my mother's youngest brother, Grand Duke Dimitri[1], a great lover of horses and a particular chum of mine, sent me a pair of lovely fat ponies. My joy and pride were boundless—I believe the ponies came from an island in the Baltic provinces called Osel. The particularity of these animals was that when driven they squealed just like pigs! They were rather wild and I was not allowed to drive them that first year, but my sister often drove them down to the sea at Phaleron. Our ponies made such a noise that they quite rivaled my sister in attracting public attention on these drives. They were dark bays with black manes and tails, very fat rounded necks, which reminded one of the marble horses depicted on the reliefs of the Parthenon on the Acropolis.

My brothers did not care much about riding, although my eldest brother, Constantine, had gone through a course at the famous Hanoverian riding school, and was an expert in this art. My second brother, George, had left home at the age of fourteen for Denmark to be educated in the Danish Naval School. He passed all his examinations brilliantly, returning later to serve in the Greek Royal Navy.

In June of 1889 we all went to Russia for my sister's marriage to the Grand Duke Paul. We went by train and passed through Warsaw, then the capital of the Russian province of Poland. My sister's fiancé came from Petersburg to meet us there. We had an official lunch given us by the Governor General of Poland, General Gourko.

The famous old Shah Nasr-ed-Din of Persia happened to be there, returning from Petersburg where he had been on an official visit to the Tsar. He spoke very little and bad French, and many funny anecdotes were told concerning him. One of them was that when the Tsar introduced his

---

1. Killed by the Bolsheviks on January 28, 1919.

children to him the Shah asked if they were all by the same mother. One of the funniest stories came from Paris, where the Shah had asked to see a guillotine. When this gruesome instrument was shown to him, he insisted upon someone being executed to see how it worked. When the French authorities naturally refused, he called one of his own suite and ordered him to put his neck under the knife, and the unfortunate man obeyed. Of course he was immediately removed. The French authorities told the Shah that such an execution was entirely out of the question, but His Majesty was much irritated and disappointed, saying it did not matter a bit if one of his subjects had his head cut off!

The Emperor and Empress came to receive my parents and sister officially at the station in Petersburg. We all lived in the Marble Palace[2], the winter home of my mother's family. This palace had been built by the Empress Catherine II for her favorite, Count Stanislaus Augustus Poniatowski, the last King of Poland. It was standing on the quay of the River Neva, where all the palaces were built, and not far from the British Embassy. It was a magnificent and imposing edifice. The rooms were all very spacious and grand, with beautiful marbles everywhere. There, too, my grandmother's apartments contained wonderful treasures.

My sister's wedding took place on June 5, 1889 in the big church of the Winter Palace. It was a very grand affair. The Empress, the Grand Duchesses and all the ladies of the Court and aristocracy were dressed in gold and silver brocades, with the well-known Russian headgear, called *Kokoshnik*, and literally covered with priceless jewels. The bride wore a thick silver brocade dress which was so heavy that it could stand by itself. It was embossed on the bodice and train with silver flowers. From her shoulders hung the court train of dark red velvet with a broad edge of ermine. On her head was a magnificent tiara, studded with diamonds, the centre diamond being a huge pink stone. This tiara was made for the Empress Catherine II, and was worn by every bride in the Russian Imperial Family. It was usually worn by the reigning Empress for the big court balls. At the back of this tiara, on the top of the head, the brides wore a small diamond imperial crown, from which was suspended the bridal veil. The earrings were very long, heavy, beautiful diamonds; diamond ornaments embroidered the bodice, and heavy bracelets were worn, all belonging to the crown jewels. I was the only bride married to a Grand Duke who did not wear this regalia, as I insisted on being married in Greece.

My sister's marriage ceremony lasted about an hour. After this there was a huge banquet, when the health of the bridal couple was toasted by the Emperor. Again, though impressed by all this grandeur, I was not really old enough to realize the full magnificence of what I saw. I only remember the horrible sensation of beginning to feel lonely and deserted by my sister, and somehow cut-off from her. She seemed now to belong to something which had nothing in common with a small person like me.

---

2.   The Marble Palace now houses a school and museum.

My sister looked radiant, and won everyone's heart. Although she was very short, she had a lovely figure and did not look a bit crushed by all the weight of her attire; she carried it off splendidly.

The bridal couple did not leave at once for their honeymoon, but went first to a charming palace, also on the quay, which my brother-in-law had bought to be their future home. They asked my parents and all of us to dinner, and it seemed very strange to me, to see my sister at the head of the table as hostess and a grown-up lady.

For several days after their marriage they had official receptions at the Winter Palace, and I remember how we all looked on from a balcony at the top of the huge hall. After this ordeal they at last left for their honeymoon, and went to a place called Ilyinskoe, a charming country estate belonging to the Grand Duke Serge, near Moscow.

After this I went and stayed with my cousin Xenia at Peterhof. There I spent quite a long time—a great comfort to me just then, as I missed my sister badly. Later, we all went together to Copenhagen with the Emperor and Empress, on board their yacht the *Polar Star*, and settled at Fredensborg. A short time before we left for Greece, my sister and her husband arrived to present themselves to our grandparents.

Our return to Athens was a sad one, as my sister remained behind and we missed her painfully. From that moment I became the constant companion of my father, and was very proud of the fact.

In October came the marriage of my eldest brother Constantine to Princess Sophie of Prussia, to whom he had become engaged in 1889 while he was studying in Germany. Princess Sophie was the third daughter of the Emperor Frederick of Germany; her mother, the Empress Frederick, was the British Princess Royal, eldest daughter of Queen Victoria.

A great many members of the family came for this occasion: the Queen of Denmark; the Tsarevich Nicholas of Russia; my aunt, the Princess of Wales, with her two daughters Victoria and Maud; and the Empress Frederick, with her daughters, Charlotte, Victoria, Sophie, the bride, and Margaret. They all lived in the palace. Kaiser Wilhelm came on his yacht, on which he remained; he only appeared in Athens for the state dinner and marriage ceremony. Many society people had put their private houses at my father's disposal for his numerous guests, and one of these had been prepared for the Kaiser, but he never used it.

There was a very great deal of work to do to get everything into shape for the marriage, and my father did most of it himself. The Orthodox ceremony took place in the Cathedral. All the clergy, headed by the Metropolitan (Archbishop of Athens) received the Sovereigns and the bridal couple at the entrance of the cathedral holding a bible, bound in gold and precious stones with an icon in the centre, which he presented to us each to kiss. Then he was followed by the procession up the aisle. When the marriage was over and my brother appeared with his bride, the enthusiasm of the people was unprecedented. This marriage seemed to them to be the realization of a great national dream because tradition said that if the next

Constantine's wife was called Sophie (which in Greek means wisdom; and is the name of the famous cathedral in Constantinople) the Byzantine Empire would be revived.

We all drove back to the palace where the Protestant marriage ceremony was performed in my father's private chapel. A few years later, Princess Sophie, to the annoyance of her brother the Kaiser, gave up the protestant faith to join our Greek Orthodox Church.[3]

On the day following the marriage the Kaiser left, so we all went down to the Piraeus to our place, *Themistocles*, to see him off. He took leave of us most affectionately, and the only one he forgot to say good-by to was his own sister, the bride! I remember the Princess of Wales being extremely put out by this, and calling him back to do so.

In April 1890 came the happy news of the birth of a baby girl to my sister Alexandra, to whom was given the name of Marie[4]. I remember being very proud of becoming an aunt, and also recollect that the Duke of Clarence happened to be staying with us just then, on his way back from India.

That June, at Tatoi, my sister-in-law, Sophie, gave birth to her eldest son who was named George[5]. His birth was hailed with tremendous enthusiasm by the Greek people. My father was alone with us then, my mother being still in Russia with my sister, after the birth of her child. She soon returned on hearing the news, and the Empress Frederick also arrived.

Later, in October, my sister and her husband came to stay with us and we were overjoyed to have her back. It was her one and only visit to Greece after her marriage, as she died in the following year.

In 1891 my mother took me with her to Russia. My sister was then living at Tsarskoe-Selo to be closer to her husband, who was in command of the Horse Guards, and was stationed at Krasnoe-Selo. She had been given a suite of rooms on the ground floor in the big palace[6] of Tsarskoe-Selo, and I stayed with her for a couple of months. My brother-in-law was only able to get home to his wife and baby for weekends. My sister missed him dreadfully, and was very lonely without him, so my visit delighted her.

My mother lived at Pavlovsk which was about half an hour's drive by carriage. My sister gave me a lovely time and we had great fun, although she was in a delicate state of health. Every afternoon we used to drive to Pavlovsk in a narrow Russian carriage drawn by one horse, the famous

---

3.　While King George had not been required to convert to the Orthodox religion on becoming king, the constitution required that his children and descendants be raised in the Orthodox faith. Princess Sophie was banned from Germany by her brother for a period of three years as a consequence.

4.　Married Prince William of Sweden in 1908. This marriage ended in divorce in 1914. She married secondly Prince Serge Poutiatine in 1917 (div. 1923). Grand Duchess Marie died in 1958.

5.　He became King George II on the second abdication of his father, King Constantine, in 1922. Died 1947.

6.　Known as the Catherine Palace.

droshky of old Russia, to call on our mother. The *droshky* had no doors or back to it, and over the horse's head there was a kind of wooden arch called *douga*. The horse, usually a stallion, had a long tail and mane, while the driver, in Russian fashion, had a kind of long padded dressing-gown of dark blue cloth with a belt. It was a very smart get-up, and as the horse was a real Russian trotter, we went like the wind. The Grand Duchesses always had white reins, which made it all look still smarter, dark blue ones being those used by the Grand Dukes.

At Pavlovsk our grandmother always gave us most excellent teas. There was a big gallery on the garden side of the Palace which was all painted in frescoes by a French artist called Gonsague, and it was called after him. My grandmother, who was already getting on in age, had arranged it to look like a room, and sat there all day and even had her meals there. There were quantities of lovely flowers, and the place looked like an arbor. She often went for drives with us when the carriage was brought up.

After we returned to my sister's home, we would tour the magnificent palace. Upstairs, all the rooms of the Empress Catherine II had remained intact. The walls of one room were of amber, the next of amethyst, a third dark blue glass, and so on. Marvelous furniture of her period stood about, just as if the Empress might walk in at any moment. In the huge marble hall leading to these apartments there were priceless Chinese plates inlaid into the marble walls. One of the members of the Chinese Mission, sent from Peking to greet the Tsar, stood speechless at this beautiful collection, and said that that kind of thing no longer existed, not even at the Palace of Peking.

Not long after my arrival at Tsarskoe-Selo, baby Marie fell ill. Her life was despaired of for a while, and my poor sister was in a pitiful state. My brother-in-law was sent for, as no one thought the baby could survive. In her despair my sister sent for the famous Father John of Kronstadt, who was deeply venerated in the whole of Russia. It was said that sick people often recovered through his intercession. He came to Tsarskoe-Selo at once and was taken to the nursery. The poor child was lying in her cot, half conscious. He gently took her up in his arms and walked up and down the room. The baby quietly fell asleep and from that moment she started getting better and was soon quite healthy again.

The Grand Duchess Vladimir[7] was living at Tsarskoe-Selo then, and had her own very charming house and garden. She had three sons: Kirill, Boris and Andrew, and one daughter, Helen, who later married my brother Nicholas. The eldest son was about my age. The Grand Duchess Vladimir had the greatest charm any woman ever possessed. She was always most sweet and kind to me, and often asked me over in the afternoons for a ride with her and her children. We used to ride in the park and usually ended-up at the farm at Pavlovsk, where we had tea. From there my cousin Kirill rode

---

7.   Born Princess Marie of Mecklenburg-Schwerin. Following her marriage to Grand Duke Vladimir in 1874, she took the name Marie Pavlovna.

with me back to Pavlovsk to meet my sister, and the rest of the family returned home by carriage.

The Grand Duchess Vladimir always had most magnificent horses for riding, usually very tall ones, which I envied. Like most short people, I love tall horses. Before we started, she always allowed me to have a canter on her horse, which filled my heart with bliss.

At the end of August I left Tsarskoe-Selo for Denmark with my mother, and as the Emperor and Empress were going too, they took us on their yacht. My sister and I were very much upset at having to part again after the lovely time we had had together.

Towards the end of September in Fredensborg, my parents had a wire from the Grand Duchess Serge telling them that my sister had prematurely given birth to a son, Dimitri[8], that she was desperately ill, and that they were to come at once. This was a terrible shock as she was just twenty-one years old.

My parents, in a miserable state of mind, left at once for Ilyinskoe. My sister lay unconscious for a week and never recognized them. When the news came of her death[9], the Emperor and Empress decided at once to go back to Russia for the funeral and took me and my brothers with them.

We went by rail so as to get there sooner. This meant having to spend a few hours in Berlin, and the Kaiser, with his well known tact, gave a huge dinner at the station for the mourning Russian Sovereigns, and we all had to be present. The Kaiser was away, so he deputed his brother, Prince Henry of Prussia, to represent him. I well remember how angry and upset my uncle and aunt were at having to endure an official dinner at such a time.

Our arrival and meeting with our parents and my poor brother-in-law was too painful to describe. My parents and all of us lived with my brother-in-law in his palace so that he should not be alone in his empty home. Everybody was kindness itself to us in our grief, but of course, nothing could make up for such a loss.

My sister was laid to rest in the fortress of Sts. Peter and Paul[10] right opposite the Winter Palace, on the other side of the Neva. There is a big Cathedral there, where all the Tsars and Empresses and members of the Imperial Family are buried. Part of this fortress was the state prison, where years later my husband and so many others were put to death.

We returned to Greece soon after the funeral, and the people there were more than touching in their sincere sympathy for my parents. The Greek people sincerely felt the death of my sister as a personal loss.

In the spring of that same year, 1891, the Tsarevich [Nicholas] went on an official cruise to the East. He invited my brother George, his great

---

8.   Born September 18, 1891, Married in 1926 to American heiress Audrey Emery. The marriage ended in divorce in 1937. Grand Duke Dimitri died in 1942.

9.   Grand Duchess Alexandra died on September 24, 1891 at Moscow.

10.   In 1938, obeying a wish of Queen Olga, King George II had the body of his aunt brought home to Greece. She is now buried at Tatoi between her mother and sister.

chum to accompany him. He came to Athens, remained a few days with us, then embarked at the Piraeus with my brother on board the Russian man-of-war *Azof*. They first went to Egypt and then to India, Siam and Japan.

In [Japan where] they were visiting a place called Otsou, one of the Japanese policemen, evidently a fanatic, attacked the Tsarevich with his sword. As he was getting out of his rickshaw, the policeman dealt him three heavy cuts on his head, the third right across his ear. My brother George, who was driving just behind him, saw this, and never losing his wits, he gave one leap and pounded the policeman on the head with a thick bamboo stick which he had just bought that day. As my brother was very strong and stood over six feet two inches in height, the man collapsed under his blows and the Tsarevich's life was saved. Our cousin Nicholas never lost consciousness, and quietly walked into a house close by, followed by my brother. A doctor was at once sent for and had to sew up the three deep wounds. The Tsarevich never flinched or said a word, but only asked for cigarettes. Nicholas bore these scars to the end of his life. When the Princes returned to their ship my brother was cheered by the officers and crew.

From Japan [Nicholas] returned to Russia by Siberia to inaugurate the new railway, and my brother returned to Denmark via America.[11]

In 1892, during the spring, we all went to Denmark for our grandparents' Golden Wedding. The whole family assembled from every country for this occasion. We were all given quarters in Copenhagen, scattered about in various palaces. There was no end to the receptions, deputations and audiences to people who came to offer gifts. On the day of the Golden Wedding, our grandparents drove in state to the cathedral where we all awaited them. That night, at the Casino, the officers of the Guard and many of the ladies present performed a very pretty torch dance.

The Emperor and Empress gave a huge lunch on board their yacht, *Polar Star*, which ended tragically. One of my grandfather's gentlemen-in-waiting fell down the steps to the dining room and died on the spot from heart failure.

We remained in Copenhagen for two weeks, and the weather was exceptionally fine and the heat great. The Prince and Princess of Wales did not appear in public just then as they were in deep mourning for their eldest son, the Duke of Clarence, who had died in the early part of the year.

During the summer of 1893 we all met at Fredensborg. It was our last *séjour*, as the Tsar died a year later, and we met at Bernstorff after that.

One afternoon the Emperor went out for a walk with my father and the Prince of Wales; as it started raining heavily, they stopped a passing cart and got in, asking the driver to take them to the palace. The man, being of an inquisitive nature, wished to know who these three gentlemen were and asked them. When the first said he was the Tsar of Russia, the next that he

---

11.   Prince George said that on passing through England, Queen Victoria refused to receive him because she had been told the incident had taken place in a 'house of ill-repute'!

was the King of the Hellenes, and the third that he was the Prince of Wales, the man gave them a commiserating look and said: "And I am Jesus Christ."

I remember my grandfather telling us that once when he was returning home on foot to the castle, the sentry, a recruit who had never seen the King before, challenged him. It never occurred to the boy that the King could walk about alone, in plain clothes like anybody else. My grandfather had to tell him who he was and the sentry, rather annoyed, answered: "Anybody can say that!" and would not let him pass. The porter had to be called before the King was allowed to enter his own house.

Another time at Bernstorff the Emperor got himself a hand pump, which he filled with water and used to pursue the boys in the garden, squirting it at them. King Oscar of Sweden[12] came on a visit to my grandfather from Stockholm, remaining only a day. After lunch he and my grandfather were standing at the garden entrance of the house, very smartly dressed in frock-coats and top hats. The Emperor's room was just over this door, and when he looked out of his window and saw them talking very seriously, he went for his pump, turned it on them, and very nearly drowned them! They were both soaking wet. My grandfather, who was a sport, laughed heartily, but not so King Oscar; he became livid with rage. As a consequence the Emperor came down to apologize, but could hardly keep his face straight at the sight of the two sovereigns. When later we asked him what made him do such a thing, he laughingly answered that he simply could not resist it.

Another time, I think it was at Fredensborg, King Victor Emmanuel of Italy [then Prince of Naples] came on an official visit to my grandfather. He had come straight from Stockholm, where he had been visiting King Oscar. He had a great scratch on his nostril, and we asked him what had happened. This is what he told us: King Oscar, who was enormously tall, and had the habit of throwing his arms around one and pressing one to his chest, had done this to the King of Italy, who is very short. King Oscar was wearing the Order of the Annunziata, and when he crushed King Victor to his chest, the decoration caught the latter's nose and nearly tore his nostril off.

My aunt, Princess Waldemar's brother, Jean of Orléans, Duc de Guise, was serving in the Danish Regiment of the guards. As a Bourbon Prince he was forbidden to serve in his own country's army. His great chum was a Siamese Prince called Kira, who also served in the Danish army. The latter was extremely short in stature and Prince Jean remarkably tall and thin. As they were always about together, Aunt Minny nicknamed the pair *la côtelette*.

In the spring of 1894, just before Easter, we had a series of earthquakes in Greece. My father and brothers went off at once on our yacht to the island of Zante, where many villages had been ruined. The earthquakes continued for a week, the last one being on Good Friday. It

---

12.   King Oscar II (1829-1907).

came on just as most of the people were in church, and a kind of panic ensued. Everybody rushed into the streets. Nothing happened in Athens itself, but on Easter Monday, my father, mother and all of us went by yacht to the north where the earthquakes had wrought havoc. We even felt the tremors on board, which was a very uncanny sensation. We left the ship in the morning and visited all the devastated regions, returning at night. Most of the villages had been entirely wiped out and the population lived in tents, many of them having lost members of their family beneath the ruins.[13]

That same year, in July, my mother and I went to Russia for my cousin Xenia's marriage to the Grand Duke Alexander[14]. The Princess of Wales and her two daughters, Victoria and Maud were there too. The marriage took place at the Emperor's summer residence, Peterhof. The ceremony was exactly the same as that of my sister's. Xenia wore the silver brocade Russian court dress with the same crown jewels and tiara.

The bridal couple left for their honeymoon by carriage that evening, for a place in the country called Ropsha. It was there that the Emperor Peter III, husband of the Empress Catherine II, had been murdered.

On the night before the wedding, my cousins Victoria and Maud and I went to say goodnight to our uncle, Alexander, in his private study where he had to work half the night on his papers. He asked me if I possessed the Russian Grand Cross of the Order of St. Catherine. I was much astonished and answered that I did not because I was too young and unmarried besides. He insisted he had given it to me for my sister's wedding in 1889. To my utter amazement he brought out a box which contained this decoration and presented it to me to wear next day for Xenia's marriage. He had just given it also to my cousins a few minutes before. Mine was the last he ever gave. This quite unexpected gift made me nearly burst with pride.

The decoration was instituted by Peter the Great for ladies only, as a sign of gratitude to his wife, Catherine I, because she had sold all her jewels to help him in the wars against the Swedes. The ribbon is red, with silver edges, and is worn across the chest over the right shoulder. It is held together on the left hip by a bow of the same material from which hangs a diamond cross; in the center of the cross is a picture of St. Catherine with the inscription, "For love and country." With it goes a star entirely studded with diamonds, to be worn on the left breast.

In August, Aunt Alix, her two daughters and myself, accompanied the Emperor and Empress to the military camp of Krasnoe-Selo. We lived in little wooden houses in a small park. The Emperor followed the manoeuvres on horseback, and the Empress, my two cousins and I rode with them. The Princess of Wales followed in a carriage. We enjoyed that week spent in the camp more than anything else during our visit, and following the

---

13.   After many such disasters the Royal Family was the principal source of relief, as there were no government or public agencies in those days to help.

14.   Grand Duchess Xenia and Grand Duke Alexander were cousins, both direct descendants of Emperor Nicholas I.

manoeuvres on horseback was the greatest fun. In the evenings we all went to the theatre, where the best artists of Petersburg came down to act. The famous Imperial Ballet also performed.

The poor Tsar was not feeling very well and he was pleased when this tiring week, for him, was over. It was also the beginning of his fatal illness. He was getting steadily worse and the doctors suggested that he should spend the winter in the south. Corfu was proposed, and the Emperor seemed to like this idea, so the Empress asked my father to make arrangements for a long stay there. My father was delighted with the proposal and at once set to work to refurnish both the palace at Corfu and *Mon Repos* to receive his brother-in-law and sister. In September the Tsar went to Poland with his family, taking my brother Nicholas with him for the shooting at Belovège and Spala. The Tsar's state of health became so bad that the plan of going to Corfu had to be abandoned, and he was taken to the Crimea instead. The household was installed at the imperial residence of Livadia.

Meanwhile I had remained with my mother at a place called Strelna, another summer residence belonging to her family. I used to ride there every morning with my Uncle Dimitri, who had sent me the noisy ponies. But at the end of September we also left for the Crimea.

On the way we went to visit a stud farm for horses belonging to Uncle Dimitri, not far from Poltava. I enjoyed this visit immensely as I loved horses, and he had such beautiful ones to show us. He only kept black ones, the colour of his regimental horses, the Horse Guards. All his officers got their chargers from his stables.

We only spent a day there then went on to Sevastopol. There we embarked in the evening in a yacht for Yalta, a small town on the Black Sea not far from Livadia. We arrived there early in the morning, and my brother Nicholas and the Tsarevich come on board to meet us.

We drove straight to Livadia where we lived in a wooden house that used to be inhabited in the old days by Emperor Alexander II and his first wife, the Empress Marie[15]. She had weak lungs and often spent months at a time in the Crimea's mild climate. She had also built a charming wooden house called *Ericlik*, on a hill about half an hour's drive by motor, in the centre of a pine wood, with a lovely view over the plains down to the Black Sea. There were covered balconies and terraces all around it too, so that during the heat she could lie outside in the cool shade.

After having washed and had breakfast we went to call on my uncle and aunt. I ran up alone to his room and found him sitting in front of his writing desk, sad and looking ever so ill and pale.

When he saw me enter he looked up with his usual dear smile. I approached and he put his arms around my neck and kissed me affectionately, saying, "Minnerly" (a pet name he used to call me), "I am very

---

15.   Born Princess Marie of Hesse and By Rhine. She was a great aunt of Grand Duchess
       Elisabeth and Empress Alexandra.

ill." I tried to cheer him up, although my heart felt heavy, seeing the terrible change in him during that one month. He had a list of names written down on a bit of writing paper of the people he knew who had recently died. The last one was that of his old dancing master, who had died on the stage during a performance of the ballet *Coppélia*. I had happened to be present that night, and I well remember the poor old man falling and not being able to rise again. The director of the Imperial Theatre came and told my mother, who was also present, that the dear old gentleman had played his part for the last time. She was very much upset as he had been her dancing master too. The performance was stopped and we all went home.

The house in which my uncle, aunt and their children lived at Livadia was also wooden and small. Their daughter Xenia and her husband, Alexander, were living in a place called *Ai-Todor*, which he had inherited from his mother, the Grand Duchess Olga Feodorovna[16]. They too came over to Livadia constantly. My brother Nicholas and I had our meals with my Aunt. The Emperor felt too weak to lunch or dine with us and had his meals next door in his own room.

The Grand Duke Serge and his wife, the beautiful Grand Duchess Elisabeth and my brother-in-law, Paul, both younger brothers of the Emperor, were also there. In the afternoons my brother-in-law used to take me out riding on funny little ambling Crimean ponies, sometimes my brother accompanied us. The Grand Duke Paul was very tall, and as his pony was diminutive, his feet nearly touched the ground, and he made a very funny picture. I remember one afternoon riding down to the beach which consisted of pebbles (there was no sand whatever) where we met my mother sitting there by the sea with the Empress. Their bench was placed on boards of wood to keep the damp out. We got off our ponies, and Paul sat by them and I lay full length on the boards below them. Suddenly, when I was looking up at them and talking to my aunt, a huge wave came up and passed right over me. I was, of course, drenched to the skin, but fortunately there was a carriage nearby, into which I jumped and drove home to change all my clothes and get dry.

A few days before the Tsar passed away, the Tsarevich sent for his fiancée, Princess Alix of Hesse. The Grand Duke Serge and his wife, who was an older sister of the future Empress, went with the Tsarevich to meet the Princess at the frontier, and brought her directly to Livadia. Although she was received officially, everything was done quietly, owing to the bad state of health of my uncle. A few days after her arrival we all were present in the tiny chapel of Livadia when the Princess was received into the Orthodox religion.

On November 2, 1894, towards the evening, the beloved Tsar passed peacefully away, surrounded by all his family. He was seated in an armchair, his arm round the shoulders of the Empress, who was on her knees by his side. I cannot describe the sense of desolation we all felt, as we adored

---

16.   Born Princess Cecilie of Baden (1839-1891).

him and considered him our best friend. Our only comfort was to behold the marvelous expression of peace and serenity on his dear face, that peace which passes all understanding.

A day or two later his coffin was taken to the big Cathedral of Livadia. He was escorted there at night by his Cossack bodyguards, torches were raised all around the cortège, which gave the sight a melancholy beauty. There the coffin remained for several days, covered with a cloth of gold, with the Imperial Eagles displayed. Prayers were said day and night, and all the populace passed by to render homage to their dead Tsar.

[Afterwards] the coffin was borne down to Yalta where a man-of-war was waiting to receive. it. It was placed on a high structure, covered with red velvet and surrounded by palms and masses of flowers. The coffin stood in the centre of the ship, from which everything else on deck had been removed. The now widowed Empress, with the young Emperor, Nicholas II, his fiancée, sisters, my grandmother and mother, remained on board to accompany the coffin to Sevastopol. As the ship slowly moved away from the pier, the military bands played a beautiful Russian hymn called *Kol'Slaven*, which in Russia replaces the ordinary funeral march and is infinitely more solemn. The departing battleship looked like the funeral vessel of a Viking. My brother Nicholas and I remained on the pier until it vanished. We two then embarked for Greece on board a Russian yacht which the Emperor had put at our disposal. When we arrived in Athens we were alone, as my father had left at once for Petersburg on hearing of the Tsar's death.

Not long after our return home my cousin, Prince Charles of Denmark, who was then serving in the Danish Navy, came on board a Danish man-of-war and remained some time. He spent most of his time with us at the palace, and we were constantly together. Years later he told me that I had hurt his feelings because when he took leave of us on his departure it seems that I said that I was sorry he was going because I hated the idea of being alone during earthquakes. He said this remark spoiled all his illusions, after I had been so charming and kind to him.

My parents returned towards December. They had stayed on in Russia for the Tsar's marriage to Princess Alix of Hesse. That winter passed very quietly because we were in deep mourning.

In May, 1896, my sister-in-law Sophie gave birth to her eldest daughter, Helen. Sophie already had two sons, George and Alexander[17], who remained in Athens as King in 1917, during his father's exile.

Those children were my greatest joy, and I often used to run over to my brother's house to play with them. Helen was my special favorite, and we have always remained the greatest friends although I am twenty years older than she.

In April, Grand Duke George of Russia arrived in Athens to propose

---

17. King of the Hellenes (1917-1920). Alexander died on October 25, 1920, as the result of a monkey bite.

to me, and was accepted. He proposed just two days before my niece's birth.

A few days later we had the inauguration of the first Olympic Games to which athletes flocked from all parts of the world.

[Editor: The revival of the athletic spirit in Greece owed a great deal to the Royal Family. In 1896, Athens was selected for the first revived Olympic Games. Crown Prince Constantine was named President, and his brother, Prince George was named Chairman of the Judging Committee, in part due to his keen personal interest in sports. He had the satisfaction of seeing a Greek win the Marathon race from Marathon to Athens, commemorating the famous run of the Athenian messenger who brought the news of the victory at Marathon of the Greeks over the Persians in 490 B.C. The winner of the race was a Greek peasant from the village of Marousi, called Louis, who became a national hero. As Louis entered the stadium Prince George, carried away by his enthusiasm, ran beside Louis as he circled the stadium before running into the tape.]

The then King, Alexander Obrenovitch of Serbia, son of King Milan and Queen Natalie, took these games as an excuse to come to Athens, but his real purpose was to lay his crown at my feet!

Though he was informed of my engagement, he insisted upon coming, hoping to cut out my fiancé. Poor boy! His looks, if nothing else, were much against him, and had he been the last man on earth, I would have turned away. He remained several days in Athens, and was present at all the games, always sitting next to me—which I did not much enjoy. Of course I was unmercifully teased by everyone about this obstinate suitor, and it was a great relief when he left.

Later, King Alexander married a rather notorious woman called Draga Machin, [and later] they were both murdered in a horrible way, and their corpses thrown out of the palace window. Years later, when I was visiting Yugoslavia I asked Queen[18] [Marie] to show me the tomb of my ex-suitor, and she answered, "You had better go there alone, I think." I could not help remarking to her that had I accepted his proposal, she would not now, as Queen, be receiving me in Belgrade.

In May 1896 my mother and brothers and my fiancé left for Moscow to be present at the coronation of Emperor Nicholas II. I refused to go and have regretted it ever since as a ceremony of that kind will never be seen again. However, I did not wish to leave my father when I knew that I would soon be married and have to leave him for good. I dreaded the thought of

---

18.   Queen Marie of Yugoslavia, third daughter of King Ferdinand and Queen Marie of Roumania.   Married June 8, 1922, King Alexander I of Yugoslavia (of the Karageorgievitch dynasty).

being parted from him and from Greece. My father did not go to Russia because sovereigns are not supposed to be present at each other's coronations. My mother and brothers returned full of wonderful descriptions of the ceremony. It must have been a splendid and imposing spectacle.

We all went to Tatoi for that summer, and my fiancé came there in July for a long visit. I was suffering from bad headaches and pains in my left arm; our doctors could not quite make out what it was, so my fiancé advised my mother to take me to Vienna to consult a famous specialist there. We left in October and travelled to Trieste on a Russian battleship called the *Alexander II*. We had a lovely smooth passage, and the whole journey was most enjoyable.

We remained in Vienna about a week, and the specialist we consulted cured me. During our stay my parents called on the Empress Elizabeth at the Hofburg. She was dressed in black satin, and looked very beautiful and tall and slender. Her dress was quite plain, and showed off her marvelous figure. Her hair, which was so long that she could cover herself entirely with it, she wore plaited all around her small head, which gave the impression of a wreath or crown, and enhanced the beauty of her pure features. Being extremely shy, she always held a small pocket handkerchief in her hand, which she constantly lifted to her mouth. The Hofburg was large and imposing, but left no great impression on me except for its darkness, and for the family portraits which hung in great numbers everywhere.

We left Vienna after saying good-by to my fiancé, who returned directly to Russia. We went to Milan for a few days, and then to Bologna. When my father and I went out walking there we were always followed by Italian detectives. My father could not bear to be watched or guarded in this way, and most of our walks were made up of attempts to dodge these unwanted protectors. When we succeeded in doing so, my father was always very happy. On the birthday of Queen Margherita of Italy, we all went to the Opera to hear Puccini's *La Bohème*, which was being given for the first time. It had an enormous success, and I well remember what a deep impression it left on me. Ever since then it has been a special favorite of mine.

EMPRESS ALEXANDRA C. 1896

GRAND DUCHESS ELIZABETH and
GRAND DUKE SERGE ALEXANDROVITCH

GRAND DUCHESS ELIZABETH (ELLA)

QUEEN ALEXANDRA

Eilers collection

Chapter IV

At the beginning of 1897, a long series of Balkan troubles which were to preoccupy our family and our people for so many years began. The first serious incidents were caused by the question of Crete.

In April I had accompanied my father to Corfu for Whitsuntide. We were having a most enjoyable time with the excursions and picnics all over that divine island, which at that time of the year looks like one great garden, when my father was suddenly recalled to Athens. The political horizon was getting very ominous. The insurrection in Crete against the hated Turk was taking alarming proportions, so we returned at once.

My father decided to send Colonel Timoleon Vassos, his aide-de-camp, to Crete. The troops disembarked at night under protection of our Royal Navy. My brother George was commanding the torpedo boats. We were in a state of terrible anxiety until we heard that the raid had been successful. After the Cretan expedition, war with Turkey began in Thessaly.

My eldest brother, Constantine, commanded the army, and my brother, Nicholas, a battery [of artillery]. My mother, my sister-in-law, Sophie, and I had a lot of work to do with the Red Cross hospitals. We were all extremely busy, because, besides looking after our own hospitals, we constantly visited all the others scattered about the town. Sophie converted an immense building which had just been finished as a military school into a hospital and worked there for the greater part of every day.

A number of Red Cross units came from various foreign countries to offer their help. I had the Danish contingent in a private house which had been offered for use as a hospital. These Danish nurses were wonderful. They were headed by a matron called Miss Reinhard, a lady of good family. We all became very fond of her and my mother kept her for years after the war as matron of her big private hospital. Although none of the Danes could speak a word of Greek, they were not long in picking up a little, and became very popular with the wounded soldiers.

In my hospital I had several Turkish soldiers and found them docile, patient and most grateful for all we could do for them. I remember one of these very particularly as he was a curious type. He came of a special Albanian race called *Gegs*, very wild and cruel. This man had been shot through both his knees. He was rather old; his height was a good deal more than six feet and he had a most interesting face—thin as a skeleton, very dark, with a nose like an eagle's beak. He would not keep his bandages on, and as soon as the nurse left him he always pulled everything off again, and would stick his fingers in the wound like a wild beast. He took a violent fancy to my brother Andrew, then about fifteen years old, because he said he reminded him of his own son. The Albanian used to stroke my brother and scream aloud when Andrew left the ward.

I remember a rather amusing episode at that time at the palace. Every night after dinner in my father's room, Papa and I used to sit at the dinner table after everything had been cleared away and play patience. My mother read her Russian papers seated in her particular armchair. As it was already very hot, and the summer well advanced, all the doors to the covered colonnade were wide open. We were silent, sad and anxious: the war was going very badly for us. Suddenly, in the dead silence we all heard a strange sound. We sat up and listened and heard again a noise like a mew of a cat. I must explain that the only animal my father cordially detested was the cat. He could not forgive the race of cats in general for eating up the birds in his garden. When I said that the noise must come from a cat, he pronounced it quite impossible, since no cat would dare come into his rooms. I was told to get up and look for the beast anyhow. I looked under every sofa, table and chair, but could find nothing. We waited. The sound came again. Against the wall, quite close to us, stood what was called a console of mahogany decorated with heavy bronze ornaments with a marble slab on top. This was a bit of the old furniture left by King Otto. On the marble slab stood a rather high, narrow ornamental vase of *Sèvres* china. It seemed to me that the sound came from there. I had to climb on a chair and stand on the marble slab to look into the vase. To my utter amazement I saw two shining yellow eyes looking up at me.

In high glee I announced this unexpected discovery. My father could not believe it and got up to see for himself. He was horrified, and with the greatest trouble we hoisted the vase between us, carried it onto the terrace, and turned it over. Out came a huge cat with six kittens. They must have been about a day old. One by one the mother took her kittens into the garden. Next afternoon my father caught the cat just as she was ready to jump back into the vase with a kitten in her mouth. She was removed by force and told never to come back. She did not appear again.

[Ed. Note: At dawn on April 17, 1897, Turkish forces commenced their attack across the frontier at Anapilis. With great skill, outnumbered by more than ten to one, Crown Prince Constantine fought a delaying action.

King George used his personal relations with the British, German and Russian Royal Families to good effect, and on May 19, 1897, they forced Turkey to grant a ceasefire.

Negotiations lasted from May until December, when, again through the King's diplomatic skill and family connections, Turkey agreed to end the war, returning to Greece all of the territory which she had lost. Turkey also

In February 1898, there was an attempt against my father's life. I was with him at the time and remember it in every detail. One afternoon, Papa and I went for a drive to the sea to a place called Old Phaleron, where it was our custom to drive or ride. In those days we used to drive in a landau, and on that day, as it was rather chilly, we had the front of it closed. We were going at a foot pace up a small hill; my father never allowed his coachmen to make the horses trot uphill. We happened not to be talking at that moment when we suddenly heard a rifle shot go off. The horses started. I remember telling my father that it was ridiculous to allow people to shoot so close to the road as it would surely end in an accident someday. I was seated on the right and being very shortsighted, I put up my glasses and bent sideways to see what was happening.

To my astonishment I saw the barrel of a rifle aimed straight at me. By this time the coachman had whipped up the horses, and we were going quite fast up the hill. "They are shooting at us," I said to my father.

Looking at Papa at that moment I thought that I would surely be killed and never see him again. The firing went on, and as we advanced we could easily distinguish two men standing about twenty paces from us in a field, deliberately aiming at us with rifles. I had a red velvet bow on my hat which my father thought would make a good target for them, so he quickly stood up, put his hand on my neck and forced me down. With his other hand he menaced them with his walking stick. As we passed, they both jumped on to the road over a small ditch which separated it from the field, and knelt on the ground to fire their seventh shot. In another second we disappeared in clouds of smoke and the two men ran [away]. The coachman was hurling curses at their heads, but he never lost his wits for a moment. The footman sitting next to him on the box was wounded in the leg, and both horses received slight wounds on their backs.

When we got to the top of the hill Papa gave orders to go slowly and calmly asked me if I thought it really was an attempted assassination!

We drove home quietly after that and arrived safely at the palace. Someone had called my brother George, who was at home that day, telling him there had been an accident. He came running onto the terrace just in time to see the wounded servant being carried away. As he saw Papa and I were none the worse for our experience and treated it calmly, his anxiety passed.

We three walked out of the terrace gate and stood talking in front of the palace on the public side. A few minutes later Constantine, who lived close by, came running up to us, as pale as a sheet. He had just been told that our father and I had been killed. By this time all the town had heard about it, and crowds came flocking up to the palace to hear what had happened. We were quickly surrounded by people both known and unknown, so we went back to my father's rooms. My mother, returning from her hospital at the Piraeus, was told by the aide-de-camp on duty that there had been an accident, and in a terrible state of anxiety she entered the room to find us all together discussing the extraordinary event.

That same evening we had a service of thanksgiving in our chapel at the palace. The following day there was an official *Te Deum* at the Cathedral. Crowds of people lined the road and cheered as we drove in state. Afterwards, we heard that one of our assailants had been in the crowd. That very evening he and his companion were arrested. For a few days we were asked not to go outside our garden until the police could find out if there had been a conspiracy. On the following Sunday there was an immense demonstration in front of the Palace; the crowd persistently asked for the King to show himself and make a speech, which he did.

When we were again allowed to drive out, my brothers George and Nicholas came with us, as they did not like the idea of Papa and me driving alone. We again went to Old Phaleron and at one moment—but in another place—we again heard a rifle shot. In a twinkling five revolvers appeared; my father's, my two brothers', mine and the footman's! We laughed at this, but I most of all, because my brother George, knowing Papa had given me a revolver, had taken the bullets away to avoid an accident!

Within three days after the attempt on his life, my father received more than five thousand telegrams. I received a lot myself, and for weeks letters of congratulation came from every corner of the earth. Someone even sent me pressed flowers from Brazil. About a week later we all went to the spot where the attack had taken place to lay the foundation stone of a church which was built in remembrance of that day.

During that quiet winter of my twenty-second year I decided to learn to ride a bicycle. As there was no ladies bicycle to be had, my two eldest brothers taught me to ride on theirs. These lessons took place in the three enormous ballrooms of our palace. Both my brothers were 6'-3" tall, and I only just over five feet, so being hoisted on to their bicycles was a hard job for me. The first time they lifted me on to the saddle they gave the bike a hard push and of course I ended sprawling on the floor. This gave them great pleasure, but we persisted, and little by little I managed to achieve balance although my feet were miles away from the peddles. Once I was able to control the machine, Papa made me a present of a ladies bicycle; and on rainy days we used to ride all round the broad corridors and ballrooms. One day [Constantine] and myself collided with an awful crash between two columns and were nearly killed. Our bicycles were useless for days.

During that winter, with the money which remained over from my war hospital, and also with the help of some rich friends, I organized a station for first-aid for street accidents. I was given permission by the government to build a small pavilion in Parliament (*Bouli*) Square. Someone remarked that it would come in handy for the next fight between the deputies in the Chamber! When I married I turned it over to my sister-in-law, Alice[1], wife of Prince Andrew. It continued to work successfully until last year, 1930, when the Republic had it pulled down in order to ruin one more charitable institution erected by a member of the Royal Family.

In July 1898 my brother Nicholas and I visited Italy with our father to see the exhibition at Turin. We only remained for two days. King Humbert and Queen Margherita were there, and we lunched with them at the palace. From Turin Nicholas and I went on to London. I was overjoyed because ever since I can remember it had been my dearest wish to visit England.

On our arrival my sister-in-law Sophie, and my cousin Victoria, were at the station to meet us. We drove direct to Marlborough House, the residence of the Prince and Princess of Wales. I shall never forget that rare and lovely feeling of a dream come true. I liked everyone and everything at once in London, and felt as if I had lived there always. Besides all this, I had a special love for the Princess of Wales, my Aunt Alix. From my very earliest memories she was always a kind of fairy godmother to me, and we loved each other dearly. As a child in Denmark, whenever I was in trouble, I always went to her, and she always understood. When I behaved badly, she was the one I asked to go to my father and plead for me; and many a time she got me out of a scrape or saved me from punishment. I was always allowed to go to her rooms whenever I chose. She, too, was delighted to be able to show me her lovely home and have me stay with her.

My cousin Victoria was a great chum of mine, and, with my aunt and her, I had a most lovely time going about sightseeing. With them I visited the Tower of London, the National Gallery, Hampton Court, and many other places of interest. At night we went to the beautiful theatres which I adored.

The Prince of Wales, Uncle Bertie, was laid up just then with a broken knee. We only remained four or five days in London, and on July 30, we all left for Cowes in the Isle of Wight for the Regatta. We lived on board the Prince of Wales' old yacht, the *Osborne*, which was still a paddle ship. As our uncle could not walk, they had arranged a room for him on the deck where he spent most of his time. Crowds of people came to visit him.

Shortly after our arrival, Aunt Alix was sent for from Denmark. Her mother, Queen Louise, was very ill and to our great sorrow she had to leave at once. My cousin Victoria took my brother and me everywhere at Cowes. We used to go out on sailing expeditions and every trip was an adventure.

The famous Guiglielmo Marconi was on the Prince's yacht; he had come from Italy to try his wireless experiments. It was considered marvellous then that wireless messages could be sent from the yacht to Queen Victoria, who was staying at her lovely place, Osborne, on the top of a hill, a few miles away! We did not see much of Marconi. I only remember visiting a cabin with Aunt Alix, where he had all his instruments, a few days

---

1.   Born Princess Alice of Battenberg (1885-1969). She is the mother of the Duke of Edinburgh, and grandmother of Prince Charles, the Prince of Wales.

before she left.

The day after our arrival at Cowes, Queen Victoria asked my brother and me to dinner at Osborne. I had never met the Queen before, and I own that I felt a bit nervous at going there without my aunt or cousin. The Duke and Duchess of Connaught[2] were staying with the Queen, with their two daughters, Margaret[3] and Patricia. Princess Beatrice, Queen Victoria's youngest and widowed daughter, was also there with her young children.

All the family met in one of the drawing rooms for the Queen's appearance. We only waited a few minutes when the doors were thrown open and Queen Victoria appeared, assisted by one of her faithful Indian bodyguards. She was already well advanced in age, and had difficulty in walking without assistance. Though she was very short in stature, she was certainly every inch a Queen.

She greeted us all with a sweet smile and I was told to go forward to present my respects. I did so, shaking in my shoes. I made a deep curtsey and kissed her hand, after which we went in to dinner. I was so awed, impressed and shy that I do not remember much of that dinner, except that it was a rather silent one.

After dinner, when coffee was being served, the Queen, who was sitting in her armchair, sent for me and talked to me very kindly. She told me she had seen my mother when she was a little girl of about ten.

This reminded me of an amusing story my mother told me of her childhood visit to London with her father, Grand Duke Constantine. He went to call on Queen Victoria and my mother went with him. She had short hair in those days and Queen Victoria asked her when she had had her hair cut, *"Depuis quand portez-vous les cheveaux coupés?"* Mama answered proudly, *"Depuis ma jeunesse".*

A few days after my aunt's departure my cousin Victoria went up to Osborne to call on her grandmother and took me with her. The Queen was having breakfast at a big round table in the garden under a shady cedar tree, surrounded by her family. She was again very kind and gracious to me. After her breakfast she retired to the house to her manifold occupations of State, and the rest of the family dispersed.

The Queen always used to drive in the morning round the park in a small cart drawn by a pony which was carefully led by a groom walking alongside. The cart was standing there just as everyone went away, and as there was no one left but my cousin, Mr. de Soveral, the Portuguese Ambassador (a great friend of all the Royal Family), and myself, the temptation to get into the cart was irresistible. I jumped into it, took the reins from the horrified groom, and started driving at full speed round the garden. My cousin was doubled-up with laughter, and could not get out a word although she tried hard.

---

2.   The Duke of Connaught (1850–1942) was Queen Victoria's third son. Married in 1860 to Princess Louise Margaret of Prussia.

3.   Princess Margaret (1882-1920) married Crown Prince Gustaf Adolf of Sweden in 1905.

I also have kept a delightful remembrance of the battleship *Crescent*, which was commanded by my cousin George, the Duke of York[4]. He often asked us on board for meals. He was very gay and lively, and we all enjoyed ourselves thoroughly. Once we went round the Isle of Wight in a torpedo-catcher which made twenty-eight knots, and as the sea was rather rough, it simply sliced through the waves in the most exciting manner. We were, of course, drenched to the skin.

The late King Leopold of the Belgians was also at Cowes, and often came to visit the Prince of Wales. In fact, he came so often that it tired Uncle Bertie a bit; so one day, when King Leopold settled himself down for a long chat, my Uncle simply handed him *The Times* and paid no further attention to him!

One day Victoria, my brother and I went out with the Captain of our yacht and some of the officers for a sailing expedition. We anchored in some out-of-the-way place on the coast and had tea. Just as we were ready to return to Cowes, the tide went down and we were stuck on the sand and nothing could make our boat move. Since it was Sunday, we could get no help anywhere. At last we got a tiny sailing boat belonging to the clergyman of the neighborhood and got away. Meanwhile, as it was getting very late, Uncle Bertie had begun to feel something had happened to us and sent out several steam launches to look for us all over the Solent. We luckily met one of them and were taken home. Our uncle was very much annoyed; there was a slight rumpus, and we never dared tell him what fun we really had had.

The Duchess of York[5] came often to visit us on board the yacht and brought her little boy, Edward[6]. He was only three or four years old then. About ten days later, the Prince of Wales decided to have a change and went for a trip in the yacht along the coast. We went to Portland, Weymouth and Plymouth where we visited the lovely estate of Lord Mount Edgecombe. There I tasted Devonshire cream for the first time and did not appreciate it—to the displeasure of all my English relatives. We also visited another estate of Lord Mount Edgecombe in the country, a place called *Conteel*, with a small but very old and beautiful castle. Then we stopped at Dartmouth, where we anchored in the river—one of the loveliest places I have ever seen. Returning by Portland, we bicycled with the yacht's officers into the country to visit the so-called White Horse. The huge effigy of a horse and rider (I believe one of the four Georges) was cut out of the grass in the slope of a hill. It was filled up with white pebbles so that one could see it for miles. It was so large that eight of us sat in the stirrup.

After returning to Cowes for a few days, my brother and I left on September 1, by way of London, for Denmark. Just the day before we left the news came of the horrible murder of the poor Empress Elizabeth of Austria,

---

4.   King George V.

5.   Born Princess Mary of Teck, (1867-1953).

6.   King Edward VIII.

which shocked the whole world.

When we arrived in Copenhagen my father and many members of the family met us. My grandmother was very ill, and as she could not walk she was wheeled about the garden in a chair, the rest of us following; even then she loved to have the family around her.

In the early hours of September 29th she passed peacefully away in the presence of all her children. It was a terrible grief to us all as we were profoundly devoted to her. She was a remarkable personality; a wonderful Queen, devoted mother and grandmother. She was the leading spirit of the whole family throughout her life.

A fortnight later Queen Louise was laid to rest in the Cathedral of Roskilde, where all the Danish Kings and Queens are buried. Both Emperor Nicholas II and the Duke of York arrived in time for the funeral.

We got back to Athens during the first days of November. On the 27th the representatives of the Great Powers came to announce to my father that my brother George had been chosen to be the High Commissioner in Crete[7]. This was the result of the war [of 1897]. The Powers refused to unite Crete with the Mother Country, since we had been beaten by the Turks. On the 20th of December my brother [George] left for his new post, and the next day we heard that he had been enthusiastically received both by the Christian Cretans and by the Mohammedans

Again that winter we were in mourning and the only times we were allowed to go to the theatre were for the performances of Madame Eleonora Duse. Although I was already twenty-two, I continued some of my studies. I took singing lessons, which I enjoyed. I often used to sing with the window open and my father, who always took a short walk in the garden after breakfast, before starting his work, could of course hear me. To tease me he would say later during lunch that the peacocks had been making more noise than usual. Papa hated the idea that any of us might suffer from a swollen head, but I suspect he really liked to hear me sing, as he always happened to stop in a place in the garden from where he could hear me. I often sang at my brother's [Constantine] house when Sophie had visitors to tea.

One spring about this time the Empress Eugenie[8] passed through Athens on one of her voyages to the south. She stayed in a hotel in town, and I accompanied my father when he went to call on her. She was still very beautiful and had a great deal of charm. The Empress and my father talked politics and touched on the subject of our unfortunate war. There were still a lot of red-shirted Garibaldians—the remnants of those who had volunteered to fight with us against the Turks. They could be seen every day walking about the streets of Athens, and I remember that the Empress warned my father that it would be best to get rid of them as soon as possible as they were not a safe element.

In September of 1899, my mother and I went to pay a visit to my

---

7.   Prince George served as High Commissioner from 1897 to 1906.

8.   Eugenie di Montijo, consort of Napoleon III.

brother George in Crete. He met us at Suda Bay, and we drove to Halepa where we had a small and comfortable house. I felt terribly excited at seeing the historic island at last liberated from the Turkish yoke after so many centuries. The troops of the Foreign Powers were still in occupation. Every day the sentinels in front of my brother's house were of a different nationality: one day Russians, next day Italians, and the third, French. The British troops were stationed at a place called Herakleion, much further away, and we did not see them. For the maintenance of order on the island, and to train a Cretan gendarmerie, there were the famous Italian Carabinieri.

My brother had a collection of animals which he at once took me to see. He had five horses to drive and ride, a monkey and several gazelles, one of which was perfectly tame and had been named *Bichette*. He had a French soldier to look after them, and all the animals loved him.

During the first days of October I went back alone [to Crete] to stay with George. I was overjoyed to be there again as I had become very fond of the island. I had taken my sidesaddle with me, but in the confusion of landing it had been forgotten on board the ship and went on to Egypt. It took quite a long time to get it back again. The wife of the Russian Consul lent me her saddle, which was much too small for me. The first time I used it on one of my brother's ponies, the results were disastrous. The pony suddenly shied and stopped short. I was precipitated over its head and landed in a bunch of cacti—which was extremely painful!

When my own saddle at last arrived, we used to ride every day all over the rough hills. Mama wrote to my brother to get a nice strong Cretan pony for me as a surprise from her. One day it was brought to me and I rode on it immediately; it proved to be a wonderful animal.

Every so often, my brother had to give state dinners at the Palace of Canea, Crete's capital. I presided on those occasions, which made me feel very important. Such dinners were for the local authorities, the representatives of the foreign Powers and the officers of the foreign troops. It was during this period that Eleutherios Venizelos started on his revolutionary career. It was in Crete that he had his general rehearsal for future action in Greece[9], for the ruin of our dynasty and of our country.

Our uncle, Prince Waldemar of Denmark, visited Crete on board the ship *Valkyrie*, of which he was commander. One evening he and all his officers came to dinner at our house, after which my brother brought every one of his animals by turn into the room, including his favourite pony!

Often during the cold days, *Bichette*, the gazelle, came up to my bedroom and slept on the carpet next to my bed. At six in the morning she used to wake me up by knocking her little horns on the door and I had to get up and let her out.

Sometime in November, the British Fleet, commanded by Admiral Paget, came to Suda Bay, and one of the captains asked my brother whether

---

9.   Venizelos became Prime Minister of Greece in 1911, and served in that office at various times until 1934.

he could give him a wild ibex from the mountains as a mascot for his ship. My brother sent a couple of Cretan gendarmes to get one, and they actually caught a magnificent specimen, which they brought back in triumph. The ibex stayed some time with us tied up in the stable yard. He used to have terrible fights with my brother. Once he ran away, but was caught and brought back again. When he got a bit tamer, he was sent on board the ship where he became as gentle and docile as a lamb. The captain took him later to Portsmouth, where our Cretan ibex walked on parade at the head of the blue-jackets for years.

On Christmas Day of that year my brother and I lunched on *H. M. S. Hood*. The whole ship was beautifully decorated for the occasion. The officers acted a comedy for us, and the blue-jackets sang various songs. Strangely enough, years later during the Great War, I had a sergeant in one of my hospitals at Harrogate who had received the coveted Victoria Cross. This man told me that he had been a blue-jacket in the old days, and had been on board the *Hood* that Christmas Day so many years before. He remembered my brother and me perfectly.

On the last day of December my brother and I left Crete on board *H.M.S. Hussar*, commanded by Captain Maecus Hill, for the island of Milos, where our parents awaited us on board our yacht *Amphitrite*. It was an extremely cold day, and I can never forget the beautiful view of Crete as we left Suda Bay. All the mountains were covered with snow in brilliant sunshine, beneath a dark green stripe of trees, and then that glorious sapphire-coloured sea. It has remained as a picture in my mind. I never saw Crete again.

At Milos we arrived in the afternoon and left that same night for Athens on our yacht. My brother had taken a month's leave to spend Christmas with us at Athens. We still kept the old style calendar[10] in Greece in those days, and our Christmas was a fortnight after the Latin one.

We had a lovely time during the Christmas season. Each of us had a table covered with the most wonderful presents given to us by our parents, especially by Papa. In a big marble hall, called the Hall of Heroes, after the patriots of the Greek War of Independence—who were depicted in a frieze round the wall—stood a huge Christmas tree covered with every sort of decoration and lighted by coloured candles. Our gift tables stood in front of the tree. We all gathered, and in later years all the grandchildren with us, in my mother's drawing room. Between this room and the Hall of Heroes was the Throne Room. When everything was ready my father put out the lights, opened all the doors wide, rang a bell, and then we all rushed to the Christmas tree which shone in the distance so alluringly.

---

10. Greece only adopted the Gregorian Calendar in 1923. Until then the Julian Calendar was officially in use, (e.g., June 12 old style corresponds to June 25 new style, in the XX Century). Grand Duchess George, as did so many writers, used dates without indicating whether they were new or old style. The editors have elected to leave the dates as written, since it would be impossible to verify many of them.

QUEEN ALEXANDRA - 1902
Royal Danish Library

PRINCESS MARIE and GRAND DUKE GEORGE

GRAND DUKE GEORGE

QUEEN MAUD
of Norway
Eilers collection

KING HAAKON VII
(Prince Chalres of Denmark)
Eilers collection

PRINCESS MARIE and GRAND DUKE GEORGE

THE CHRYSTAL HALL - WINTER PALACE
THE HERMITAGE THEATRE
Photos by G. Tantzos

Private dining room of the
Imperial Family - Winter Palace
Photo by G. Tantzos

Баца 188²

GRAND DUKE GEORGE

Chapter V

During Easter week in 1900 we all went to Corfu where my fiancé, Grand Duke George Mikhailovitch, joined us. Both my sister and I married our mother's first cousins. My father's second sister, the Empress Marie Feodorovna, was the sister-in-law of Grand Duke Paul, my sister's husband, who was the youngest brother of Emperor Alexander III; therefore, my sister became her own aunt's sister-in-law! My husband's father was my grandfather's brother. I think I became my own aunt!

Early in May my future father-in-law, the Grand Duke Michael Nicolaievitch, arrived on board a Russian battleship. It was then decided, with the Emperor's permission, that our wedding should take place at Corfu. I was grateful not to have to wear all the grand clothes and jewelry worn by the imperial brides of Russia. My wedding gown was of ordinary white satin, and on my head I wore a small crown which my mother had ordered especially for the occasion. It was made of red velvet on wire; some of her diamonds were sewn onto the velvet and on top of this a small diamond cross was placed, which belonged to me. It was so pretty that we all regretted having it taken to pieces again after the wedding.

From the crown hung my lace bridal veil. We had all worn this priceless veil to our christenings. It was unfortunately burnt a few years later in the Athens palace fire[1].

The marriage took place in a small church in the old Venetian fortress. I drove with my mother in an open carriage over a drawbridge, as the weather was warm, while the bridegroom drove with my father. My train was carried by my brother Christopher, then twelve years old, and my nephew Prince George[2], who was ten. They were both dressed in white sailor suits. The streets were lined by Greek soldiers and Russian sailors; bunting hung everywhere, and the people were enthusiastic.

After the ceremony we went to kneel at the tomb where the relics of St. Spyridon, the patron saint of Corfu, are kept. Then we drove to the palace to receive congratulations from the government and the court, after which there was a state banquet. In the late afternoon we returned to *Mon Repos* to change our clothes and rest. In the evening we had a family dinner.

---

1. The old palace was destroyed in a mysterious fire in 1910, which some thought was an attempted assassination.
2. Later Crown Prince, then King George II of the Hellenes (1890-1947).

I received the most gorgeous jewelry from all the members of my family and from my husband. The gifts were placed on a billiard table and were greatly admired.

That same evening my husband and I left for Sorrento on board my father's yacht. It was an awful moment, leaving my family and my country, to both of which I was passionately devoted. We had an awful passage and everyone was seasick. The trip from Corfu to the Bay of Naples took nearly thirty-six hours.

At Sorrento we stayed at the Hotel Victoria. Every day we made excursions to Amalfi, Capri and Pompei. After ten days we went on to Naples and Rome where we remained for a week. At night we used to go the opera to hear the famous Italian dramatic tenor, Tamagno. We also went to the *Quirinal* to pay our respects to King Humbert and Queen Margherita. I remember the King coming down in the lift to meet us the moment we arrived. They were both most charming and very kind to us. When we left them we went for a drive to the beautiful park of the Villa Doria-Pamphilli where we met Their Majesties driving, too. In those days it was the fashion for everyone to drive in the afternoon through this park in smart carriages. The pleasant custom has been abandoned now that carriages have been discarded for motors.

We also went to Tivoli one day with an Italian friend of ours. We drove there in a landau guarded by two carabinieri on horseback, as the Campagna was not very safe. We visited the lovely Villa D'Este, which still belonged to the Emperor of Austria in those days.

From Rome we travelled to Florence, where we stayed three days before proceeding to Vienna. We also spent a couple of days at Gmunden, which is about five hours from Vienna, to visit my aunt and uncle, the Duke and Duchess of Cumberland, and their children. I had never seen Gmunden before in the springtime and found it very beautiful. We had always been there in the autumn, when it rained constantly.

When we returned to Vienna, we went to see the procession of the Corpus Christi. It was a magnificent sight and I was much impressed. The old Emperor Francis Joseph walked in the procession followed by all the archdukes. Then came the troops; the Emperor's magnificent Hungarian Guard in gorgeous uniforms on white horses, wearing leopard skins flung over their shoulders.

After another five days we left for Russia by way of Warsaw, where we were received at the station by Prince Imeritinsky, Governor General of Poland. The following morning we arrived at Gatchina, a magnificent palace where my widowed aunt, the Empress Marie Feodorovna, resided. As it was seven o'clock in the morning, only my youngest brother-in-law, the Grand Duke Serge Mikhailovitch, was at the station. We drove directly to the palace to change our clothes, and when we were ready were taken in to see the Empress, Aunt Minny, as we called her, with two of her children, Grand

Duke Michael[3] and Grand Duchess Olga[4]. My mother and my [father-in-law] had [also] come to meet us there.

We remained at Gatchina for two hours, and then with my mother and Grand Duke Michael we left for Peterhof, where we were officially received at the station by the Emperor and Empress, and the entire Imperial Family. There was a guard of honour from my husband's regiment, the Lancers, and a military band. I was introduced by the Emperor to various ministers and courtiers. From the station we drove to the Church of Alexandria with Their Majesties for a short service. When this was over we left for my father-in-law's lovely country house called Mikhailovskoe, also on the Baltic coast, where we were to live.

This house, in Italian style, had been built by an Italian architect in the 1840s, when my husband's parents married. Every facade was different, with a lot of terraces and fountains, pergolas and balconies both open and covered. The rooms were charming though a bit old fashioned. Both my daughters were born there. The view from our windows on the garden was very pleasant; there were masses of different kinds of trees, and a lot of lilac bushes, which are particularly lovely in Russia, and beautiful flowers everywhere all around the house as well as in all the rooms. We had a wonderful fruit garden there, too, and every morning the gardener sent us small round flat baskets containing every imaginable luscious fruit. We ate fruit all day.

Not far from the house were the stables, a huge building for a hundred horses, with apartments for all the stable men and their families at the top. In the park, not far from the house, stood a charming chapel.

On our arrival at Mikhailovskoe my grandmother, the Grand Duchess Constantine, came to greet us, bringing me a lovely jewel as a wedding present. My father-in-law gave me a magnificent tiara representing a laurel wreath. The leaves were in diamonds and the berries in rubies. Besides this, he gave me four ropes of pearls with a clasp consisting of a huge, ancient sapphire surrounded by twelve big diamonds. These had belonged to his wife, Grand Duchess Olga, who had died so dramatically ten years before at the station of Kharkov on her way home from the Crimea. From my husband I received a marvellous diamond tiara, representing a wreath of ivy, and a lot of other jewelry which had belonged to his mother.

The next day we went and called on all the relations who lived along the coast, and each presented me with a handsome gift. In the evening we were asked to dinner by Their Majesties who gave me three ropes of pearls,

---

3.   Brother of Emperor Nicholas II, and named Emperor by Nicholas on his abdication in 1917. Grand Duke Michael was probably murdered by the Bolsheviks at Perm, about July 11, 1918.

4.   Sister of Emperor Nicholas II, (June 1, 1882-November 24, 1960). She married first, Prince Peter of Oldenburg, which was annulled in 1916. She married secondly morganatically, Col. Nikolai Koulikovsky, by whom she had two children. Grand Duchess Olga died in Toronto, Canada.

also with a sapphire and diamond clasp, and a big diamond and sapphire brooch to go with it. I was quite overwhelmed by all these riches. Certainly I had had a few brooches of my own before, and one beautiful rope of pearls which had belonged to my grandmother, Queen Louise, which my father gave me.

A fortnight after our arrival in Russia we had to go to Petersburg for an official reception at my father-in-law's palace on the quay. It was on this occasion that I wore for the first time the Russian court dress with the *kokoshnik*. First we received each ambassador and his wife, then the rest of the *Corps Diplomatique* together. They all stood in a row with their secretaries and attachés behind them. They were introduced to me by the Master of Ceremonies of the Tsar's court, Count Henrikov. We had to speak to each person in turn. I remember playing a joke on Count Henrikov. I told him that I was terribly shy and frightened and would very likely have a nervous breakdown and run away. I got him into an awful state of anxiety and he did his best to calm and encourage me. As a matter of fact, I was terrified, but having done this kind of thing before I knew I could live through it. When it was over and I had done my best to air as many languages as I possibly could (even speaking a bit of Danish, which I had only learned by ear), Count Henrikov came and paid me a compliment; so I had to own to him that as I had been dreading the ordeal myself it made me feel happier to know that he was equally terrified[5].

After the Diplomatic Circle, I stood with my husband in the large hall at the top of the marble staircase while ladies of the society, officers and various other people, passed by and kissed my hand. I remember one lady, the wife of Admiral Makarov, who was terribly shortsighted. She passed in front of me and went straight ahead, ignoring me completely. I burst out laughing in the face of the lady following her and she did the same. Count Henrikov rushed after Madame Makarov and brought her back again, to everybody's amusement.

During all that summer we lived a quiet family life, meeting our relations very often. My Cousin Xenia, who was now also my sister-in-law, was living at Peterhof in the Park of Alexandria, not far from her mother's cottage, in a house called *The Farm*. It [was formerly] inhabited by Emperor Alexander II, and my father, on one of his earlier visits to Russia, had seen this house and liked it so much that he had built a replica of it at Tatoi. This helped to make Xenia's house like a second home to me. I frequently drove over there as well as to her mother's cottage.

In August, the Emperor and Empress invited us and my brother Nicholas, who was staying with us, to the military manoeuvres at a place called Luga. We lived in the Imperial train, which was most comfortable and great fun. Near the train was built a long wooden platform on which we could sit in the afternoons as the train was very hot. In the mornings we all started on horseback to see the troops and the movements of the army. I

---

5.   By the end of her life, she spoke seven languages.

78

rode my beloved cob, Champion, which had come from home with my brother. Though he had never heard a shot in his life, Champion never flinched and behaved beautifully throughout. That precious friend—because he was truly a personality—lived to be more than twenty-five years old. He had the most perfect action; never did I have a horse like that again. He did not like other people to ride him, and at home in Tatoi both my father and eldest brother had had unpleasant experiences with him. He only really liked me and my youngest brother Christopher.

During these manoeuvres we usually had lunch under an enormous tent put up for the Tsar, his guests and the officers of high rank. The plates and mugs to drink out of were all of silver so that nothing could break. In the afternoon we would go for walks with the Emperor and Empress in the lovely woods nearby. One day we discovered a lake and got hold of a boat and rowed about in it. After five days we left, and I was awfully sorry as we really had enjoyed ourselves.

In early September my husband and I went to Denmark on a visit to my grandfather. Many members of the family were already there: my father, his three sisters, Aunt Alix, Aunt Minny, Aunt Thyra[6], the Duchess of Cumberland, along with a number of cousins. As it was my husband's first visit to Denmark, the family insisted upon showing him everything of interest. We remained about three weeks and then travelled to Spala, the Tsar's shooting-box in Poland. At the station we were received by Grand Duke Michael, and my brother Nicholas, who was shooting with them. The house was about six miles away, through a lovely pine forest. That same evening we left with Their Majesties and their children, in the private train, for Sevastopol.

It took us three days to get to Sevastopol, where we immediately boarded the imperial yacht *Standart*. There was a tremendous reception at the station, as was always the case when the Tsar appeared anywhere. The yacht was most luxurious and comfortable and we sailed for Yalta in the early morning and saw some naval manoeuvres taking place in the Black Sea. That afternoon, at Yalta, we drove to *Ai-Todor*, Xenia's house, where we remained until November. The next day my brother George arrived as a guest of the Tsar.

My husband had bought a small bit of land not far from *Ai-Todor*, on a high cliff just above the sea. The view over the whole of the Black Sea was glorious, but I must honestly confess that when my husband took my brother and me to show us the place, I sat on a rock and cried with despair at the thought of having to live there. This bit of land was an enormous mass of rocks and stones, with here and there a small crooked oak tree, sprung up from the original trunks which had been hewn down by the Tartars, to whom the place had belonged. One risked one's life if one attempted to get

---

6.   Youngest daughter of King Christian IX, sister of King George I, Queen Alexandra and Empress Marie, (1853-1933). In 1878, she married the Duke of Cumberland, de jure King of Hanover.

down to the sea by a steep narrow path used mostly by goats. In later years we turned this wild place into a lovely garden.

Towards the end of October we left with my mother and Christopher for Athens. When we arrived my brother Constantine and his family welcomed us, as my father was still abroad, and Constantine was acting as Regent during his absence. It is difficult to describe my joy at being home again among my own family and all my old friends. Those three months I spent in Athens passed all too quickly. It was a gay winter, and we went about quite a lot to dinners and dances in town.

When we left in January 1901, my sister-in-law Sophie came with us on her way to Friedrichshof, at Kronberg, not far from Bad Homburg, to visit her mother, Empress Frederick, who was very seriously ill. The Empress died only a few months later. My father started from Athens with us this time on his way to Corfu; but just as we passed the Isthmus of Corinth we received news of Queen Victoria's death, so Papa had to disembark at Patras and return to Athens, [to go on to London] for the Queen's funeral.

My husband and I, with Sophie, remained a few days in Vienna where I again saw my Aunt Thyra. The Cumberlands lived in Vienna in winter at their palace, called Penzing.

I had never been out of Greece in the winter before, and I could not quite picture to myself what the North would look like under frost and snow. I had a good exhibition of it as we approached the Russian capital. We arrived very early in the morning, and Xenia and all my husband's family, with our court, received us at the station of St. Petersburg. We drove straight to my father-in-law's palace.

To see this big town under snow was very exciting. Streets were full of funny little low sleds drawn by one horse; and everybody seemed to be smothered in furs of all descriptions. All the coachmen wore long beards like so many Father Christmases as even their swarthy beards were covered with hoar-frost. In various corners of the streets people stood around warming themselves at big cauldrons filled with red hot coals. What struck me most of all was the silence which cloaked the great city; in the snow-filled streets even the horses' hoofs made no noise as they struck the stone pavements.

When we arrived in our new home my father-in-law took us to our new apartments. I had seen them, of course, in the summer; but now they looked very nice with their winter carpets and furniture. I had to work hard though for quite a long time to make the rooms really liveable, and it was lucky that this was so: if I had not been so busy I should have suffered even more than I did from homesickness. Our palace—also on the quay by the Neva, not far from the Winter Palace—was a colossal building. In fact, my husband's youngest brother Serge, who lived quite at the other end of the house, always bicycled from his rooms to ours. There was a grand marble staircase leading to our floor, and opposite our apartment were the numerous state rooms. The furniture was rather Victorian looking and stiff. The apartment had been furnished in 1857 for my father-in-law's marriage.

All the state rooms had the most beautiful parquet floors like those of the other palaces of Petersburg, inlaid with rarest woods of different colours in lovely designs.

Two of my husband's unmarried brothers, as well as my father-in-law, lived in this palace; they were the Grand Dukes Nicholas and Serge Mikhailovitch. We always had meals with my father-in-law. Dinner was a family meal without the ladies and gentlemen in attendance, and we gathered for it in my father-in-law's rooms. Luncheon was a state meal with all the court in attendance in a huge dining room, the walls of which were covered with beautiful Cordova leather. From this room one had a superb view of the Neva with the fortress of Sts. Peter and Paul on the other side. I did not much enjoy those luncheons because I always had to sit opposite my father-in-law and had various old generals as neighbours—which was not very amusing. At home in Athens we always had our meals *en famille*.

On the day of our arrival we went for tea to Aunt Minny, in her palace of Anitchkov, on the famous street called Nevsky Prospekt. This was a charming palace with a big courtyard. The Empress' rooms were filled with beautiful pictures and wonderful objets d'art. I would visit her often because I loved her and felt that she, as well as her children, belonged to my private family. She was just like a mother to me, and made no difference between me and her own children.

Aunt Minny was not very tall but she held herself in such a way that she could never have been taken for anything but a Empress. Though not strictly pretty, she had wonderful velvety brown eyes, dark hair, and a personal charm that captivated every one she met. Although extremely feminine, she was a woman of enormous courage, as she had abundant opportunities to prove during the Bolshevik revolution. She rode splendidly, and drove a four-in-hand or a pair with equal facility. Aunt Minny was really human, like all the Danish family, and consequently was most popular and beloved in her adopted country.

The first few days after our arrival in St. Petersburg were spent in calling on our relatives, which was a considerable undertaking, as the family was so numerous. After our first visit to my Aunt Marie, we went to the Emperor and Empress at the Winter Palace.

This palace was a real labyrinth, with endless suites of rooms of every description and size. Most of the private apartments of the preceding Tsars had been left exactly as they were when they were last lived in, so that one could easily picture their taste and mode of living.

The Emperor and Empress' rooms were magnificent in every way. They were very large with huge windows, and the walls were covered with pictures by famous artists old and new. The Tsar had the right to take any picture he fancied from the Hermitage Museum and hang it in his apartments. Besides these, one saw at every turn the most priceless treasures and objets d'art of every kind which defy description. The young Empress, who had a passion for flowers, surrounded herself by them in every room—and beautiful they were indeed, as the imperial hot-houses and gardens were incomparable.

In the midst of all these treasures and luxuries Nicholas and Alexandra lived an ideal family life, as homely and simple as that of any ordinary person. They were utterly devoted to each other and adored their children. When I arrived in Russia, they had three daughters, the eldest, Olga, being five years old. The Emperor, as I have mentioned before, was my first cousin, and my favourite one as well; we had been great friends since our earliest childhood.

Emperor Nicholas II was short in stature but very well proportioned. He had brown hair, but his beard was much lighter; his eyes were the most wonderful I have ever seen. All his soul seemed to be in them and he captivated everyone by the look in his eyes. I sincerely believe that there never did live such a kind, good, generous and patient man. He was the prototype of the perfect gentleman. People have said that he had no will and was weak in character. This was solely the result of his inveterate modesty. He always thought that his advisors knew better than he did. His first opinion or decision was always correct; but thanks to this modesty he often changed his opinion and followed the lead of those who counselled him. He loved his country above anything on earth and sacrificed everything he valued on its altar. This he proved for all time by his unspeakable death. He had the softest heart of anybody I have known and the good he did, right and left, unknown to anyone, was quite incredible.

The Emperor also had a great sense of humour and enjoyed the funny side of life—which was fortunate, as it helped him to bear his heavy responsibilities. He loved sport, especially riding, tennis and swimming, and was a very good shot.

The Empress, Alexandra Feodorovna, was tall, with light hair, darkish blue eyes and a very pretty face. Her character is very difficult to describe. Of a most retiring nature and rather silent, she was extremely shy and self-conscious and owing to this she was often misunderstood. She was over sensitive, and in a way haunted by the notion that she was unpopular and unloved. She persisted in this fixed idea even with members of the family. She was a most devoted wife; indeed, she so loved her husband that she even disliked hearing him go over his childhood memories with his sister and myself, since she had not been present.

Yet, sometimes, in the intimate circle of the immediate family, she could be quite gay and amusing. I know that in most publications concerning the Empress she has been accused of many thoughts and deeds which probably never entered her mind. So sad was her own disposition that people in distress appealed more to her than did happy folk. Her devotion to her children was extraordinary—especially to her sick boy, the Tsarevich—and she gave most of her time to them. She did not like the worldly part of life. Balls, receptions and audiences were a real ordeal to her. She occupied herself a lot with charity, and no one ever asked her help in vain.

Whatever has been said to the contrary I am absolutely certain that the Empress adored her adoptive country. She spoke and even wrote the Russian language perfectly; she loved the Russian culture and the Russian religion, and she had no interests outside of Russia.

My eldest brother-in-law, Nicholas, was a strange mixture. He was a highly cultured man, and a mischievous child at once. He was very tall and bald, with a short dark square beard, and on the whole rather good-looking. In his youth he had wished to marry his cousin, Princess Victoria of Baden[7], but as marriages between first cousins are prohibited in our Church, he had to give her up. He never married. He was a great historian and wrote a biography of the Empress Elizabeth Alexeievna, wife of Emperor Alexander I, besides other books. I remember him showing me a lot of the documents he had taken out of the Imperial Archives for studying, and how very interesting they were: intimate letters and personal papers of the Empress.

My youngest brother-in-law, Serge, who was one of my best friends in Russia, was more than six feet three inches in height and, unlike the other brothers, was very blond with blue eyes like his father. He was a soldier and worked very hard at military affairs; art and history did not interest him much. Serge was extremely clever; but he was decidedly ugly though very attractive. I once asked him why he was so ugly and he answered, "That is my charm!" His sense of the ridiculous was extremely keen, and many a time [he and I] got into trouble because of our love of laughter. My husband and Serge had a dreadful habit of walking up and down in my room while they were talking. I [moved] chairs and tables in such a way that the two of them had to manoeuvre unconsciously as they talked to keep from bumping into the furniture. But even this did not break them of the habit.

There was a huge palace just outside Petersburg called *Smolny* which the Empress Marie, wife of Paul I, had turned into a *Pension de Jeunes Filles* for daughters of the nobility. Here the two elder daughters of the Prince of Montenegro, later King Nicholas, were brought up. The eldest, Militza, was married in 1889 to the Grand Duke Peter Nicolaievitch, and the second, Anastasia, to Prince George of Leuchtenberg, whom she divorced to marry Grand Duke Nicholas Nicolaievitch. These two ladies were not very popular in the family and were of a quite different mentality. They were extremely well read and clever, but very ambitious. For some years they were great friends with the young Empress, but their influence was not for the best.

My husband and Peter, his first cousin, had been inseparable friends since their childhood and youth, but after the latter's marriage, the friendship cooled off, owing to Militza, and they seldom met, much to my husband's disappointment.

The Grand Duke Nicholas Nicolaievitch was a good-looking man of huge stature, and wore a short, pointed beard on his slightly protruding jaw.

---

7.   Princess Victoria married King Gustaf V of Sweden in 1881. Their eldest son, Gustaf Adolf, was married to Princess Margaret of Connaught, while their second son, William, married Grand Duchess Marie Pavlovna of Russia (daughter of Princess Alexandra and Grand Duke Paul), Marie's niece.

I cannot say that I knew him very intimately, because he was much older than I was and we never really met very often. When we did it was usually on official occasions or rare visits. He was a real soldier and did not care about social life. Sport, hunting and shooting were his passions, and whenever he could get away from his military service he used to go to the country. His great hobby was collecting old china, and he possessed a large number of unique pieces. One could not describe him as being particularly brilliant, nor was he very popular while he commanded the Guards, before the war, because he was terribly severe and rather hard. His loyalty to his sovereign was deeply rooted and unquestionable in spite of rumours to the contrary, which were spread during the war for purposes of propaganda.

The most lovable of the Grand Dukes was my cousin Michael, the Emperor's youngest brother. He was only four years younger than myself and we were the best of friends. He loved sport in all its forms and was very agile and athletic. Extremely musical he played several instruments. He always lived with his mother, being a bachelor, and he only married—morganatically—a few years before the war. When I used to stay at Gatchina, Misha, as he was called, and I used to ride a lot together and he also drove me about in his tandem. He drove over everything, bogs, fields and bad roads, to see what I would do. I only asked him to remember that I had two small children at home and was still needed. He and his younger sister, Olga, were inseparable chums and it was touching to see them together. He was most amusing, had the kindest heart imaginable, and was a general favourite. He was murdered by the Bolsheviks.

My husband could not serve in the army because of a bad leg, so the Emperor made him Director of the Museum in memory of Emperor Alexander III. In organizing this new institution my husband had a great deal of work to do. The Museum itself was an old palace which had belonged to the Grand Duke Michael, son of Emperor Paul, and had been bought by Emperor Nicholas II for this purpose. It contained pictures, sculptures and ethnologic collections. It was a more or less private institution and belonged to the court, though it was open to the public. Since his boyhood my husband had been interested in old coins, and for many years he collected them assiduously. When we married he already possessed a very large and well-known numismatic collection which he kept in our palace, but as it was continually augmenting there was eventually no more room for it; so he transported the entire collection to his museum. This did not keep him from working at it constantly and cataloguing it himself. He used to work at the coins for hours at a time. The collection consisted of only Russian coins and medals, and some of them were unique.

All the Grand Dukes were personal aides-de-camp to the Tsar and several times a month they had to be on duty at the Winter Palace or at Tsarskoe-Selo for twenty-four hours. On those days the Grand Duchesses were usually invited to lunch, tea and dinner by Their Majesties. I always looked forward to those days as we used to have great fun. I was especially pleased when we had to go to Tsarskoe-Selo, as I loved the country. In the mornings I often played on two pianos with the Empress; and in the afternoons we all went in small sleds in the park, or, when the long winter was over, we drove and walked.

The winter of 1901 passed quietly; there were no receptions at court owing to the death of Queen Victoria, who was the young Empress' grandmother. I had Russian lessons every morning, but I did not enjoy them very much as they reminded me of the schoolroom. The one thing I did find delightful was my first drive in a sled. I had never even set eyes on a vehicle of that kind before. The sleds in Russia were very low and the driver sat on a seat practically on one's knees. The horses were covered by a large flowing net to keep them from kicking the snow and ice into one's face.

The winters, especially that first one, seemed interminable to me. I shall never forget my first Easter in St. Petersburg. In our Church we always have midnight mass for Easter, and I remember that while I was dressing to go to this service at the Winter Palace, it started snowing hard. I was so upset that I cried. At home, in Greece, Easter is always the beginning of spring, with quantities of flowers everywhere, and all the lilacs are blooming. In Greek, the lilac is named after Easter, and here I was still in the midst of winter!

The service at the Winter Palace was magnificent and the Imperial choir quite heavenly. Those who have not been lucky enough to hear the Tsar's private choir have heard nothing in church music. No words can ever describe those voices.

The Grand Duchess Serge[8] happened to be staying in St. Petersburg the first winter I spent there. Her husband was Governor General of Moscow and they did not come very often to the capital. A few days after my arrival the Grand Duchess called and took me out for a walk on the quay. I had a special love for her ever since I first met her in Athens at the time of my sister's engagement. She had been particularly kind and sweet to me, and we remained friends ever after.

Grand Duchess Serge, Ella, was one of the loveliest women of her time. She had the most perfectly shaped head, just like a statue, and perfect features. Her complexion was like a rose petal, and she never used cosmetics or powder. When she appeared at a ball she was simply radiant, always beautifully dressed, and wearing her wonderful jewelry as nobody else possibly could. I was devoted to her and through all the years I knew her she was always the same kind and dear friend. Staying with her at her husband's beautiful country place, Ilyinskoe, near Moscow, was a delight. She made one feel completely at home and one was always free to do what one wished. She was simplicity itself, took part in all the fun and did everything in her power to give her guests a good time.

The Grand Duke Serge was not very popular, I am afraid; but I personally liked him, as he was particularly nice and kind to me always. He

---

8.   Elisabeth, known as Ella, was the wife of Grand Duke Serge Alexandrovitch, and sister of Empress Alexandra.

was tall, fair and good-looking, but inclined to be a bit unbending; this gave the impression that he was grand and 'stuck-up'. This did not keep him from being a very good friend to those he loved. He adored children, and as he had none of his own, I believe it had a hardening effect on him. I speak of the Grand Duke Serge as I knew and liked him, and not of the stern disciplinarian who was feared by all who came under his authority. The public Grand Duke Serge—the autocrat feared and hated by the revolutionaries—was not the Serge I knew.

During my first winter in Russia my niece, Marie Pavlovna, and her brother, Dimitri, would come and spend Sundays with me. Marie was ten years old and Dimitri nine. Sometimes I took them to the circus, which we all three enjoyed very much.

We used to go nearly every night to the theatre. There were many superb theatres in old Russia, including the Marie (Mariinsky) Theatre for opera and ballet; the Alexander Theatre for the Russian drama; and the Michel Theatre for the French drama. Every Saturday night a new French piece was given, and it was our habit in the family to meet there. Many of the best known French actors and actresses started their careers in the Michel Theatre: Lucien Guitry, for example, his son Sacha, André Brulé, Suzanne Meunte, and others. On Sunday nights the famous Imperial Ballet Corps, the pride of the Russian stage, gave performances.

In April we went for a short stay at Gatchina with [Aunt Minny]. After her husband's death, the Empress spent the spring and often all summer there. Earlier, Gatchina was only used as a shooting-box; and strangely enough the family chose to live in the entresol, which was originally intended for the servants. I suppose they wished to have a complete change from all their luxurious apartments in their numerous palaces. These rooms were very cosy and attractive, with ceilings so low that Emperor Alexander III could easily touch them by stretching up his arms. Guests were lodged in the usual big rooms above this unpretentious entresol. There was a huge courtyard in the centre of the castle, open on one side to the park. There too, as at Pavlovsk, stood a life-size bronze statue of Emperor Paul. As in the other palaces, the apartments of that Emperor and his wife, Marie Feodorovna, were left just as they were in the old days.

The Empress Marie Feodorovna (not to be confused with my aunt, who bore the same name) was a Princess of Württemberg. She was very gifted and used to draw very well; she also worked in ivory, and quite a lot of her things were still standing about at Gatchina. There was also a beautiful *Sèvres* toilet set given to her by her contemporary, Queen Marie Antoinette, when Emperor Paul and [she] travelled to Paris and Italy under the names of Comte et Comtesse du Nord.

The park at Gatchina was simply magnificent. There were several lakes with small islands in them; on some of these were built lovely little pavilions where we sometimes had tea. The prettiest was called *Pavilion de l'Amour*, and was delicately painted throughout, with a big marble table in the middle.

My aunt and cousins loved fishing in these lakes, and we used to stand for hours on the bridges or in the grass angling for carp, pike and various other kinds of fish, which to my way of thinking tasted of mud.

Later on in the summer we [would] go for picnics in the woods all around Gatchina, and on these occasions we cooked our own food. Often we would invent new dishes which sometimes turned out very well. I remember being told to peel the onions; they were rude enough to insinuate that I, as a Greek, would be accustomed to them! One cook, generally the Empress' chef, was allowed to supervise us for safety's sake.

In May of that same year we went to our country place, Mikhailovskoe. My mother and my brother Christopher arrived from Athens to stay with us. That summer, I remember, was terribly hot and we practically lived out of doors, having all our meals on the balcony.

On June 18, 1901, the fourth daughter of the Emperor and Empress was born, and was given the name of Anastasia. She was born at Peterhof in that same *Villa Baboon* where I had stayed as a child in 1886. And two days later, on the 20th of June, my daughter Nina made her appearance.

My baby was a lovely child with big brown eyes, wonderful eyebrows and dark hair. A fortnight later she was christened. In church, the parents are not supposed to be present at their children's christening and the godparents take their place. I dressed up smartly and waited upstairs in my room on the sofa. Later all the family came up with my baby to congratulate us. The Emperor and his mother were the chief godparents, the others being my grandmother, Grand Duchess Constantine; my brother-in-law, Serge; my sister-in-law, Grand Duchess Anastasia[9]; my sister-in-law, Sophie; my father; and my grandfather, the King of Denmark. The three last named were unable to be at Mikhailovskoe for the occasion. They all presented me with beautiful gifts of jewelry. Our baby was very much admired by everybody, and I felt very proud.

In August, my father-in-law, Papa Michel, as Xenia and I called him, had to go to the Caucasus for the centenary of its union with Russia. As he had been for some twenty-five years Viceroy in that country, the Emperor sent him as his representative for the festivities. We decided to accompany him because my husband was born near Tiflis and loved the Caucasus more than any other province. My mother, my two younger brothers, Andrew and Christopher, came too, as well as the Grand Duchess Helen Vladimirovna, who later married my brother Nicholas.

We went from Novorosiysk to Batum across the Black Sea in one night. From Batum we took a train to the big estate of my father-in-law called *Borjom*, about three hours distance from Tiflis. This estate, which was

---

9.   Grand Duchess Anastasia Mikhailovna, married to Grand Duke Friedrich Franz III of Mecklenburg-Schwerin. They had one son and two daughters: Alexandrine, who married King Christian X of Denmark (son of Grand Duchess Marie's first cousin, King Frederick VIII) and Cecilie, who married Crown Prince Wilhelm of Germany, son of Kaiser Wilhelm II.

about the size of Holland, had been given to my father-in-law by his brother, Emperor Alexander II, as a recompense for all the Grand Duke's work in the union and pacification of the Causasus.

Borjom was a magnificent place in the mountains, with healing waters which drew people to it from all parts of Russia. The house, a large two-storied structure of wood, was quite comfortable. For the suites there was another wooden house in the garden nearby.

Our house stood on a small hill above the public road; on a lower level still was the river Kura. The scenery was magnificent with dense woods and mountains, a bit like the Semmering in Austria, only on a much grander scale.

There was splendid shooting at Borjom—stags, buck and ibex. The latter were to be found on a high rocky hill, just at the back of the house. We could often see them disporting themselves on the rocks. They were terribly wild and shy and extremely difficult to get at.

My brother-in-law Nicholas had a villa standing in a small valley, just above a bend in the river, built in Italian style with a tower. He had a powerful electric lamp on this tower to attract butterflies and other insects, and had a wonderful collection of them.

After a short stay at Borjom, we all went to Tiflis for the festivities. We stayed at the Palace, where my husband had lived his childhood and youth. This place was always inhabited by the Governor General of the Caucasus. It was a charming and roomy house in a beautiful garden. The festivities started by a grand *Te Deum* in the famous old cathedral of Tiflis, and all the Caucasian clans, of which there are, I believe, over one hundred, had gathered for the occasion. They wore the most extraordinary and varied national dress. Unfortunately, except for the neighbourhood of Tiflis, no women of the Caucasus came.

There were so many people that huge tables had to be erected on a field, just outside the town, for them to have a grand meal. Each clan occupied one or two tables. We all went out to see them. An entire ox's skin was brought along in a kind of barrow on wheels, filled with a special Caucasian wine called *Kahetinsky*. A man with a long silver ladle, *Asarpesh*, gave wine to all the guests. My father-in-law drank to the health of all those present, and the enthusiasm and excitement of these wild-looking people was intense.

I remember one clan which was particularly interesting because they were supposed to be direct descendants of the Crusaders who had passed by the mountains of the Caucasus and become stranded there. They were called *Hefsury*, and wore their historic costumes, consisting of a kind of rough dark blue and red stuff with small white crosses on their chest, underneath their armour. On their heads small metal helmets surmounted by a cross, and chain-mail over their faces. They were armed with a short flat sword and shield. They even gave us an exhibition of a fight, which was weird.

These various festivities ended with a gala performance at the opera when all the clansmen were invited and the sight was very picturesque indeed. During a state ball, I saw the *Lesguinka* danced by members of the Tiflis society; it is an extremely graceful dance. I took some lessons in it, but had to give it up as a bad job.

Soon after the festivities, my mother and two brothers returned to Greece from Batum on board their yacht. My husband and I and our baby Nina returned to Borjom, where we remained until the end of November for the shooting, when my husband used to start at four o'clock in the morning and stalk stags all over the mountains until the afternoon. I got myself a Caucasian pony and accompanied by a Cossack explored the country.

Towards the end of our stay it became very cold and the country was covered with snow. One afternoon we went sledding and on our way home my husband, who was never without his rifle, saw a huge stag standing at the edge of the wood. He aimed and down came the glorious animal. Our baby, who was just going by at that moment with her English nurse, also in a sled, seeing this started a terrible uproar, and although she was only five months old she would have nothing to do with her father for a couple of days.

We returned to St. Petersburg by train, passing by Baku, famous for its oil-wells. I thought it a horrible place, it reminded me of Gustave Doré's illustrations for Dante's *Inferno*. Everything was black and shiny and the all-pervading smell of the petroleum very obnoxious.

GRAND DUKE CONSTANTINE - 1915
(Uncle of Author)

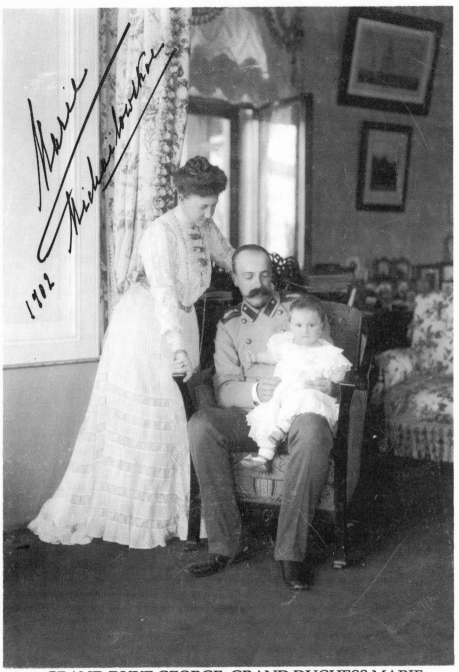

GRAND DUKE GEORGE, GRAND DUCHESS MARIE,
with PRINCESS NINA

PRINCE NICHOLAS (brother of author)
and PRINCESS HELEN
Eilers collection

GRAND DUCHESS MARIE PAVLOVNA
Niece of Author

PRINCESS NINA, GRAND DUCHESS MARIE, PRINCESS XENIA

Chapter VI

The Christmas of 1901 was the first I ever spent away from Greece. It all seemed very different in Russia, and I missed my family more than ever. One great compensation was that we had our baby. I can never forget her excitement on seeing her first Christmas tree, with all its twinkling candles and gay ornaments.

On New Year's Day there was a great reception at the Winter Palace, where Their Majesties received congratulations. We all had to appear in court dress, with the *Kokoshnik*, before eleven o'clock in the morning, which was rather an ordeal. We all met in Their Majesties' private drawing room. From there we walked in procession to church for mass. It took quite a time to get there, as we had to walk through endless halls crammed with people who bowed and curtseyed to us as we passed the Malachite Hall. The walls and columns of this vast room were entirely covered with malachite, a bright yellowish green stone from Siberia.

On official occasions—the first of January, as at marriages or christenings—we all had pages to hold our trains. Each Grand Duchess had one and the Empress had two. These pages were young men of the Russian nobility, future officers in the army. The final, or graduating class of the military school was called the *Corps des Pages*, and supplied these young gentlemen in attendance. At the end of a year they became officers, and each Grand Duchess presented her page with a gold watch bearing her monogram.

The season started after New Year's Day; receptions and balls succeeded each other at the Winter Palace in a series of splendours that seemed like a fairy-tale. All those magnificent halls, beautifully illuminated by huge crystal chandeliers were filled with exquisitely dressed ladies and resplendent officers in the uniforms of the Guards and other regiments. Supper was generally in a spacious room called the Nicholas Hall. The whole place was turned into a grove of palm trees, under which stood small round tables for six or eight people, covered with flowers and priceless silver.

At the palace balls the ladies sat at supper with their cotillion partners. The Tsar did not sit down at once, but went from table to table talking to his guests. After a while he joined a table, next to some lady previously decided upon, where his place had been kept for him.

On other occasions during the season there were performances in the lovely little theatre of The Hermitage Museum. This theatre was built in a semicircle with seats going upwards in the style of the ancient Greek amphitheaters. After the performances there we used to dance.

In the days of the Empress Catherine II, and even before, the waters of the River Neva were considered very healthy for drinking. Every morning a special courier was sent from St. Petersburg to Tsarskoe-Selo, or wherever the [Tsar] happened to be, with Neva water. This tradition was kept up till the fall of the Empire. Count Benkendorff, the Master of the Grand Court, told me personally that he had done all in his power to put a stop to this ridiculous habit, but was unable to do so. Another tradition was that whenever there was a great reception or feast at the Great Court, a bottle of vinegar was always kept handy, because one of the Empresses had, centuries ago, felt faint and asked for some. After a wedding banquet, when the polonaise was danced, a card table, with candles and cards, always stood at the end of the room because Empress Catherine had once expressed the wish to play cards on a similar occasion, and the soldiers of the first battalion of the Paul Regiment of the Guards—named after Emperor Paul I—were all chosen from men whose noses had an upward tilt, because the Emperor's nose had been that way!

I had to give audiences several times a week to ladies of St. Petersburg society. I used to receive them one at a time, unless it was a mother with her daughters, in one of the state rooms opposite our apartment. I hated these rooms because they were so old fashioned and stiff. My father-in-law had told me to rearrange them in my own way, but when he saw the changes I made he was very much upset, and everything had to be put back again as before. I only insisted upon having the part where I had to sit with the ladies arranged as I pleased.

These audiences lasted for a couple of hours; and sometimes the two or three hours seemed like as many years. I remember one day, just before my lady-in-waiting came to tell me that the audiences were to begin, I got up onto a small settee in my room to arrange something on a bracket on the wall. At the foot of the settee I had a large wolf-skin, given to me by Prince Youssoupov. Getting down from my perch I involuntarily put my foot on the animals enormous head, lost my balance, and fell in such a way that I sprained my ankle very badly and could not get up. At that very moment my lady-in-waiting appeared at the door; she was frightened at seeing me on the floor, ran to help me, tripped, fell and also hurt her foot. With much pain and trouble we managed to get up and drag ourselves to the audience room. By the time the last lady left, my foot had become so swollen and painful that I had to be carried to my sofa and a masseur sent for. I was on crutches for two days.

In the spring of 1902 we spent Easter at Athens with my family. While there we took a passenger ship which plied between Egypt, Greece and Odessa. It always stopped for a day at Constantinople and the passengers were able to visit the fascinating old Greco-Turkish city. The Emperor sent word to my husband that as we were going to Constantinople we should pay an official visit to the Sultan, Abdul Hamid II, of notorious memory. He was one of the cleverest and cruellest sovereigns of modern Turkey. The Sultan had been informed of our arrival and sent one of his generals on board to greet us. My husband had to don his full dress uniform and I one of the smartest gowns I had with me, and we left for the Yildiz-Kiosk in an elegant carriage.

It took us about three quarters of an hour to get there through very dirty and muddy streets. I remember passing by some barracks where the guard came out to salute us; the men stood in the mud up to their ankles, and the officer on duty stood on a board in front of them, but as the board was too narrow he had to stand sidewise to fit on it. It was a ridiculous sight, but also rather painful because the poor fellows' uniforms were in rags.

As soon as we entered the beautiful park which surrounded the Yildiz-Kiosk we found cleanliness and order. The troops here, at the Imperial household, were splendidly dressed and smartly drilled. We drove to the palace where the Sultan was awaiting us in a great hall, surrounded by hundreds of generals and courtiers in full dress; all were wearing the Turkish headgear, a red fez. We shook hands with His Majesty, who offered me his left arm and took me round the hall, introducing all the people present. It was most awkward shaking hands under such conditions, since my right arm was clasped in the Sultan's.

After this promenade we were taken into a private apartment and offered Turkish coffee with excellent cigarettes. We had to talk through an interpreter as His Majesty could not, or would not, speak any foreign language.

Abdul Hamid II was not very tall, but he made a very striking figure with his dyed beard and hair, his painted cheeks, cruel dark eyes and a nose hooked like that of a bird of prey. He wore, of course, the usual fez. It was July and the heat intense; nevertheless His Majesty was muffled in a thick military coat and galoshes to which were attached golden spurs. Under his uniform he wore a coat of mail as protection against possible assassination that was the terror of his life. His every movement made this armour creak in a most audible fashion.

After a short interview, we were driven to another palace in the vicinity, where we were told to await the Sultan on his return call. A few minutes after our arrival there His Majesty appeared in a barouche drawn by a superb pair of Russian trotters, a present from the Emperor, which he drove himself. We met him at the entrance and the same ceremony as before was repeated. He asked us to dine with him and then went away. We were told to consider this palace as our own and to take a rest there. Just before we were ready to proceed to dinner, His Majesty sent us decorations, his Grand Cross, a ribbon and star. Of course we were expected to appear wearing these, which we did.

All the guests met in a small drawing room on the first floor. The furniture was atrocious gilt stuff covered with bright red or green brocade.

Both the Russian and Greek Ministers had been invited for the occasion. After a few minutes the Sultan arrived and gave me his arm—the right one this time—to go into dinner. I was the only lady present. My husband and I sat on either side of our host behind whose chair stood the interpreter. The table was covered with marvellous gold plate and flowers; the servants were in gold-braided red liveries and wore the inevitable fez. There were a great many guests, but of course I knew none of them. The Greek Minister told me that the food was brought in from an hotel. The Sultan kept no cooks for his guests and only a special, trusted chef for himself, as he was in constant fear of being poisoned. One servant brought special dishes for his Royal Master; each of these had been tasted before it was brought in.

The Sultan was most amiable and inquired after my parents; then he asked if I had any children. When I told him we had a twelve- month-old baby travelling with us, he asked whether he might send her some presents. Naturally I accepted with thanks. He invited us to return two days later to see the usual Friday ceremony, the *Salaamlik*.

When dinner was over he gave me one arm and tucked his napkin under the other, and we walked downstairs preceded by the Master of Ceremonies, who had to crawl backwards down the steps, salaaming to his Sovereign. I expected to see this unfortunate man topple over at any moment, and told the Sultan so, but he only grunted and did not seem to care what happened to him.

We drove back to the ship soon afterwards. Early the next morning, the same delightful old general who had originally received us, arrived with a huge cypress-wood box containing the Sultan's present for my child. We were terribly excited to see what was in it. Our astonishment was equal to our disappointment when we found it full of smaller boxes containing Turkish delight and hard sweets. This was the last gift expected for a child. Since we had asked the captain of our ship to postpone his departure for three days, the passengers were naturally dissatisfied; so we offered them all the Sultan's sweets, with the result that content was restored all round.

That day we went with our Turkish general visiting all the Sultan's magnificent palaces and treasures of the crown. These latter were kept at a palace on a hill called *Topkapi*. There were cupboards full of the old costumes of all the preceding sultans and their glorious turbans plastered with precious stones of every colour and dimension. At Topkapi we were taken on to a huge terrace from which one could see the whole Bosphorus and the Golden Horn. I have seldom beheld such a glorious natural spectacle.

They served us coffee in cups set into wonderful gold filigree vessels like egg cups, with precious stones all over them.

Later that day we went to call on the Greek Orthodox Patriarch in his palace. To me personally this visit meant more than anything else in Constantinople. The Patriarch of Constantinople has existed as the head of the Greek Orthodox Church since the Emperor Constantine the Great, and also bears the title of Pope.

In the year 1453 when the Byzantine Empire was conquered by the Turks, the Patriarchate was never touched, and its spiritual leadership over the Christians in the whole East was never contested. The Patriarchs were always respected by the Sultans, and even had interviews with them when necessary. Only in the year 1821, when the Greek War of Independence began, the ruling Patriarch, Gregory V, was hanged by the Turks at the entrance door of his palace. He was succeeded by another prelate, and the Oecumenical Patriarchate has continued to the present day.

Unfortunately, each country in the Orthodox communion—Greece, Roumania, Serbia, Bulgaria—when in turn it threw off the Turkish yoke, became autocephalous, that is, named its own head of the Church. The Oecumenical Patriarch thereafter found his actual functions restricted to that of leading the Christians who still remained under Turkish rule.

I was the first member of the Greek Royal Family to pay a visit to the Patriarch. In memory of the terrible death of the martyred Gregory V, the door in front of which he was hanged had been closed forever. We, therefore, entered the palace from the back and were greeted by His Holiness surrounded by all his bishops, whom he introduced to us.

I was very deeply impressed by the wonderful simplicity and dignity of this noble prelate as well as by the whole atmosphere of the Palace of the Phanar. Here was no luxury, no *éclat*, no resemblance to the Vatican of Rome, but only a deep mystic sentiment of sincere Christianity and asceticism. His Holiness took us up to his reception room, where he made a very touching speech, hailing me as the daughter of the King of free Greece. None of those present, myself included, could keep back our tears. The patriarch accompanied us to his private chapel where he said a few prayers. I was shown the very spot where Gregory V, canonised in 1921, one hundred years after his execution, was put to death; the thought of that martyrdom moved me very deeply. I left the Patriarchal Palace of the Phanar carrying with me ineffaceable feelings, an abiding emotion which remains as one of my most sacred memories.

On that day we also visited the splendid church, now, alas, a mosque, of St. Sophia[1]. No Greek can see the historic mother church, the masterpiece of Byzantine religious art, without being profoundly stirred with pride, reverence and regret. The name of the church means in Greek, "God's Holy Wisdom," and it occupies a very special position among the churches of Orthodox Christendom.

On Friday our old friend the Turkish general came early in the morning to take us to Yildiz for the feast of the *Salaamlik*. We were led to a pavilion just outside the private park of Yildiz, where we stood on a flowered terrace overlooking the road by which the procession would pass. The whole *Corps Diplomatique* stood with us. From the entrance gate the road led down rather a steep hill to the mosque where the Sultan went on these occasions to pray. The road was lined by very smart-looking troops.

---

1.   Today it is a museum.

The procession was started by the harem ladies who drove in closed landaus with curtains drawn, their eunuchs sitting with the coachmen. I do not remember the exact number of these carriages, but the impression remained that there were a great many.

The ladies of the harem were followed by many generals and officers on horseback; and then at last the Sultan himself seated in an open carriage drawn by four magnificent horses ridden by postillions. Next to the Sultan sat his aged Grand Vizier, a man of diminutive stature, who sat all huddled up in the corner, looking absolutely terrified. This carriage was followed by the Sultan's private bodyguard of fair-haired, blue-eyed Albanians, dressed in white uniforms covered in brown braid.

While the Mohammedan service was going on in the mosque, we were offered coffee and cigarettes on our terrace. About half an hour later the Sultan returned, heading the processions, but this time less officially, as he was driving his own barouche. He still had the terror-stricken Grand Vizier by his side, but he was no longer followed by his bodyguard. Instead there trailed after him on foot all the old generals of his suite running full tilt up hill behind the carriage, and puffing and panting in their effort to keep up. I can only describe this sight as ludicrous.

As soon as His Majesty got back to his palace he sent for us to take leave, as we were sailing in the evening. He tried to induce us to stay one day more as he wished me to hear one of his sons play the violin. As we were leaving one of the courtiers came up to me to ask in Abdul Hamid's name if I would like to visit the Harem or the stables. Without an instant's hesitation I chose the stables.

There was also in the park of Yildiz, a great white building with an enormous horse-shoe, like an archway, to serve as an entrance door. His Majesty's Arab horses were really magnificent animals, and I did not regret having chosen to see them instead of the fat old ladies of the harem. The Grand Duke George and I were offered horses, and I gave myself the great pleasure of choosing a beauty. When these horses arrived in Russia a few months later, they were not even the same colour as the ones given us by Abdul Hamid, and I strongly suspect that they never even came from the royal stables. They looked more like broken-down cab-horses than anything else.

In August, 1902, my brother Nicholas was married to the Grand Duchess Helen, only daughter of the Grand Duke and Grand Duchess Vladimir Alexandrovitch. Their wedding took place with the usual magnificent ceremonies in the church of the big palace at Tsarskoe-Selo. The walls of this old church of the time of the Empress Catherine II were all painted a kind of corn-flower blue with gold ornaments. My parents and my other brothers came from Greece for the event, which was surrounded with all the pomp and splendour of the Imperial court.

In the autumn my husband and I and Nina went again to the Caucasus for the shooting. Soon after we got back to Petersburg, the young Crown Prince William of Germany arrived on an official visit to the Tsar.

My father-in-law had a special love for the Prussian Royal Family, his mother having been a sister of the old Kaiser William I; and the family ties were to be made closer later on, although we did not know it then, by the marriage of the young Crown Prince to our niece Cecilie.[2] Grand Duke Michael decided to give a ball in our palace for the Prussian Prince. This was my first experience of playing hostess on such an important occasion and I felt rather alarmed. I am glad to say that it all went off without a hitch, and the whole world of St. Petersburg appeared to enjoy itself enormously. The Prince was charming and had great success among the ladies.

During the winters in St. Petersburg my youngest brother-in-law, Serge, in addition to carrying out the duties of his military service, occupied himself with music. He organized a full orchestra of amateur players and also a male choir in which he sang himself with his fine bass voice. Concerts took place twice a week in the great banqueting hall of our palace. I used often to sit next door and listen. One evening Serge told me to arrange a private dinner for the Emperor and Empress in our apartments as he was going to ask the famous basso, Chaliapin, to sing for us. Chaliapin's voice was then at the acme of its glory, and he was one of the idols of music-loving Russia.

Their Majesties accepted our invitation with joy, and after dinner we all proceeded to the hall to hear the men's choir. During an interlude Chaliapin appeared, smiling and debonnaire as usual, announcing in his great deep voice, *Vot i ya!*, which means "Here I am." When he recognized the Tsar, about whose presence he had not been informed, he nearly ran away, Serge caught him just in time. He sang divinely that evening.

After the great basso had finished singing, we took tea in the next room, and the Emperor wished Chaliapin to be presented to him. They had a friendly talk, and afterwards the Emperor handed him a glass of champagne and drank to his health. Chaliapin drained the glass and put it into his pocket, asserting in a loud voice that he intended keeping the goblet as a souvenir. It was one of my best Bohemian glasses, and I never saw it again. Ever after that Chaliapin and I remained very good friends. He often came to visit me, and I always managed to manoeuvre him to the piano and make him sing. He could not play the piano properly, but accompanied himself, after a fashion, playing with one finger. He never brought any music with him, and consequently I never played any of his accompaniments.

During one of these first winters in St. Petersburg the Archduke Franz-Ferdinand, who was murdered in 1914 with his wife at Serajevo, came on an official visit to the court. I found him perfectly charming and we met a good deal during this visit; with the result that we became great friends, and many a time did we dance together at the balls given in his honour. This was the first and last time I ever saw the ill-starred prince whose tragic death

2.   Daughter of Grand Duchess Anastasia Mikhailovna of Russia and Grand Duke Franz Friedrich III of Mecklenburg-Schwerin (1886-1954).

brought on the great tragedy of European war.

It was in the winter of 1903 that the famous costume ball took place at the Winter Palace. This festivity was one of the most brilliant moments in the social history of the old régime. It was a subject of endless discussion and ever since remained as a characteristic picture of Tsarism at its most magnificent. When the Emperor and Empress decided to give a fancy dress ball with costumes confined to one period, they hit upon the Muscovite 17th century as one of the most splendid epochs in the development of Russia. The exact point in history which was celebrated by the great ball was the ascent of the Romanov family to the throne of Moscow in 1613.

All St. Petersburg society was informed of the project several months ahead of time so that costumes could be made perfect in every detail. Court dress of that period was prescribed for all the men except army officers, who were to wear uniforms of the same period. Everybody set to work feverishly to make the ball a success; and a success it certainly was, in every sense of the word.

We all kept our costumes a secret, so as to add the element of surprise to the event. Old pictures and prints were examined, museums searched, and famous artists consulted on every detail of the dresses worn three hundred years before. I had a special costume painted for myself by a connoisseur, which consisted of an apple-green satin garment embroidered with silver, and a loose shirt of gold brocade, of which only the sleeves and neck were visible, embroidered with white silk flowers. Over all this was a short-waisted jacket of white velvet bordered with gold and worked here and there with a coloured flower. On my head I wore a very big golden *kokoshnik* on which seven stars were embroidered in pearls. In the centre of these I placed the diamond buttons from my court dress. Around the edges of this great gold crown were chains of diamonds. On my forehead hung a net of seed pearls attached to the *kokoshnik*, and from the back hung a tulle veil embroidered with small gold motifs. Ropes of pearls were looped under my chin from the sides of the crown, and a collar of pearls, with broaches and other ornaments of diamonds and emeralds completed the effect. My shoes were of gold brocade with double-headed eagles embroidered in pearls. The points of these shoes turned upwards. The whole costume was designed after that of a rich merchant's wife of the 17th century.

We all met at the Winter Palace that night in a great state of excitement and curiosity. The Tsar wore the identical costume, as well as the crown, of the first Romanov Tsar, especially brought from Moscow for the occasion. The dress was all of thick gold brocade.

The Empress' costume was also of heavy gold. Her jewels were glorious; most of them came from the peerless collection of the Russian Crown. Suspended from her neck was a huge, flat, square-cut emerald surrounded by tiny diamonds. The stone was larger than an ordinary match-box, and I could not help remarking when I saw it that it must have been the identical emerald through which Nero looked on at the burning of Rome.

It would take too long to describe all the marvellous costumes and priceless jewels worn by the ladies of Petersburg that night. We all stared at each other in utter amazement; some mysterious magic seemed to have changed all these familiar figures into splendid visions out of Russia's oriental past.

From the ballrooms of the Winter Palace we walked in procession to the Hermitage Theatre, where a performance of the period we were evoking was given. The orchestra and actors were all dressed in costumes of the time. At the end of this entertainment we all danced our usual waltzes, and I must say they looked extraordinarily inappropriate in Muscovite dress!

The great ball was repeated once more because my aunt, the Empress Marie, wished to see it, as did the *Corps Diplomatique*. Empress Marie, who did not want to wear a heavy costume like ours, came in a beautiful amethyst velvet gown with marvellous sables and jewels, and looked quite lovely. The diplomats, unfortunately, did not think of wearing the costumes of their respective countries of the seventeenth century, but came in their usual twentieth century evening dress. They looked so out of place and so odd that they felt quite shy and uncomfortable. It was indeed strange to see a foreign diplomatic lady in a décolleté dress dancing with a bearded Russian Boyar!

As was inevitable with an event of such extreme magnificence, this ball became a matter of history at once; the photographs of all present were collected and made into a wonderful printed *edition de luxe*, which was offered for sale even outside of Russia, and prized by collectors.

As in all countries, the people loved a show and were always hoping to get a glimpse of their sovereigns and family in their regalia. I sincerely think that if monarchs appeared more often in their crowns, there would be fewer republics!

The summer after that historic occasion we spent quietly at Mikhailovskoe; and in August my second daughter, Xenia[3] was born, just two years, two months and two days after her sister Nina. Her christening was the same as Nina's; her godfathers were my cousin Michael (Misha), brother of the Tsar, my eldest brother, Constantine, and my own godfather, the Grand Duke Alexis Alexandrovitch. Her godmothers were the Empress Alexandra Feodorovna, my mother, my sister-in-law (and cousin) Xenia, and Princess Victoria of England.

A few days later my poor father-in-law was found one morning on the floor in front of his bed when his valet went to waken him. He had had a stroke. We were all terribly upset and grieved, but the crisis passed, and little by little Papa Michel recovered and lived until 1909, although his left side always remained paralyzed. He was fortunate enough to keep his speech and his lucidity of mind. As soon as he was well enough he was taken to Cannes, where he remained through the winter.

---

3.   Born August 22, 1903, died 1965.

GRAND DUCHESS MARIE, PRINCESS XENIA (behind),
PRINCESS NINA, GRAND DUKE GEORGE C. 1909

HARAX

TOMMY
(Princess Xenia)

EMPRESS ALEXANDRA C. 1896

GRAND DUCHESS MARIE -1900

PRINCESS YOUSSOUPOV
Born Princess Irina Alexandrovna, daughter of
Grand Duke Alexander and Grand Duchess Xenia

PRINCE ANDREW and PRINCESS ALICE
Eilers collection

Chapter VII

In 1903, Grand Duke George and I went to Darmstadt for my brother Andrew's marriage to Princess Alice of Battenberg. She was the eldest daughter of the Admiral of the British Fleet, Prince Louis of Battenberg, who was given the title of Lord Milford Haven during the war[1], and of Princess Victoria, who was the eldest sister of the Empress Alexandra and of Grand Duchess Serge. There was a great family meeting at Darmstadt for the occasion. The Emperor and Empress came, as well as the Princess of Wales and her daughter Victoria. My parents were there, of course; so were several of my brothers and my mother's only sister, the Grand Duchess Vera, widow of Prince Eugene of Württemberg.

As a child, Grand Duchess Vera had been extremely nervous and difficult to manage; her mother (my grandmother) sent her to her sister-in-law, Queen Olga of Württemberg, who kept her and educated her and loved her as her own daughter, having no children of her own. When she grew up she married Prince Eugene, the heir to the throne of Württemberg.

Aunt Vera had a son and twin girls[2]; the latter were two days older than myself—which led to a slight misunderstanding at the time of our birth. When these twins were born the Queen of Württemberg at once informed my grandmother by telegram. Two days later my father telegraphed to my grandmother that mama had given birth to me. My grandmother got so mixed up in this quick succession of events that for a moment she thought that her daughter Vera had given birth to a third baby after two days!

Prince Eugene and their baby son both died soon afterwards and my Aunt Vera never married again. She was a most amusing, clever and original type, extremely popular in her German home. Four years younger than my mother, she was diametrically her opposite in every way. She was short, stumpy and extremely plain with a strong resemblance to my mother, though without a touch of her beauty. We did not meet Aunt Vera often, but we were all very fond of her and we used to tease her shamefully. She was so kind and droll that she never minded and answered us back without the slightest hesitation. She wore her hair cropped and curly. She also had to use a pince-nez, being terribly short-sighted like most of us.

My brother Andrew's marriage took place in two churches, as his

---

1.   World War I.
2.   Karl Eugene (b.d. 1875); Elsa (1876-1936), and Olga (1876-1932).

English fiancée was a Protestant. They were first married[3] in the Orthodox Russian Church, and afterwards in the Protestant church of the Schloss. By coincidence the German clergyman was the one who performed my [bother Constantine's] marriage in Athens in 1889.

In the afternoon following the wedding, [the entire] family [gathered] at the entrance of the Schloss to speed the young couple on their honeymoon. Every one of us was given a small packet of rice to throw at the newly weds, but instead of using the rice for the appointed purpose, my two brothers [Constantine and George], seeing Aunt Vera standing close to them, deliberately emptied the contents of their packets into her short hair, and rubbed it in. This was not enough; they got hold of a man's soft hat and pulled it down over her head and face, which caused her glasses to drop and smash on the stone pavement. Before she could get the hat off, her two tormentors wisely disappeared.

When she at last pulled off the hat, she saw only one man standing by her and being short sighted she thought it was one of her nephews. In another second she had given her neighbour a resounding box on the ear. The victim happened to be Admiral Mark Kerr, A.D.C. to Prince Louis of Battenberg. As he had watched this performance and waited close by to see how it would end, Admiral Kerr only laughed when Aunt Vera attached him and said, "I quite understand, Ma'am."

Next day we all left for various countries; my husband and I went to Cannes to my father-in-law. At Cannes we lived at the Villa Wenden, which belonged to my husband's sister, the Grand Duchess Anastasia of Mecklenburg-Schwerin. Both of our babies had come to Cannes from Russia with their grandfather and it was a great joy to see them again. Papa Michel was staying in a small villa close by with his suite, and we usually lunched there.

I did not remember much about the Riviera, as I had only been there once as a child of ten. On that occasion we were returning from abroad and embarked in our yacht at Villefranche; one day my parents took my brothers and sister and me to Monte Carlo for lunch. Later we all went to the Casino, but as children are not admitted the officials wished to keep me out. My father did not know where to leave me, so he had to say who he was, even though he was travelling incognito. I was then allowed to enter.

We took our children to Athens for Christmas then came back to Cannes again in the spring. On our return we stayed at the Villa Kazbek, which belonged to my brother-in-law, the Grand Duke Michael, and his beautiful morganatic wife, Countess de Torby[4]. They had three delightful

---

3. September 24, 1903. Prince Andrew was Captain of Cavalry, aide-de-camp, à la suite 23rd German Dragoon Guards (1st Grand Ducal Hessian), and 1st Russian "Neva" Infantry.

4. Countess Sophie de Torby was the eldest daughter of Prince Nikolaus of Nassau and his morganatic wife, Countess Natalia von Merenberg.

children, Zia[5], Nada[6], and a son, Michael.

Cannes was very nice in those days; a lot of well-known and charming people had villas there and gave most amusing parties. After the casino was built, Cannes—at least to my mind—lost a great deal of its charm. At that time, when there was no casino we used to drive to Monte Carlo; all my husband's family were great gamblers. My eldest brother-in-law, Nicholas, used to win and lose enormous sums. When he won he always made me and my girls gifts of lovely jewels. I did not care much about gambling, and used to go off by myself to explore all the streets and shops of the town. My husband loved gambling too; but he was always careful and never lost his head. I often stood behind his chair to watch him play roulette. The casino was really very smart in those far away days and at night all the visitors had to wear full evening dress.

Soon after our arrival at Cannes this second time, we heard the news of the outbreak of the Russo-Japanese war, whereupon we immediately returned to Russia.

[Editor - In 1895 the newly westernized Empire of Japan occupied several Chinese territories which Russia coveted, among them the warm water port of Port Authur. Russia intervened, declaring that this would constitute a perpetual menace to the peace of the Far East. Japan withdrew rather than risk war. In 1900, during the Boxer Rebellion, Russia occupied Manchuria. The only remaining Chinese prize left was Korea. A group of Russian adventurers resolved to steal it by establishing a company there, the Yalu Timber Company, and began moving Russian soldiers into the area disguised as workmen. Witte, then Finance Minister, opposed the policy, but Emperor Nicholas, impressed by the leader, a former cavalry officer named Bezobrazov, approved, and Witte resigned in 1903.

The Russian seizure of Korea made war with Japan inevitable. In 1901, the Japanese statesman, Marquis Ito, came to St. Petersburg to negotiate. He was ignored, and finding no one to talk to, he put his requests in writing. Delays followed, and finally he withdrew. Through 1903 the Japanese Minister, Kurino, issued urgent warnings and begged in vain for audience with Emperor Nicholas. On February 3, 1904, bowing grimly to fate, Kurino left Russia.

Emperor Nicholas believed that Russia's overwhelming superiority would prevent war, and that he could make his decisions at leisure. Japan, however, made his decisions unnecessary: on the evening of February 6,

---

5.   Married Sir Harold Werhner, Bt., and known as Lady Zia Werhner.

6.   Married George Mountbatten, 2nd Marquess of Milford Haven.

1904, Emperor Nicholas received the following message:

> ". . . About midnight, Japanese destroyers
> made a surprise attack on the squadron
> anchored in the outer harbor of Port Arthur.
> The battleships *Tsarevich*, *Retvizan* and the
> cruiser *Pallada* were torpedoed. . . ."

Emperor Nicholas recorded in his diary, ". . . This
without a declaration of war. May God come to our aid."]

During the years I spent in Russia I met several interesting
personalities whose names have now become historical. Ministers such as
Witte[7], Pleve[8] and Stolypin[9]. These last two were murdered. The opinions
on Count Witte were very contradictory. I only know that he is one of the
few people who could not get on with the Tsar. Although he did not like his
Tsar, the Count always said that the Tsar's first decisions and judgments
were correct.

Of the foreign ambassadors I only knew a very few, as these were
only met on official occasions. One whom I liked very much was the Austro-
Hungarian Ambassador, Count Aehrenthal, who later became Premier of his
country. In Russia they never forgave him the stand he took in the
Herzegovina and Bosnia question.[10]

At first the news from the front seemed good; but little by little,
everything went from bad to worse, and the war ended disastrously for
Russia. One curious thing was that bad news always arrived in St.
Petersburg, by some mysterious route, long before the official reports of the
Commander-in-Chief, General Kuropatkin.

The ladies of St. Petersburg society began working feverishly for the
Red Cross and for the hospitals. In this we were led by the Empress, who
arranged regular workshops in the Winter Palace. I also arranged a
workroom in our palace, mostly composed of the ladies of my husband's
regiment and some of my friends. As I was not very good at sewing, I made
sheets and used a sewing machine. My daughter Nina often sat on my lap
and turned the handle, which gave her enormous pleasure.

---

7.   Sergius Witte, gave Russia its first constitution and its first parliament. He persuaded
Emperor Nicholas II to sign the Imperial Manifesto of October 30, 1905, which
transformed Russia from an absolute autocracy into a semi-constitutional monarchy.
He was born of humble origins in the Georgian city of Tiflis in 1894, and died in 1915.

8.   Vyacheslav Pleve (Plehve), Minister of the Interior in 1904. Assassinated in July 1904.

9.   Peter Stolypin, (1863-1911). Minister of the Interior in 1906, then Prime Minister from
July 7, 1906 until his assassination in September 1911, while attending a performance
at the Kiev Opera House in the presence of Tsar Nicholas II.

10.   In 1908, Austria had summarily annexed these provinces over the protest of the
Powers, England, France and Russia.

All the Imperial Family was much occupied by charitable works and institutions, such as hospitals, schools, kindergartens, crèches, etc. The Empress Alexandra founded a training school at Tsarskoe-Selo for children's nurses. All these various institutions were extremely well-run. Most of the hospitals were admirably organised and the physicians and surgeons were among the best men of their day.

Later on my husband rented a small house just outside the town, and we arranged it as a hospital for soldiers who had lost their legs or arms and equipped them with new ones. We often went to visit them. My husband supplied them with every kind of musical instrument; and as Russians cannot exist without some kind of music, they all could play to their hearts content.

During the summer the whole family, headed by the Tsar, went to see the launching of various new battleships. I remember particularly the launching of the battleship *Alexander III* because of the ghastly incident which took place. Grandstands had been erected, on the one side for the Emperor and Imperial Family, and on the other for the naval cadets. It was blowing a gale, and just as the great ship was sliding down to the water, a huge pole with a flag got loose from the scaffolding and came crashing down on the heads of the cadets standing in the front row. Three of these unfortunate boys were killed on the spot, and I could clearly discern how their heads were crushed. It was such a horrible sight that none of us could get over it for many a day.

The summer of 1904 was marked by one happy event, the birth of the little Tsarevich[11], who was given the name of Alexis[12]. The baby was fair with yellow curls and blue eyes. The country had waited in vain for nearly ten years for an heir to the throne, and when he made his appearance at last, the rejoicings were great. Sadly, he came during an unfortunate war, and much of the glamour which his advent would have had in normal times was dimmed.

As soon as we heard the happy tiding we all went to Peterhof to present our congratulations to the Tsar. I can never forget the intense happiness in my cousin's wonderful eyes. His most sacred wish had been granted at last, now, when he was most in need of comfort and courage. Notwithstanding numerous publications to the contrary, the Tsar suffered agonies over this unfortunate war. I, who constantly saw him and knew him well, can vouch that he felt despair in his heart and soul, but was much too proud to show it, always bearing a courageous smile with the idea that by doing so he would help others. He adored his troops and the death of every man was a personal loss to him.

11.　　Born August 12, 1904.

12.　　His Imperial Highness Alexis Nicolaievitch, Sovereign Heir Tsarevich, Grand Duke of Russia.

115

The christening of the long expected heir[13] was very imposing, but simple to what it might have been. The precious baby was driven to the church[14] in a gilded coach with his nurse, accompanied by the Empress' Mistress of the Robes. The coach was preceded and followed by a military escort. The route was lined with troops. At the big palace the Imperial Family had collected round the Tsar, all the men in full dress uniform, the ladies in court dress. The Tsarevich headed the procession, being carried on a cushion covered with golden cloth by the Mistress of the Robes[15]. At the church entrance we were received by the Metropolitan and clergy dressed in their marvellous chasubles and mitres. The Tsar's choir—the best I have ever heard—sang divinely. In honour of all his fighting troops in the Far East, the Tsar made his son godchild of all the army and navy. After the christening ceremony[16] the baby was carried back to his mother with the same ceremonial.

It was only much later that we heard, as a great secret, that the poor little Tsarevich was suffering from that terrible and incurable disease called haemophilia. During all his short life he suffered tortures owing to this illness. It had the saddest results on his unfortunate mother's character, and her life became one long agony of despair beholding his sufferings.

Later we had to go to Homburg, where the doctors ordered me to take a cure, because I had a heart attack in winter. My brother [Constantine] and his wife [Sophie] and their children were staying at Friedrichshof. This beautiful place had been inherited by Princess Margaret of Hesse from her mother, the Empress Frederick. We often went to visit them. One day we were asked to lunch because King Edward was expected and also the Kaiser. There had been some political misunderstandings between them, as so often happened, and it was decided to bring them together again, a visit to Princess Margaret being used as an excuse. Princess Margaret was King Edward's niece and the Kaiser's sister.

It was a very large lunch as the English and German suites were invited. Afterwards everybody talked and both the British and German ministers of foreign affairs tried their best to get the King and the Kaiser to have a private conversation. Somehow they kept on avoiding each other, like children who have quarrelled. At last, after much manoeuvering it became possible to get them both on the terrace. As soon as this happened everyone melted away like mist. We all ran upstairs, and in a twinkling all the windows looking down onto this terrace were crammed with eager and expectant faces. The two monarchs were strutting up and down like fighting cocks, and, to judge by the loud voice of King Edward, were having a rather

---

13. Tsarevich Alexis was named for the second Romanov Tsar, Alexis I (1629-1676), the Peaceful, and was the first Tsarevich born "in the Purple" since the seventeenth century. "In the purple" referred to children born to a reigning monarch.

14. Peterhof Chapel.

15. Princess Marie Golitsyn.

16. Father Yanishev, confessor to the Imperial Family performed the ceremony.

hot and excited argument. What the results of this meeting were, I never discovered.

The winter of 1905 we spent as usual at St. Petersburg. Since the beginning of the Russo-Japanese war the Emperor and Empress had retired to the Alexander Palace of Tsarskoe-Selo, and no court functions took place any more at the Winter Palace. The last one was on January 6, 1905, Epiphany-day. All the Imperial Family met as usual in the Winter Palace for Mass, after which the Tsar, followed by all the male members of the family, went out on the quay for the blessing of the waters. A pavilion was erected right in front of the palace, where the Imperial Family stood. The Metropolitan blessed the waters of the Neva by dipping a cross into the river. At the very moment this ceremony took place a salvo of guns was fired from the opposite shore. On this particular day, either on purpose or through bad luck, one of the guns was charged and the shrapnel poured into the midst of the assembly. No one of the Imperial Family was hurt, and I believe only one policeman was slightly wounded.

The Empress and all the Grand Duchesses were standing at the windows of the Malachite Hall looking down on the ceremony. Strangely enough none of us remarked anything unusual; but in the hall next door to us, where the diplomats were assembled, a bullet crashed through the double window and caused something of a commotion. When the Emperor and the Grand Dukes returned, one of them came up to me and showed [me] a bullet and a bit of broken wood from the pavilion which he had collected. I could not imagine what it was he was showing me, till he explained. We were all naturally horrified and thanked God for their marvellous escape.

This uncanny event seemed to mark the beginning of the revolution which lasted openly for a year. One can now call it the *répetition générale* of what was to come in a few years' time. This strange attack on Epiphany day was never proved to be an attempt on the Imperial Family, even after the investigation and the severe punishment of the responsible officers.

To me Russia always represented something vast, broad and enormous. There were few restrictions of any kind, and far fewer conventions than among the other nations of the world. Over this immense mass of humanity the shadow of the Emperor and the Imperial Family brooded like the Gods of Olympos. The possibilities were immense in every branch of life, both mental and physical. Things happened in Russia which could happen nowhere else. There was, of course, a great deal of the Orient about it still, notwithstanding Peter the Great's efforts to turn it into a Western Power. The mentality of the people was still largely Eastern and childlike. There were no caste hatreds. These were introduced at first by the Nihilists and later by the Bolsheviks.

Coming as I did from Greece, a constitutional country, I felt at first that there was an enormous gap between the upper and lower classes. It was only later that I began to understand it all and be able to appreciate the patriarchal ways of my adoptive country. I felt the particular quality and characteristics of Russia most by contrast later when, during the Great War and after, I spent eleven years in England. The freedom one feels and enjoys in that country comes from the great order and discipline which has become an institution, following centuries of hard work. But in Russia one felt free for another reason, because everything there was on such a vast scale. With a small effort and a little persistence anything could be obtained.

To give an example of the democratic ways of the Russians, I can cite a happening which occurred in our own family. My father-in-law had an old valet who had served him for years, and in his old age looked like a marquis. This man's son went into a military school and in due time became an artillery officer. Eventually he served in my brother-in-law Serge's regiment, and was invited to lunch with his brother officers at our palace. Such a thing could never have happened in England.

The aristocracy lived on a familiar footing with their subordinates, and treated them as equals. The peasants, there were no tenants, treated their masters in a familiar way, often calling them by their Christian names. When sick or in trouble they always came to their landowners and asked for help or advice just as children would do, and on the whole—barring a few exceptions proving the rule—the landowners were extremely kind and thoughtful to their peasants. They built schools and hospitals for them, and tried to improve their mode of life.

Dissatisfaction was visibly growing and a strong feeling of general unrest was perpetually noticeable. The strangest rumors were going about which left a feeling of uneasiness and apprehension. On the famous "Red Sunday" so named by various foreign papers, all the workmen of every description were convened by the notorious Father [George] Gapon and various other revolutionary chiefs to the Winter Palace. They were purposely told that the Tsar would appear on the balcony and talk to them. As a matter of fact, the Tsar was at Tsarskoe-Selo and knew nothing about it. I remember seeing all these men marching past our palace along the quay in their Sunday clothes.

When they had [gathered] in the big square in front of the Winter Palace, some one, evidently on purpose, caused a panic, and the troops which were standing there to keep order, thought there would be an attack on the palace, and shot at the crowd. The results were entirely disastrous and there were many casualties. We could plainly hear the shots from our rooms, but I did not realize what was happening. I can still remember the terrible state in which my husband was, because he was very liberal, and feeling more than knowing what had happened, he was certain that this deplorable event would have far reaching consequences, which it did.

One thing they could not bear in Russia was injustice. This rankled in their brains and it worked them up to a state of dumb rage, which eventually found an outlet in cruelty. As a whole though, I found them a long-suffering people, kind-hearted, extremely hospitable and fatalistic. Their devotion to their masters sometimes reached a state of fanaticism, and they would smilingly sacrifice their lives for them. In England, I found that the gap between master and subordinate was much greater, in a way, because the difference of education between the two was smaller than in Russia.

So, many unexpected events took place in Russia; one was never quite sure what would occur from one day to another. For instance, when I arrived in my new home in 1900, I bought myself a French dictionary, a *Larousse*, and I found the words "constitution" and "revolution" were blackened by the censor. This was typical proof of the childish way in which the population was treated. Three years later these fatal words were on everyone's lips. It was just like keeping secrets from inquisitive children. . . . [The] propaganda against the government assumed vast proportions. . . . [It] had been decided [by revolutionaries] long before the Great War upon the disintegration of the Russian Empire. Leaflets were published not only in the numerous languages of the country, such as Polish, Finnish, Swedish, German, etc., but in every dialect. These were clandestinely distributed from hand to hand.

This unpleasant atmosphere continued to hang over us. In August my husband, myself and our children went to the Crimea, and lived as guests with Xenia at Ai-Todor. They did not have room enough for us in their own house, so they gave us a delightful flat, built over the wine-cellar in their vineyard. It was built on a height and we had a marvellous view over the Black Sea.

Xenia and her husband had turned two small villas in another part of their park, near the sea, into convalescent homes, one for officers, the other for privates. We used to visit them and try and cheer them up.

Later in the autumn, Xenia's brother, Michael, and her youngest sister, Olga, then married to Prince Peter of Oldenburg, whom she divorced in 1916, arrived. We all met there for meals. We did not feel very gay, just then, because we were constantly hearing of new revolts all over the country.

All these cousins and their suites had arranged a small amateur orchestra of *Balalaikas*—the Russian mandoline—and played at the big house every evening after dinner. Music, of course, was the dominant passion of their lives. They had music for every occasion; misery or happiness was always expressed by music. I do not believe it is easy to find a Russian without a musical ear. They all seem to be born musicians. All the regiments had their choirs. These sang at the regimental churches and in the mess rooms after meals. The troops on march always sang; they invariably had good voices, and all their national tunes were lovely.

As the army was still loyal in those days, a certain order could still be counted on. We felt, though, that things were coming to a head and expected the crisis [at] any moment.

[Editor: Emperor Nicholas had inherited Witte along with the throne. Witte said of Emperor Nicholas, ". . . I knew him to be inexperienced in the extreme but rather intelligent and he always impressed me as a kindly and well-bred youth."

119

The Tsar disliked Witte's cynicism and arrogance, but admitted his genius. The constitution which Witte had forced upon the Tsar, saying in a memorandum, that only two alternatives existed: a military dictatorship or a constitution, and the latter was the best way to calm the situation. Having forced a reluctant Tsar to sign the document, Witte was expected to make it work, and was installed as President of the Council of Ministers. To Witte's surprise, instead of getting better the situation grew worse.]

At Sevastopol, the port of the Black Sea fleet, things were taking alarming proportions, because one of the big battleships, the *Potemkin*, had revolted openly. The crew imprisoned all the officers on board, and [took] possession of the ship. They started making a tournèe of the Black Sea, bombarding several places on the coast.

A little later another man-of-war followed this example, but just as it was about to leave port it was sunk by the loyal part of the fleet. Then we had news of skirmishes in the Crimea and in our neighbouring small town of Yalta. Even the scholars began to revolt against their masters and refused to continue their studies. The postal and telegraph offices went on strike as well as the trains and passenger ships. For a week we knew nothing of what was going on in the rest of the country or the world in general.

My sister-in-law's children and ours were never allowed outside the house, unless accompanied by armed soldiers. One afternoon, my husband and I were quietly sitting at home reading when suddenly we heard the *Marseillaise* sung in chorus under our windows. I must own that this incident tickled my fancy and I could not help laughing, imagining that I had turned into Marie Antoinette and was living in Versailles. My husband got up in a towering rage, opened the window and gave these people a bit of his mind in very expressive language. As usually happens with cowards, on hearing him they fled.

One evening we were told that we would be attacked during the night and the guards were doubled round our abodes; but nothing happened. In a village close by a priest was murdered during the service in church, which caused a panic. After a week things calmed down a bit, and the post-office, trains and ships started to work. We then heard that the Tsar was safe at Tsarskoe-Selo, but separated from the rest of the family.

As soon as it was possible my cousin Michael and his sister left for Petersburg to join their brother, the Tsar. They arrived safely but had a perilous journey across the country. They were not allowed to have any lights on the train because the mob had bombarded previous ones with stones.

Just as we heard of their safe arrival, the strikes started anew. I remember one of our gentlemen coming to tell me that if I wished to give news of myself to my parents I was to wire at once, seeing that in an hour it would be too late. Then we remained for three long weeks in utter ignorance of what was going on in the rest of the country and world at large. Meanwhile, a Republic had been proclaimed in the Crimea and our "President" rejoiced in the glorious name of Pergament I! This very same man played a role in the Bolshevik revolution.

(Editor: In parts of Russia, the Manifesto stripped local police of many powers and led directly to violence. In the Ukraine and Byelorussia, bands of Ultras, calling themselves "Black Hundreds", turned against the Jews. In Kiev and Odessa pogroms erupted, and in the Trans-Caucasus similar attacks were made on Armenians. The Manifesto was seen by all factions as a sign of weakness, and that the Empire was crumbling.

In December, the Moscow Soviet led a revolt, proclaiming a Provisional Government. The Tsar acted at last, bringing in the Semenovsky Regiment of the Guard, which cleared the streets with artillery and bayonets.

During this trouble, Lenin slipped back into Russia to lead the Bolsheviks. The police soon found him and he was forced to slink about from one place to another. He was still pleased with the results, "Go ahead and shoot," he said.]

Christmas came in between, and on the eve as we were not allowed to go to the village church as usual, the priest was sent for to have a service in the house. This unfortunate man had been told he would be killed so he lived in constant anxiety. He was driven to the house in a closed landau, under escort of a cavalry posse, and returned home the same way. Xenia invited all the wounded officers to our Christmas tree, and what with our children and them, we spent quite a happy evening.

Before all these disagreeable events had started, my husband and I laid the foundation stone of what was going to be our future home. We had got hold of a very clever and gifted architect, who had already built two charming villas for the Grand Duke Nicholas and his brother Peter, both cousins of my husband.

As I always had a passion for everything English I insisted upon building an English cottage. We had the plans ready since the previous year and decided to build at once. We made a regular feast out of it and asked all the wounded officers in addition to the family. After laying the stone, we had a grand lunch for all our guests. There were so many rocks in the place that the stones were used for building our cottage, another for the suite and for our guests, the kitchen, stables, garage, and a special house for the servants and their families, besides the walls that surrounded the property. In this way we were able to start planting trees at once and also laying out the garden. My husband and I went there every day to supervise the work. We always suspected that it was our workmen who came to sing the *Marseillaise* under our windows later on.

In January 1906, we received the unexpected and sad news that King Christian IX[17], our grandfather, had suddenly died. Xenia and I were terribly upset as we were deeply devoted to him. We decided to leave for Copenhagen at once, to be present at the funeral. As the revolution seemed to be quietening down a bit, we all left together for Petersburg. From there Xenia, Michael, Olga and her husband and myself left together for Copenhagen.

There I met my father who had come from Athens, and my three aunts. Empress Marie had spent the winter with her father, staying with him [at the] Palace of Amalienborg. My grandfather was already eighty-eight years of age and had always enjoyed wonderful health. He rode every morning and walked like a young man. On the day of his death he gave an audience to seventy people; at lunch, he remarked [to Marie] in a casual manner, "It is curious that an old gentleman like myself should not feel tired." During lunch he was seized by a pain in his chest and he told [Marie] that he would go to his room and rest on his bed; that she was not to worry, but was to go for her usual drive.

My aunt felt rather anxious, as her father never rested, and when she was ready for her drive she went to his room to see if all was well with him. The moment she opened the door she heard him draw a long breath and hastening to his bed she realized that he had breathed his last.

The Kaiser announced his arrival for the funeral which slightly upset everyone, as he was not popular with the Danish family. The funeral took place in the Cathedral of Roskilde, where all the Danish kings have been buried for centuries. My grandfather was laid to rest in a tomb next to his wife, Queen Louise.

---

17.   Died January 29, 1906.

KING CHRISTIAN IX
Grandfather of author
Eilers collection

QUEEN LOUISE
Grandmother of author
Eilers collection

GRAND DUKE NIKOLAI CONSTANTINOVITCH

GRAND DUKE SERGE MIKHAILOVITCH

GRAND DUKE ALEXIS MIKHAILOVITCH c. 1890

Chapter VIII

The first time I met Kaiser William II was during my eldest brother's marriage at Athens, and then later at Friedrichshof and Homburg.

I only really came to know him on his visits to Corfu, where we constantly met. The Kaiser bought the Villa, *Achilleion*, in 1904, but did not live in it for several years because of repairs and changes which had to be made. He used to come in the spring, with his wife, his delightful daughter Victoria Louise—who later married my first cousin Ernst-August of Hanover—and accompanied by an enormous suite.

They all came together on board their huge yacht *Hohenzollern*, which looked like a liner. The yacht was escorted by the German fleet, and the peacefulness of Corfu vanished when the Kaiser appeared. There was a kind of nervous tension in the air and a general sense of hurry. He was here, there and everywhere, tearing about the island in his motorcars, inspecting his ships or excavating. Twice Alexandra, the Princess of Wales, happened to be there at the same time on board her yacht *H.M.S. Victoria and Albert*, with her two younger daughters. Their visits were always the greatest joy to us.

In those days, as we were very numerous, we, the Greek family, lived in town in the big palace, *Mon Repos* being too small. The Kaiser often asked us to meals at his villa and also on board his yacht. My father gave luncheon parties for him too, either in the palace or at *Mon Repos*. It was then that I came to know him quite well. He was always particularly nice to me and we used to have endless talks, mostly on politics. He fascinated me by his intelligence and quick comprehension and wit. He was a very interesting personality with his steely blue eyes and rough moustache; what always struck me, although we got on so well, was that he had not much heart. It was all brain with him. All those who surrounded him were in mortal fear of him. Irritated by witnessing exhibitions of this kind, I own that I was sometimes extremely rude and impertinent to him, but he never seemed to mind. I remember my father telling the Kaiser once that he was ashamed of the way in which I treated him, but His Majesty laughingly retorted: "We are such good friends that it does not matter in the least."

The Kaiser always brought with him a wonderful string orchestra. They were all wonderful artists. Every morning from our palace we could hear the band playing on board the *Hohenzollern*, which was most enjoyable. Sometime, too, the Kaiser sent them to play for us after dinner. While on board, they all had to wear naval uniforms. On another occasion the Austrian fleet made an appearance, and the Kaiser invited all of us and the Austrian officers for a dance on his yacht.

In the course of one of his visits to Corfu he developed a mania for excavating antiquities. The well-known German archaeologist, Dorpfeld, was invited as an expert, and for a while the Kaiser spent most of his days at these excavations. He had a tent put up close by where he had meals with his suite. We often went to see how he was getting on.

One day Aunt Alix and her daughter Victoria came along with us. The Kaiser was resting just then and, taking a chair, he sat astride it to talk to his cousin Victoria, who sat opposite. Suddenly the earth under the Kaiser's chair—which was on a slope—gave way, and down came His Majesty, sprawling on the ground. Everyone ran to his help, but he was up immediately, and turning to me said: "Why did you not take a snapshot, as it was a most unusual position for me!"

My father had a cupboard in his dressing room at *Mon Repos*, of which the front was a mirror. On this glass my parents and all the family, his sisters, etc., had written their names with a diamond. One day we discovered to our utter amazement that the Kaiser had written his name down too, in huge letters. He apparently had visited the house when we were all away.

The Kaiser seemed genuinely fond of Corfu, but he behaved rather as if the whole place belonged to him, which was irritating. After four visits there he was never able to return again, and *Achilleion* was confiscated by the Greek government during the Great War. The Kaiserin[1], I believe, did not care for the place much, as she only felt at home in Germany. She was a dignified lady, very plain and somewhat stiff and distant, and we never felt quite at ease with her.

In November 1906, my father went to Rome on an official visit to the Italian Royal Family. As I [was on my way] to Greece with my children, I joined him there. In those days the feud still existed between the Quirinal and the Vatican, and we could not drive to the Pope in the Italian royal carriages. We were driven in them as far as the Greek Legation, where we got into an ordinary landau and drove on to the Vatican, being escorted all the way by detectives on bicycles. In the Vatican courtyard the Swiss Guards stood on parade, their band playing the Greek national anthem.

All along the passages and rooms stood the picturesque guards in their costumes designed by Michelangelo. In a marble hall next to the room where we were to be received were the guards of the Black Roman Nobility. As we entered, the Pope appeared through the doors facing us. With a terrific clatter of arms the whole guard went down on one knee. His Holiness, after giving us his hand to kiss, led us into a private room. The Pope was tall, rather stout and full of dignity. He asked after King Victor Emmanuel, whom he had known in Venice when he was Archbishop there a

---

1.   Princess Auguste Victoria of Schleswig-Holstein (1858-1921).

few years previously.

In the autumn of 1907, we went to the Crimea to live in our own house at last. My husband and I had been longing for this since our marriage because up to then we always stayed in his father's houses. We were terribly excited to see what it really looked like as we only knew it from photographs. From the station at Sevastopol we had to drive two hours and a half by motorcar. We first crossed the battlefields of the Crimean War with the monuments erected by the different nations that had fought there, until we came to a road that led over the mountains. Halfway was a place called Baidare, where a triumphal bronze arch had been erected. Driving through this, you suddenly saw the whole of the Black Sea at your feet. It was indeed a breathtaking view. From there the road continued down a steep hill. We arrived at Harax, the name of our estate, in the early afternoon. We were agreeably surprised by all we saw, and my husband, our children and myself at once fell in love with our new home. All the houses were built of a stone found on the estate, a blue-gray granite and the roofs were of red tiles. It looked exactly as I had hoped, like an English cottage. A lot of work had of course still to be done to make it as we wanted it, and this took up a great deal of time.

In one part of the garden my husband built a tiny kitchen for the children. Next to it were two diminutive plots, one for each child, and each had a little fountain. They also had a small enclosure for Bantam fowls, and later a big cage full of canaries. This place was the children's private playground. On Saturdays their English nurse—who stayed with them for 20 years—used to cook the most excellent English cakes which we ate for tea. My husband, who loved trees, started planting them everywhere, and in a very short time this small estate became a kind of paradise.

Quite a lot of members of the Imperial Family had villas along that coast. The Emperor's estate was called Livadia, where Emperor Alexander III had died, and next to this was a beautiful place which had formerly belonged to my Russian grandparents, named Oreanda. After my grandfather's death, my uncles, not caring much about the south, sold it to the Emperor. The house, which was built in the old Greek style, had been burned down, only the walls remaining. It had never been rebuilt. The ruins were covered by creepers and wistaria, which, though charming and artistic, looked sad. In the atrium in the centre of the building there was still one fountain intact, and I still hear the drip, drip of the water.

This atrium consisted of twelve columns, and a year or two after we had settled at Harax I begged the Emperor to make me a present of them. He kindly agreed, and I had the whole thing transported to our garden and built up again. It looked just like an ancient Greek Temple. As a background for it we planted cypresses with roses at the front. After Harax came *Ai-Todor*, then *Chair*, belonging to the Grand Duke Nicholas Nicolaievitch, then *Dulber*, belonging to his brother, Grand Duke Peter. Further on was *Koreis*, a property of Prince Youssoupov.

The Crimea is much like the Italian Riviera with the same temperate climate. Sometimes there were terrible storms and the waves would dash over the big rocks along the coast in a most imposing manner. There was unfortunately no sandy beach on our coast, only rocks and at times stretches of pebbles. One time my husband arranged a fishery by the sea, but the smell was so nauseous that I begged him to have it removed.

All seasons were delightful in the Crimea, except the beginning of summer, when it became unbearably hot. Unfortunately, there is very little water in that part of the country, and at first we could not get enough for the house and the garden, but later my husband discovered a marvellous spring in the hills about eight miles away, and arranged to buy it. He had a line of pipes laid down from this spring to our estate and was able to supply other places with water on its way to us. Round the spring was a lovely big orchard of apple and pear trees and we were able to sell the fruit. Later we built a farm not far from our own house, where we had beautiful black and white Swiss cows. The milk and butter were also sold to our neighbours. My husband, who was a first-rate organizer, wished to turn Harax into a model place. This he succeeded in doing and when our neighbours saw our estate and farm, they immediately started to work hard to put their property in order.

When we travelled through Italy we bought marble benches, fountains and other things for the garden which added greatly to its effect. Roses and flowers grew everywhere in profusion. We also built a lovely little church which was an exact reproduction of a very ancient and historic church in the Caucasus. A couple of years later the Emperor decided to build himself a bigger house at Livadia. His grandfather's house, which was wooden, was pulled down and a huge white Italian villa was erected in its stead. In the centre was an open courtyard with a well. When it was ready the sovereigns entertained quite a lot there. They were both very fond of the Crimea and came there either in the spring or autumn.

The Tsar had a passion for walking and he would make excursions on foot that lasted three or four hours at a time. His aides-de-camp who accompanied him grew thinner by the hour, to the Emperor's great amusement. One year the Ministry of War decided to give new equipment to the troops, and the Emperor, who loved his soldiers, decided to try this new equipment himself before signing the decree. He wore the uniform, arms and cap of the ordinary private and went on long marches to see whether it was comfortable and practical. One day he telephoned that he would come to us on foot in this garb next morning, and would we give him some breakfast. We made our preparations in time and went out to meet him in the garden. We could see him coming from far down the woody hill, as his bayonet shone in the sun. As soon as he got to the house he gave his rifle and kit to the servant, who looked at the Tsar aghast seeing him in this garb. He came in and had breakfast and said he felt like a poor relation coming home on leave!

The Tsar came two or three times a week, when living at Livadia, to dine with us. The Empress sometimes came too, but not very often, as she was in ill health during the later years. The Emperor would bring his two eldest daughters, Olga and Tatiana. After dinner we played all kinds of games. The Emperor always told me he loved coming to us because he could be himself and it was such a change to the usual routine of his daily life. He really enjoyed himself like a boy on those occasions and never would leave before one o'clock in the morning.[2]

During one autumn when we were all together in the Crimea, a lot of balls were arranged, and society was very gay. There were several balls given at Livadia, and we ourselves were responsible for two. As our house was rather small, we had to use our children's rooms for supper and they had to spend that night in the house for guests. They were considerably upset about this and did not enjoy it a bit.

My brother Christopher often came and stayed with us at Harax, which was always a great joy to me. We used to do a lot of music together, and often when we dined with our various neighbours, we took our music with us, and Christopher accompanied my singing. During our first autumn in Harax, the Grand Duchess Serge came with my niece Marie and my nephew Dimitri. When the Grand Duchess left, my niece and nephew lived at Livadia and I saw them often. Marie was just engaged to be married to Prince William of Sweden. She was full of life and very jolly, but inclined to be self-willed and selfish, and rather difficult to deal with. She had, of course, been greatly handicapped by the great change in her life when her father married again and she was taken from her home. Her Aunt Ella and she were so diametrically different in character that they only really understood each other when they came to part. Dimitri had a much easier character and had taken more of his parents' natures. These two children adored each other and could never be parted, which was very touching.

We lived entirely a country life in the Crimea, taking long walks, drives and rides. We spent a lot of time arranging the garden, where every tree and flower had become a personal friend. The children were really happy there as they were out most of the day, free to do what they liked. The house being built on a slope, their rooms, which were on the first floor, communicated directly with the terrace which was a continuation of their balcony. Their great joy was when it had rained to run about the puddles barefooted. They went every morning to the farm with their father, and were taught to milk the cows which they soon learned to do. They also had riding lessons, but were not very fond of this kind of exercise.

During one winter we had deep snow, and for a week we were able to toboggan down the steep slope leading from our church to the high road. It is astonishing what a difference it makes in life to have one's own house and garden. We, all of us, felt this the moment we took possession of Harax, and preferred living there to anywhere else. We often had visitors. Once an old General and his wife came to lunch and when we showed them around I

---

2.   The Guest Book for Harax shows numerous signatures of the Emperor, his daughters, and other of society.

asked the General how he liked it, and his answer was that he thought it very nice but was not accustomed to see a Grand Duke living in a house, as he was used to seeing them in palaces. I had always wished to live in a house and I was delighted to see this dream of mine come true.

As most of our servants came from Petersburg and my husband feared they would be lonely so far from their families, we had a special house built for them, their wives and children. During the autumn many workmen who had finished their agricultural labour in the northern provinces came south to look for work during the winter. They usually passed by our place and my husband invariably found work for them, making them plant trees and finding various other jobs for them. He loved these simple people and always did his utmost to help them. He seemed to understand their mentality better than anyone else and had long talks with them, inquiring about their families and homes.

At the same time he realized perfectly all that was going on in the country and the daily growing dissatisfaction that was caused by the terrible propaganda going on underhand; the future frightened him, and he always tried to enlighten the Tsar and Ministers. What could one man do when those who were responsible would not see things in the real light? The men at the top never knew what was really going on at the bottom, or perhaps they knew but, realizing their impotence, simply closed their eyes. The Emperor had a terrific amount of work to do as not a single officer or clerk was promoted or changed without his signature. He spent all his evenings and most of the night reading endless reports and papers. He often told me that if he had less of these papers to examine he would have more time to occupy himself with at least one essential branch of the administration. There were so many layers of clerks between the Tsar and his people; that was the great trouble.

The Emperor, knowing the unselfish sincerity of my husband, always believed him and was grateful to know that he at least would always tell him the truth. Since the 1905 revolution, my husband always feared that things in Russia would end badly. The peasants' one and only desire was to possess the ground they tilled, but this very natural sentiment was fanned incessantly by the propagandists with results which one can now see in that luckless country. The peasants were like children, never realizing the immense responsibility this entailed and the enormous work it represented.

Nothing was ever done by the governments to explain things to them in the proper way and enlighten them. They loved their "little Father," the Tsar, but had no confidence in the men who surrounded him. They felt somehow that their grievances never got to the ears of the "little Father." I often witnessed the joy in these people's faces when they saw the Tsar, and one could see that they longed to get near him. It is entirely impossible to compare the Russian mentality with that of any western country. Russians see things in an entirely different way from other peoples. One of the great misfortunes was that a lot of young men of the lowest classes went to the universities without any kind of education, and having no sense of proportion immediately became nihilists or bolsheviks, and imagined they could free their country from the landlords.

Emperor Alexander II made an enormous amount of reforms and gave many liberties to his country, and had even prepared a constitution. All this did not prevent him from being murdered, which proves that they were more anxious to rid themselves of the autocracy than receive any number of reforms. The truth is, that owing to the vastness of the Empire, the administration was not in a fit state to control the people. My husband always used to say that Russia ought to be governed like the United States, [but] with a Tsar instead of a president.

It was in 1907 that rumours started concerning the notorious and mysterious person called Rasputin. He was not—as many publications insist—a monk. He was a Siberian peasant. In those years his influence, which during the Great War took alarming proportions, was not very noticeable. People spoke about this man as having great curative capacities, and that he was the only person who seemed to ease the sufferings of the poor little Tsarevich. None of us every really knew what the man had in mind, as the Empress had a horror of talking of her private affairs. We only knew that Rasputin was constantly called to the palace, and that Their Majesties treated him as a friend.

His reputation was of the worst, and all this secrecy concerning him undoubtedly only served to aggravate matters. None of us ever set eyes on him, except my cousin Olga, who saw him twice. She told me herself that he made a most disagreeable and uncanny impression on her. He was an utterly illiterate man and could hardly write. He came several times to the Crimea during the Sovereigns' stay there, but I never happened to meet him, though I tried hard to do so. He lived at Yalta and came to the palace in the evenings.

I know though as a certainty that the Empress' great love and veneration for him was because she was absolutely certain that his prayers alone relieved her sick boy, whom she adored above everything. Seeing this poor little boy suffer was too pathetic for words. But he was not always ill, and could look quite strong and healthy at times. He was a very handsome child, and when well, was a regular boy and took an interest in everything. He often came with his sisters to play with my girls at Harax. He only talked Russian as a child, but later had a Swiss and an English tutor. His two eldest sisters, Olga and Tatiana, were pretty and delightful girls. Olga had her father's beautiful eyes and was fair. Tatiana was dark and resembled more her mother's family.

The Empress, who had always suffered so terribly from shyness, did all in her power to ensure her daughters having more confidence, and in this she was successful. They were perfectly natural and talked to everyone with ease. They loved sport, played tennis and rode very well. When they came of age, their father made each an honorary colonel of a cavalry regiment. Olga had a Hussar regiment and Tatiana, Lancers. During parades in uniform, but on side-saddle, they rode past the Tsar at the head of their

135

respective troop. I remember the general commanding their brigade telling me he was very proud of having two pretty lady-colonels riding behind him.

In 1909, the sad news reached us of my father-in-law Papa Michel's death at Cannes. Only his son Nicholas was with his father when he died. The Emperor immediately sent a man-of-war to bring the coffin back to Russia. We all went to Sevastopol to meet the ship. The coffin was taken [from there] by special train to Petersburg, where the body was laid to rest in the Cathedral of St. Peter and St. Paul, in the fortress next to [his] wife. I have rarely met so kind a man and such a perfect gentleman, a *grand seigneur* in every sense of the word.

He was the last of the Emperor Nicholas I's sons. He had been for many years President of the Council of the Empire, and was respected by the whole country. Deputations came from all over Russia to assist at the funeral, the majority, however, arriving from the Caucasus where Papa Michel had been Viceroy during the reign of his brother Emperor Alexander II. Some of these visitors had never been to Petersburg before. I remember asking one of them what had impressed him most in the capital, and he answered, "The Tsar and the Nevsky Prospect," this being the principal street of St. Petersburg. He also very crudely told me he knew at once I must be Greek by my accent in Russian!

GRAND DUKE MICHAEL MIKHAILOVITCH
(Uncle Bimbo)

24th March 1912

KING GEORGE I - 1912

FUNERAL OF KING GEORGE I
Benaki Museum

1912

GRAND DUKE GEORGE, PRINCESS NINA,
GRAND DUCHESS MARIE and PRINCESS XENIA - 1912

Chapter IX

In 1910, the doctors decided that it would be good for my children to have an entire change of air, so it was decided that I should take them to England, and we chose Harrogate in Yorkshire. A short time before leaving Harax, the Grand Duke Nicholas called me to the telephone to tell me that King Edward had just died. This was a terrible shock, and though I knew he was ill, I did not expect this sudden end. I think it was in July when we arrived in London and Aunt Alix asked me and my girls to stay at Buckingham Palace on our way to Harrogate. There I met the Empress, Aunt Minny, who had gone to her sister the moment she heard of King Edward's death. Xenia was also there, having come from Paris. It was indeed a sad meeting for us all.

We did not remain very long, and soon left for Harrogate, where we had taken a small house. My cousin Victoria, who was heartbroken over her father's death decided to come with us and lived in a house next door to ours. My brother Christopher was also with us. My cousin and I took the cure, and every morning early had to go to the Pump Room to drink the horrible sulphur waters. In the afternoons we took long motor drives in the country to visit all the places of interest around us.

Our favourite drive was to Fountains Abbey, a magnificent ruin of an old monastery of the 5th century. This place belonged to Lord and Lady Ripon, better known by their former name, Lord and Lady de Grey, who were both intimate friends of Queen Alexandra. There was a magnificent park and the gardens had been laid out by the famous Lenòtre, who had designed the gardens at Versailles. Their house was called Studley Royal. There were quite a lot of old abbeys around Harrogate which had been standing in ruins ever since Cromwell's reformation. These places were all perfectly beautiful and very interesting.

One day my cousin and I went to Ripon, and driving along the High Street, she saw in a shop window a photograph of her father which she did not possess. She stopped the motor, and entering the shop, asked the man to show her the picture. As he had no idea who my cousin was, he started telling her what a wonderful person King Edward had been, how beloved, and how the whole country regretted his death. Victoria was touched to tears and bought the picture, saying sadly, "He was my father." The man stared in silence, then turning to me tapped his forehead as much as to say, "Poor soul, she is not all there!" I had the greatest trouble to keep my face straight, but I explained to him that my cousin was telling him the truth.

During our stay at Harrogate we were told that King Manoel of Portugal was coming there for a cure. It was shortly after his exile from Portugal. I did not know him but Victoria did, and so she asked my brother and me to ask him to our house and be kind to him, after all he had gone through. He came to dinner with his Portuguese gentleman-in-waiting. After dinner we started playing bridge, but somehow, not knowing each other, we were all rather distant and stiff. At last I could bear it no longer and got up to have a drink. As I was holding the soda water syphon, I do not know what possessed me, but I turned it on to King Manoel and drenched him. This broke the ice at once; he rushed at me, snatched the bottle out of my hand and disappeared with it under the table. From this safe place he drenched us all and the room became a pool. From that moment we became the best of friends and remained such until his death in 1931. After this little episode we met constantly and had very pleasant times together.

After our cure we went to Sandringham. This estate in Norfolk belonged personally to King Edward, and he always spent winter and Christmas there with his family. The house was lovely—large, roomy and extremely comfortable. Aunt Alix showed me Uncle Bertie's private rooms, which she always kept untouched. Everything remained as it was during his lifetime. As I had never been to Sandringham before it all interested me. Aunt Alix's rooms were delightful, with a lovely view of the lawn and garden. She had such an endless amount of possessions that one could hardly move in her rooms. There were hardly any chairs left to sit on, as most of them were used to put albums and various other things on. Her desk always amused me, as there was little space left on it for writing.

She adored all her objects, and woe to anyone who tried to change the place of anything. I pitied the housemaids who had to keep her rooms tidy. My aunt never threw away anything that was given her no matter what it was, and she kept the most incredible things. We often tried to persuade her to get rid of some of these useless objects, but her invariable answer was, "So and so gave it to me and I cannot throw it away." I used to look around for hours at all the old photos and groups she [had] kept since her childhood. She had a wonderful collection of Russian *objets d'art* by the famous jeweller Fabergé, besides other priceless jades and so forth. She also had lovely pictures which she understood, being a very good painter herself. She was also very musical and played the piano extremely well. If any famous musician or singer came from abroad she always invited them to play or sing for her. In her dressing room she had a paper weight of Liszt's hand in bronze.

In her youth she had been a fearless rider and hunted a good deal. As her right knee was stiff owing to rheumatic fever, she always rode on the right side, but this made no difference to her. At Sandringham she had her special kennels with various breeds of dogs. She had, like my father, a passion for animals. Every Sunday at Sandringham, after lunch, she went to the stables where she gave her horses carrots and sugar, then to the kennels. Here the man in charge tied an apron round her waist, and gave her a basket containing neat little squares of white bread. She went from one kennel to another flinging handfuls of bread to her dogs who surrounded her, barking and yelping, nearly pushing her over. Then on to the farm to feed the cows and she would end up at the racing stud. This last visit I enjoyed most of all because those racing horses were very beautiful. It was delightful seeing all the mares going about with their foals, which were quite tame.

The gardens at Sandringham were a real dream of beauty. The first time I saw them I stood in ecstasy as before a glimpse of paradise. Never did I see such a profusion of flowers. There was, I believe, half a mile of herbaceous borders which consisted of every imaginable flower and colour. It really was a marvellous and never-to-be-forgotten sight. The lawns, too, were wonderful, and looked just like huge green carpets. They were so extensive that they had to be mown by a small motor.

Not far from the big house King George and Queen Mary had a small one called York Cottage.

Queen Alexandra, and all her children, loved Sandringham, and it was here that she spent the last three years of her life. After a short time at Sandringham, I left with my children for Russia.

That winter of 1910-1911 has remained a nightmare in my memory. Just before Christmas all the Tsar's children fell ill at Tsarskoe-Selo with chicken pox. Unknown to those looking after them they wrote letters to my children and sent them Christmas presents, little knowing the risk they were taking. Just after New Year my children, of course, fell ill with the disease and had to be put to bed, our visit to Athens being consequently abandoned. My children got the chicken pox very badly and Xenia, for some unknown reason, contracted internal blood poisoning, which developed into peritonitis and later pericarditis; she lay for weeks between life and death. By a miracle she was spared and in March, though she still had a temperature, we took her to Cannes. She was so weak that she could not walk. She had become an absolute skeleton. Nobody will ever know what that child suffered.

["All parties during that season were concerned. Grand Duchess Serge sent a telegram to the anxious parents:

'I have obtained permission for St. Seraphim's holy relic to be brought to you. Make all arrangements for reception.'

It was the first time that the relic had left Moscow.

The palace is in the deepest gloom, the numerous specialists have just left and 'no hope' is their verdict. The child is slowly sinking. Then a telephone message . . . the relic has arrived and the priests are on their way to the palace. The child is to receive the Holy Sacrament and as a concession the parents will receive communion at the same time. . . . Now the priests approaches the little one and she received our lord. The parents are likewise given the Maker and Healer of the World; the relic is placed on an altar arranged for the occasion. Slowly the procession leaves the sick room. The little girl gazes at the casket and slowly her eyes close. The frightened parents do not stir—has she flown away? Then they hear a faint breathing. She sleeps! Two days later she is still alive; the doctors wonder. The holy relic is still guarding the child. Then a faint voice from the bed says, 'Mama you can send the Holy Saint home; I am cured!' From that moment she was saved." *Not All Vanity* (1952), by Baroness Agnes de Stoeckel.

Baroness Agnes de Stoeckel, whose husband was Grand Duchess George's gentleman-in-waiting, quotes of Xenia's English nanny.]

In 1911 we all went to Wiesbaden, where I underwent a cure for my eyes. There was an oculist there called Count Wiser, who had, so he assured everyone, discovered a new way for curing myopia. The first thing he did was to take my glasses away. As a result I could not read or write and had to be helped when walking in the streets. I was in utter despair and after my first walk in this lamentable state I returned home and cried bitterly. After a fortnight of a strenuous cure, I began to be able to read all the large inscriptions on the shops and could distinguish things. Unfortunately, the effects of this treatment did not last long, and though Count Wiser repeated his cure three times, I had to go back to glasses again. This shortsightedness, which nearly all of us in the Greek family suffer from, was inherited from my Russian grandmother. All her children suffered from it, as also their children. My poor grandmother who died at the age of 81, went quite blind during the last years of her life.

From Wiesbaden I went to Denmark with my children on a short visit to my Uncle Freddy. We lived at his country place called Charlottenlund. I had not been to Denmark since my grandfather's death in 1906. Both my aunts, Queen Alexandra and Empress Marie, were living in their own villa by the sea called *Hvidore*. This was a very charming place and belonged to them both. They had furnished it with much care and very good taste. It was here the Empress Marie died in 1928, in exile. They both loved this place and were very proud of it. Queen Alexandra had sent for her English gardener to arrange the grounds, so there was a profusion of flowers reminding one of English gardens. Hours were spent on the beach looking for bits of amber of which my aunts had made quite a collection.

After a fortnight at Charlottenlund the whole family, except my aunts, went to Fredensborg Castle. To me it was most painful going there again after so many years and with so many members of the family missing. I felt completely lost in that enormous place and every corner of it reminded me constantly of our happy childhood. This time it was not haunted by ghosts but by innumerable recollections of the precious past. After a week I left with my children and my brother Christopher. We returned to the Crimea, staying in Petersburg on our way south. It was the last time I saw my Uncle Freddy, as he died the following year.

He had a very sad end, dying suddenly in the street in Hamburg. He was on his way back to Copenhagen from the Riviera and he and his family spent a night at Hamburg. He went out for a short walk as was his habit after dinner. As he did not return his people became anxious and started searching for him. At last they discovered his body at the morgue. He was recognized by the crest on his gold pocket watch. It appears that he had felt suddenly ill and sat on a doorstep and collapsed. The police seeing a dead man there, took the body to the morgue. His death was a terrible blow to my father who was deeply attached to his brother. This death was indirectly the cause of a fatal accident. Prince George Wilhelm, the eldest son of my Aunt Thyra, the Duchess of Cumberland, wished to go to Copenhagen to his uncle's funeral. He left Gmunden by motor with his valet. He was driving himself and on the way skidded and rushed into a tree. He was killed on the spot and his unfortunate mother, who was also on her way to Copenhagen, had to return halfway for her own son's funeral.

It was in October of this year that my father wired to me that Greece with her allies, Serbia, Montenegro and Bulgaria had declared war on Turkey. My eldest brother, Constantine, was named Commander-in-Chief of all the army. What was my pride and joy to hear that my brother led the army from one victory to another. About a fortnight after the first engagement my father and brothers, riding at the head of our army, entered Salonica. My pride knew no bounds. My husband—we were at Harax—laid out big maps of the Balkan front and by using small flags on pins of the respective nationalities, we could follow the movements of the troops.

I started a fund to be able to send equipment to the Greek Red Cross, of which my mother was president. As there were a lot of Greeks in the Crimea they all made contributions, as did a lot of Russians, and I was thus able to send a quantity of useful things to Greece. My mother and my four sisters-in-law worked unceasingly for the hospitals. My brother George's wife, Marie[1], hired a yacht, which, at her own expense, she turned into a floating hospital and transported a great quantity of wounded from the front to the Piraeus. Although she suffered badly from seasickness, she never missed a trip.

When Salonica fell into the hands of our army my parents and the rest of the family settled in that town during the rest of the campaign. My brother Nicholas was named Military Governor of Salonica and the surrounding country. Unfortunately, all the letters which my father wrote to me during this interesting and exciting time were lost with the rest of my belongings in Russia during the Bolshevik revolution. His pride and joy knew no bounds because after fifty years of reign, he at last saw the

---

1.   Born Princess Marie Bonaparte, daughter of Prince Roland Bonaparte.

realization of his dreams of a greater and united Greece come true. His happiness to see his son and heir victorious can easily be imagined.

In February we had to return to Petersburg to assist at the festivities of the 300 years jubilee of the Romanovs' reign. Just as I was dressing to go to the Winter Palace for a gala lunch, I received a wire from my brother Constantine from Janina, capital of Epirus, telling me that he had captured this town on that day, which happened to be my birthday! It is useless to describe my joy. When I arrived at the palace the news was already abroad, and I was received by all the family with abundant manifestations of delight, and many congratulations. Both the Tsar and the Grand Duke Nicholas expressed themselves in highest terms of admiration for the leadership of my brother and valour of the Greek army. It was one of the happiest days of my life. When I was leaving the palace a lot of the public standing in the street surrounded my car and cheered for my brother and his new victory. A few days later I returned to the Crimea to join my children. My husband had to remain in Petersburg on business.

A couple of days after my arrival at Harax, the crushing news came of my beloved father's murder. I thought my heart would break. I decided to leave at once for Greece and returned to Petersburg. From the station where my husband met me, I drove directly to Anitchkov Palace, where I found Aunt Minny in a terrible state of mind. The next evening I left for Athens with my Uncle Dimitri, my mother's youngest brother, whom the Tsar sent to represent him at the funeral. We travelled via Vienna to Trieste where we embarked on an Austrian passenger ship. There we met several of my Danish relations, and Prince Roland Bonaparte, my brother George's father-in-law. We disembarked at Patras and travelled by train to Athens. At the station my brother Constantine, now King, and the family received us. There was a guard of honour. Even through my misery and tears I could not help being impressed by the sad expressions of these men straight back from the front. There seemed to be a dark cloud over everything, and a general silence everywhere, although wherever or whenever my brother appeared, crowds of people collected. They all stood in respectful silence, trying to communicate to us all their sympathy and commiseration. They felt they had not only lost their king but their father.

My brother drove me to the palace where my poor mother awaited me. A great quantity of foreign princes arrived for the funeral. My father's coffin lay in state in the Cathedral and all day people passed by to pay a last tribute to their Sovereign who had given his precious life for their country. On the day of the funeral the coffin was carried from the cathedral to the awaiting gun-carriage by my brothers and nephews. No one else was ever allowed to touch it. From the cathedral to the station the streets were lined by our glorious troops, looking sad and forlorn on this heartrending occasion.

Our beloved father was laid to rest at Tatoi, the place he loved so well. His tomb stands among cypresses and pines, a place he chose himself for the family burying ground. Not far from his grave are two more, one of my baby sister Olga, the other of my nephew Alexander[2].

A couple of weeks after the funeral I returned by sea to the Crimea. I travelled on a Russian passenger ship, and I remember the captain telling me it was a very risky journey, as the Turks had put floating mines outside Smyrna, where we stopped for a few hours, and in the Dardanelles. We were lucky, however, and got by safely. Shortly afterwards I heard that an American ship was blown up there.

Passing by Constantinople, I received a wire from Constantine announcing the birth of his youngest daughter, Katherine. As a proof of admiration and special love for his brave troops, my brother made all the army and navy her godfathers as the Emperor Nicholas had done for his son when he was born during the Russo-Japanese war. Following is a translation of my brother's message to his army and navy:

> "On the occasion of my youngest daughter's christening tomorrow, I name as her godfathers my victorious army and navy in feelings of deep love to them, and also with the wish to draw tighter the bond between them and my House, which has been indissolubly forged in the fight for our beloved Motherland, in the fields of Macedonia, Epirus and the Aegean. As owing to present circumstances it is impossible to have deputations from the army and navy, your respective Ministers will represent you. Constantine R."

As my ship only went as far as Odessa, the Tsar kindly sent me his Black Sea yacht, *Almaz*, to meet me there. I went on board at once, but owing to a terrific storm we were unable to start for Yalta before the third day.

In June it was decided I should return to Germany to continue the cure for my eyes with Count Wiser, the oculist who had treated me in Wiesbaden. My husband went to Marienbad and came over to see me and the children several times during this cure. Before going to Germany, the Grand Duchess Serge asked me to come to Moscow, as she wished me to take her place as President of the Philharmonic Society. Having become a nun, she gave up all work which was not exclusively philanthropical. This Philharmonic Society had existed for many years, and the first president was the Grand Duke Nicholas, son of Tsar Nicholas I. After his death it was given to the Grand Duchess Serge.

On my way from Moscow to Petersburg I received a wire from my mother from Athens saying that our Bulgarian Allies had attacked the Greek and Serbian troops at the front. Although this news horrified me, it was not utterly unexpected, because the Bulgarians had been behaving in a strange manner for quite a long time. My brother did all in his power to avoid a conflict, but now it was impossible not to retaliate as he had been openly

---

2.   Today, all of the children lie beside their parents.

attacked. I read in my diary of 1913:

> "Our troops are fighting gloriously and victoriously, the Bulgarians retreating everywhere in disorder."

During my three weeks stay in Germany I had continual news from Greece with descriptions of the splendid victories of the Greek troops pursuing the treacherous Bulgarians.

On my name day in July, I received the following telegram from my brothers:

> "Best wishes and congratulations from the blood-stained fields of Macedonia."

signed with all their names. In August, my mother wired to me in England that peace had been signed. On our way back to the Crimea we remained a few days at Moscow to see the Grand Duchess Serge, and stayed at the Nicholas Palace in the Kremlin.

I visited Ella at her lovely convent, which was the most peaceful place imaginable. There was quite a large garden with neat little paths under shady trees and clumps of flowers here and there. Ella had just built a lovely church in the centre of the garden, which she showed me with pride. Her rooms at the convent consisted of a small anteroom, then a little room where she received. These rooms were very simply furnished, and looked cool and clean. She slept in a tiny, narrow kind of cell, on a hard board. All the walls were covered with beautiful ikons and gave the impression of a tiny chapel. I will never forget what a picturesque and peaceful sight it was to see the nuns all in grey, walking about the garden among the trees. We then sat together in her little workroom and talked for hours about everything. She was so human and understanding. Sadly, I never saw that dear kind friend again.

We spent all that winter in the Crimea. In February I left alone for the Riviera and stayed at Cap d'Ail for a third treatment for my eyes. Count Wiser was then at Monte Carlo, and I had to go to him twice a day. My husband and children joined me later, and we went to Athens. My niece, Marie, who had just got her divorce from Prince William of Sweden, wrote to ask me if she could go with us to Athens, so I gave her a rendezvous at Brindisi. We embarked on a ship for Corfu, where we spent a few hours. My niece, never having been to Greece before, was very interested to see Corfu, as her mother was born there. For me this visit was extremely painful, as it was at Corfu I had seen my beloved father for the last time in 1912. He had hoped to be able to visit me in the Crimea that autumn, but instead had to rush back to Greece from abroad when the Balkan complications led to war. A few days after our arrival at Athens we had all to go officially to the cathedral for a memorial service on the anniversary of my father's death.

At Easter we assisted at a most unusual and stirring ceremony. Our glorious troops decided to offer the field marshal's staff to King Constantine, their leader during the wars of 1912-1913. The ceremony took place in the ballroom of my brother's palace; the throne was placed on a low dais, and my brother stood in front of it, with the princes at his side. All the commanders of the divisions were present, along with deputations from every regiment. The "baton" was presented to the King by the Minister of War, Venizelos[3], who addressed my brother in a moving speech. My mother and I looked on from a small balcony. We were all moved to tears over this touching ceremony, and my brother Constantine most of all.

It was during that spring that the well-known painter Philip de Laszlo came to Athens to paint a life size portrait of the King. He posed in full dress uniform, his military cloak falling from his shoulders, wearing all his decorations and holding his field marshal's staff. The portrait was an immense success, and the likeness striking.

De Laszlo also painted a beautiful picture of my mother in her widow's weeds, wearing the Grand Cross of the Redeemer. The ribbon, being sky-blue, looked particularly beautiful on her black crepe dress. When my brother posed, I usually sat with him to keep him company, and also because it was most interesting to see de Laszlo paint. Two or three times, when my brother was too occupied to pose, the artist made me take his place, making me wear the long military cape, and hold the cap and baton. It was most tiring as the cape was heavy and the only consolation de Laszlo found was to tell me that it was good for me to feel the weight a King had to bear! My brother Andrew had to pose for the uniform and decorations. We all teased de Laszlo terribly and played tricks on him. My nephew George bought a horrible, cheap, gaudy illustration of the Royal Family, nailed it on the wall of the painter's studio and copied the artist's signature in coal below, a joke which infuriated the artist.

I must here relate an amusing anecdote told us by de Laszlo concerning the old Grand Duke of Weimar, Charles Alexander. This old gentleman was a cousin of my Russian grandmother, and although very cultured, was terribly absent-minded and vague. He once expressed the wish to see a criminal, like any other person would have wished to see a wild beast from the zoo. He was told that this being his wish he would have to go to the state prison. This shocked him at first, but his curiosity overcame his objections. He went to the prison and, in the director's room, one of the interned murderers was brought to him. After looking at him intently he asked this man in an awed voice what he had done. The answer came, "I killed my mother." The Grand Duke, profoundly shocked, replied, "Oh, but you ought not to have done that."

Another anecdote about the same Grand Duke was that he one day asked his wife's lady-in-waiting how many brothers she had. She replied she had three. When he later met one of her brothers he asked the same

3.   Venizelos was Prime Minister, but held several other post in the government as well.

question. When the man answered he had two, the Grand Duke said, "This is very curious because your sister just told me she had three!"

In the beginning of May we, my husband, children and niece, left for the Crimea on board the Russian Imperial yacht *Almaz*, which the Tsar sent for us. We remained two days at Constantinople, where we again visited, but this time luckily, unofficially. This time we went to the bazaar which was most amusing. We also went to visit Skutari and the country on the opposite coast.

When we arrived in the Crimea we at once went to Livadia to call on the Emperor and Empress, who, with their children, were in residence there. During that season we had quite a lot of people staying with us at Harax: my niece Marie, Baron Alexander de Stoeckl, my gentleman-in-waiting, with his wife and daughter; Mr. Brantingham, an American, and others.

An agreeable surprise was awaiting us: electric lights had been installed everywhere during our absence. The Tsar again came two or three times a week to dinner with his two eldest daughters, and we played all kinds of games. We also asked the choir of the Tsar's Cossacks to come and sing and dance for our guests. Mr. Brantingham went quite wild with excitement over the Cossack's weird dances, which they executed holding sharp daggers. He would not believe that they were really sharp, so a Cossack was asked to show him how he cut a single hair with his dagger. I presented Mr. Brantingham with one later as a momento. This American friend was especially delighted to make the acquaintance of the Tsar, whom he had heard much about, being a personal friend of my husband's family. They became great friends and Mr. Brantingham often repeated to me that the Tsar was quite different to what he had expected and was struck by his enormous charm, knowledge and general understanding.

PAGES FROM HARAX GUEST BOOK

3ᵉ Ноября

Signatures from top: Princess Zinaida Yusupov (Felix's mother); Prince Felix Yusupov;
Center of page: Nicholas II, Alexandra, Olga, Tatiana, Empress Marie, Prince Christopher;
Bottom: Tatiana, daughter of Grand Duke Constantine Constantinovich

Queen Marie of Roumania

COUSINS
Standing: Grand Duchess Olga, Princess Nina, Grand
Duchess Anastasia, Grand Duchess Tatiana,
Front: Princess Olga (of Greece and Yugoslavia),
Grand Duchess Marie, Princess Xenia

EMPEROR NICHOLAS II

Chapter X

In May 1914, the Empress organized a huge bazaar for all the charitable institutions of Yalta. It was very prettily arranged on the large mole, the Emperor's two yachts, *Standart* and *Almaz*, being moored close to the pier, so that one could get on board quite easily, and look down from the deck onto the bazaar. A small pavilion had been erected for the Empress, and there she sat all the afternoon selling to the public various things she had worked or painted herself, and also postcards of the Emperor, herself and their children. There were flowers everywhere, and little booths all around. We all participated in work for this bazaar. I painted a lot of nursery rhyme pictures on rough tussah silk made into cushions. When I was bored, I went up to the deck on board the *Standart* and conversed with the Emperor, walking to and fro. The bazaar lasted for three days, with wonderfully good financial results.

On May 30, their Majesties left for Roumania on an official visit to King Carol and Queen Elizabeth. We went to take leave of them at Livadia during the afternoon, and then hurrying back as fast as we possibly could, were just in time to see them pass our part of the sea, followed by an escort of the Black Sea Fleet. We all, with our house party, stood on the terrace just above the sea and waved to them with sheets. It was a beautiful sight seeing those ships going by just at sunset on a perfectly calm blue sea. Little did any of us suspect that it was our last glimpse of the beloved Tsar on this earth. He silently glided out of sight—and out of our life forever.

The last thing he told us all was, "Remember that whatever happens we must all meet again here in the Crimea in October." It was never to be. None of us standing there that day ever saw the Crimea again.

Shortly after Their Majesties' departure, our guests gradually left us. The only ones who remained were Baron de Stoeckl and his family, who accompanied me later to England. In June the heat became intolerable, and there was not a breath of air anywhere. I felt quite ill and so did my youngest child, who lost her appetite and was getting so alarmingly thin that we had to send for our doctor from Petersburg. I had no wish whatever to travel that year, and my husband seemed loath to let us go.

The doctor, after thoroughly examining my daughter, said that she was to go at once to Harrogate for the bracing air, or else he could not answer for the consequences. We therefore decided that I should take the children to England for only three weeks, and [then] return to Harax;

meanwhile, my husband would go for a cure to Marienbad.

About a fortnight before we left, the news came of the horrible murder of the Archduke Franz Ferdinand and his wife at Sarajevo. Although everyone was much shocked and horrified, no one really realized, at that early date, the terrible consequences it would entail. The thought that we, my children and I, would never return to Russia, or see our precious Harax again, never crossed our minds.

We left for Odessa on board the *Almaz* on July 12. The heat was ferocious and the dust at Odessa quite indescribable. After a night spent on board, we left next day for Warsaw, where the Governor General was at the station for our arrival. We visited the beautiful palaces of the former Polish kings, where my grandparents had lived while Grand Duke Constantine was Governor General of Poland in 1863. My mother used to tell us about that time, which must have been rather anxious, as they had a revolution and my grandfather was shot at, but only slightly wounded. Later on, we had tea in the garden of the Palace of Bellevue, the residence of the Governor General. At Warsaw we had the first inkling that the atmosphere in Europe was becoming dangerous. We took leave of my husband that evening at the station on our way to Paris. Little did we dream that we should never see him again.

We arrived in London the evening of July 17, and stayed at Claridge's Hotel. I went to dinner that night at Marlborough House with Aunt Alix, her daughter Victoria and Aunt Minny, who was on her yearly visit to her sister. We only remained four days in London and then left for Harrogate. The Sarajevo murder was on everyone's lips, and the talk was all of the dangers arising on Europe's political horizon. Everyone hoped though that a catastrophe would be averted, and there was so much confidence that this would be the case that I decided to go off to Paris with Baron and Baroness de Stoeckl and their daughter for a few days, after settling the children at Harrogate. When we got to London and went to Marlborough House, I found both my aunts in a terrible state of anxiety, and the Empress begged me not to go to Paris, as the political news was very alarming. She even said she thought of returning to Russia in a few days.

On the 30th of July, the Russian Ambassador, Count Benckendorff, begged the Empress to leave at once as war was quite inevitable. They were afraid she would not be able to get through Germany, as all the trains there were already mobilized by the army. She proposed to take me and my children back with her, but there was no time to do this, as they were at Harrogate, and the Empress left on the 31st. I was perfectly sure that I would be able to follow her quite easily in a couple of weeks as had been decided.

When the Empress arrived at Berlin she was told it would be impossible for her to go any further, as war had started between Germany and Russia, and that she could either return to England or go to Denmark. The Kaiser sent two men to the Empress—one was Count Mirbach, later assassinated in Moscow—to tell her that Russia had declared war on

Germany, to which she replied that it was just the other way round! Meanwhile, the Russian Ambassador arrived in a nearly demented state, and told the Empress what was going on in Berlin, the awful way Russians were being treated, himself and his staff included. The Empress then left for Copenhagen, and the people at the stations where her train stopped were rude to her and shook their fists at her car, and used bad language. The Empress gathered crowds of Russians in Denmark, who had got out of Germany in the most miraculous ways, after abominable treatment, and took them all with her to Russia. The Russian Ambassador told the Empress that he had wired to her in London that her travelling through Berlin was out of the question, but she never received this telegram, which most probably was purposely kept back by Germany.

Meanwhile, my husband had wired that he had abandoned his plan of going to Marienbad owing to the alarming situation, and urged us to return as soon as possible.

On August 4, I returned to Harrogate, and on the way there we heard that Great Britain had declared war on Germany. The general excitement everywhere and the elation were tremendous. I must honestly own that I felt nothing of this, but, as I wrote in my diary, "Feel completely crushed and so anxious. A real hell of a position. May God have pity on His World".

Events were following each other in indescribable rapidity. I then decided to organize a small hospital for twelve beds to be of some small use to the country we were stranded in. Baroness de Stoeckl and I set to work at once to look for a convenient house. We discovered a very nice little nursing home and made our propositions to the Matron. She at once accepted. We arranged a committee consisting of the Mayor of Harrogate, as chairman; Mr. Bain, ex-Lord Mayor of Leeds; the surgeon, Mr. Herbert of Franklin; Mr. Stephensen, director of the Bank; and Mr. A. Haserick. As ladies, I had Mrs. Boyd Carpenter, daughter-in-law of the well-known Bishop of Ripon; Mme. de Stoeckl and Mrs. Whitworth. These ladies and gentlemen proved the greatest help to me during the five years that my hospitals worked. Their energy and interest never slackened for a day. Thanks to all of them, these hospitals proved a success.

I made an appeal to the residents of Harrogate, asking them to participate in our work, and help us with donations instead of sending their offerings to unknown funds. They responded generously. Meanwhile, lectures started in town for first aid at which we assisted. We also had a nurse come to my house to give us special practical nursing lessons, and later a doctor came from Leeds and put us through an examination. The doctor was satisfied and we received certificates as British Red Cross Nurses. I went to London for a few days to let the War Office know that my modest hospital was ready and at their disposal. At Marlborough House I met my cousin Margarethe, only daughter of Prince Waldemar of Denmark, who had arrived in London quite unexpectedly. She was staying at Chantilly, near Paris, with the Duchess de Chartres, her grandmother, who, hearing of the

Germans' approach on Paris, sent her off to England to Aunt Alix. Princess Victoria suggested I should take her back to Harrogate with me, an idea I accepted with joy, as Margarethe is a great favourite of mine. Her Danish lady-in-waiting came with us. They both at once started learning nursing too. At last, on September 24, I was notified from Leeds that we were to be ready to receive fourteen wounded soldiers. As I had asked for twelve to start with, there was a terrible commotion to get more beds and fit them all into this small hospital. We were all extremely busy and excited at the thought of at last beginning our work, after waiting three long weeks. Our first patients were not very bad cases, in fact, they were nearly all convalescents sent from the big military hospital at Leeds.

Besides our new Matron, we had an excellent professional nurse. As probationers I had my cousin Margarethe, her Danish lady-in-waiting, Miss Rumsing, and Mlle. [Zoia] de Stoeckl. They worked hard and conscientiously, and became very efficient.

I found another place, quite large, which was a convalescent home belonging to a big hospital at Sunderland. I asked the Committee of this hospital if they would be willing to give me this home for war work. They very amiably consented to do this for a few months. Later, I was lucky enough, with the King's help, to secure it for the duration of the war. This was a charming place in a garden with big and airy wards. We turned one big room on the ground floor into an operating theater. I had, of course, to get a lot of new beds and various equipment in order to turn it into a regular hospital.

At the end of December we finally got our first contingent of fifty wounded straight from the front; the hospital train bringing the wounded to York and Leeds stopped at Harrogate, and the cases which were destined for my hospital were taken off there. The ambulance service was admirably organized by Mr. and Mrs. Titley, who were indefatigable in their work. Mrs. Titley had herself instructed the stretcher bearers in their work, and the results were perfect.

During the meals, Baroness de Stoeckl and myself used to talk to the wounded. Their conversations were sometimes most amusing. I was told by one of the nurses of a discussion between some of the men as to how they were to address me. One man said they were to call me "Sir" because that was the way they addressed their commanding officers! Another time, when my cousin, Victoria, was staying with me at Harrogate, she was present when the wounded arrived. She and I went from ward to ward and passing the dining room where the "sitting cases" were eating, we heard the wife of our Surgeon, Mrs. Franklin, telling the men who we were, whereupon one of them exclaimed: "My word, we are among the nuts"!

As my first hospital could only contain comfortably twelve beds, I decided to give it up and take a bigger house. We were lucky to find one nearly next door to Heatherdene. This I hired and named it St. Nicholas, after the Tsar's patron saint. As quite a considerable sum of money was sent to me from Russia, both from my husband and the Russian Red Cross, through its President, the Empress Marie, I put up a small white enamelled board above every bed with the names of the Emperor, Empress, Grand Duke George, and my daughters. This was also done for the King and Queen of England, Queen Alexandra, Princess Victoria, the Prince of Wales, who kindly endowed a bed each for one year. Several people at Harrogate having done the same, their names were also put up.

One member of my Committee, Mr. Haserick, endowed five beds in each hospital. This gentleman was constantly at the hospitals, bringing books and illustrations to the men, talking to them and doing all in his power to make them happy. For many of them, who could no more return to the army, he found work and helped them for years after the war was over.

My daughters, being much too young to nurse, although my eldest, Nina, was longing to do so, visited the wounded constantly, bringing flowers and trying to cheer them up. Nina helped Mrs. Boyd-Carpenter every Saturday to look after the bills.

When St. Nicholas was ready, Miss MacRae recommended as Matron for it a Miss Croll, a friend of hers. She, like Miss MacRae, was Scotch, and was a charming and very capable matron.

When the Germans got through Belgium, England was overrun by refugees from that country, and even at Harrogate we had numbers of them. They were very ungrateful people, with few exceptions, and gave the authorities quite a lot of trouble. There was a small hospital started for the Belgian wounded soldiers, but they, unlike the refugees, were quite nice and behaved well. We visited them quite often, and my first lot of soldiers used to go and see them sometimes. These meetings were very funny as they could not talk each other's language and their conversation was mostly by signs.

We all had such a lot to do that we really did not have much time to worry about the war and the political situation. My children and I daily received wires and letters from my husband, who gave us news from the Russian front, which was brilliant at first. Several times I asked for permission to return to Russia as I felt that my place was really there, but each time I was told to wait, as travelling by land was out of the question, and the North Sea was too dangerous because of the German submarines. Both King George and the Admiralty strongly dissuaded me risking a return to Russia just then.

At the end of December 1914, my husband wired that the Emperor had taken him on his staff. He had been out of the army for so many years that he did not feel justified to ask for a command. The Emperor sent him constantly on inspections to the troops at the front, and at the rear also, to various Red Cross Units and hospitals.

In order to be able to get more cases from the front, I took another house which we turned into a kind of convalescent home. This place I named St. George's, after King George's patron saint. To this hospital, which could hold about 40 men, many of the Harrogate soldiers were transferred.

Besides my three hospitals there were several others at Harrogate, and I often used to visit them. I also went several times to York and Leeds, which were close by. We also went to lord Galway's estate, not far from Doncaster, where they had arranged a charming little hospital for forty men. Lady Galway received us in military uniform, and instructed her nurses to give us a military salute. Her butler, at lunch, was attired in a sergeant's uniform. My cousin Margarethe and I did all we could not to laugh at this extremely military demonstration.

For my birthday and Christmas, my soldiers offered me the most charming presents, which touched me deeply: small silver jewel cases, silver frames containing their photographs, silver cigarette boxes, etc. I use them all to this very day, and value them among my most treasured possessions. I also have a leather album in which I pasted all their photographs, many autographed with touching inscriptions.

I used to correspond with most of them for years, and I have kept all their letters, one of which I will copy here, as well as a poem dedicated to me by a Canadian:

To H.I.H. The Grand Duchess George of Russia.

Madam,

I write these few lines to Your Highness to thank you with all my heart for the care and kindness you have given me during my seven months stay in Your hospital in Harrogate. I am taking this liberty in writing to you as I was very much disappointed when I left St. George's without seeing you; we had to come away very sudden, it caused me more pain than all I had gone through to leave as it was leaving home but I knew it would have to come some time. I would willingly go through everything again if I knew I was coming under your care again. The remembrances of St. George's will live long in my mind. I have had many unhappy weeks in France but I have been paid ten fold back for them in Harrogate. If I have to go back to the Front I would go with a good heart if I knew I was to receive the same reward when I returned. I have often heard people say how they pitied the wounded but ask the boys who come from Your Highness' Hospital I have met a few down here who all wish they were back so now I must close thanking Your Highness again for your care, kindness and the happy times I have received at your Hospitals St. Nicholas and St. Georges'.

I remain your sincerely,

Sapper Walsh

The following is a poem dedicated to me by a Canadian:

>   Grand Duchess George of Russia, you have played a
> noble part,
>   And I am sure that all your doing its from your very
> heart,
>   The cause it is a worthy one, for our wounded boys
> we know,
>   Who are fighting fumes and gases against our
> German foe,
>   You've selected a fine mansion in a quite little spot,
>   And the treatment that we receive will never be
> forgot,
>   And when we're back in Canada which is far across
> the sea,
>   I am sure there's many soldiers who's thought will
> be of Thee.

During one of my short visits to London in July 1915, I went with Aunt Alix and Victoria to Windsor where we lunched with their Majesties. It was then that King George gave me the decoration of the Red Cross instituted by Queen Victoria in 1883. It came as a complete surprise as it is an honour rarely conferred on foreigners. King Edward had given my mother, my sister-in-law Sophie and myself the order of St. John of Jerusalem for hospital work in 1897 during the Greco-Turkish war, so I felt very grand possessing two British orders for war work.

That same summer my cousin Victoria came and stayed with me for a couple of months. She took the greatest interest in my hospitals and visited them daily. She left in a hurry in October, because she received the news that her brother, King George, had had a bad accident in France. While inspecting his troops at the front, he was thrown from his horse, which fell on him and very nearly crushed him. The King was immediately taken to the hospital for first aid, and then was brought over to England by hospital ship like the rest of the wounded. He arrived in London in the hospital train, and was moved to Buckingham Palace in an ambulance. He had to remain in bed for quite a long time.

I went to London with Victoria and visited him, and he said that as I saw so many wounded soldiers he would show me his leg, which he did; and I was horrified to see that it was perfectly black from the bruise. He had a very narrow escape and took quite a long time getting over it.

While in London, I accompanied Queen Alexandra to quite a number of hospitals. The Queen was quite wonderful during these visits because she spoke to every single man, shaking hands and asking them where they had been wounded, about their families and comforting those who were in pain. The joy of seeing her was visible on every face.

After a short stay in London, during the Russian Christmas to be able to go to the Russian Church with my girls, we returned to Harrogate.

Early in March 1916, after dinner, all the electric lights were lowered three consecutive times, which meant that a Zeppelin was coming. This being the first air raid, the excitement was indescribable. Everyone rushed out-of-doors to look, but nothing happened. We later heard that three Zeppelins had passed over Hull. One event which happened at one of my hospitals, and which filled our hearts with pride, was that a wounded sergeant there was notified that he was the recipient of the coveted Victoria Cross. It was the very man, who years ago, had served in the Royal Navy and was with the ship in Crete in 1898 when my brother George and I spent Christmas on board.

In July, Queen Alexandra came to Harrogate to spend two days with me and to visit my hospitals. I was awfully proud and happy to have her there, and the joy of the soldiers to see her was quite touching.

As my girls were now growing up, Nina was fifteen and Xenia thirteen, it was decided we would establish ourselves in London for their further education. We took a house in Grosvenor Square. It was a very pretty and comfortable place, but somehow none of us ever felt really at home or happy there. News both from Russia and Greece got worse daily, and we all felt low and worried. Besides this, both my girls fell ill with measles. My only consolation was going to my beloved Aunt Alix at Marlborough House. She was always so full of sympathy in my troubles and anxieties, and invariably saw things in the right light and never misunderstood.

My two nationalities, Greek and Russian, proved most unfortunate, and even painful just then. My position was at times very awkward. I was even accused of being a spy, but I was quite unable to discover in what way. I was not supposed to be seen in public then with any member of the Royal Family, as my poor eldest brother was dubbed a traitor, as was the Tsar.

One lady in London society, who had always professed to be a friend of mine, actually asked the Foreign Office to turn me out of England because, as she said, I was a dangerous element. People I had known for years and cared for, turned against me, and kindness, sympathy and help, as is usual in such times, came from quite unexpected quarters, and from people I hardly knew. I was often treated as an unwelcome alien which was very trying. One day a telephone message came from a member of the court saying it would be wise for me to leave at once for Harrogate, because the mob intended stoning my house. As I did not believe this extraordinary message, I sent my Russian Chamberlain to Scotland Yard to discover if this was a fact. As I suspected, he returned to say that there was not a atom of truth in it.

I was also accused of making pro-Greek propaganda in my hospitals, and at one time there was even a question of the authorities closing them, but this luckily never took place. I had to go and see General Bedford, Surgeon General in York, who had replaced General Kenny, and he promised his help, and saved the situation.

Feeling more and more worried, I asked Count Benckendorff, the Russian Ambassador, to come and see me. I explained to him how matters stood and asked him to give me his opinion frankly. He said that it would be best for me to return to Harrogate for awhile until all these painful rumours blew over. I therefore left with my girls for Harrogate where we remained a month, returning to London early in January.

Being established in London did not prevent me from being in constant communication with my hospitals, and I often went to Harrogate to see my soldiers.

In London, I frequently went to Marlborough House to see Queen Alexandra. I used to dine with her nearly every evening. She never had any servants to serve, but the food was put on the table in silver tureens with hot water underneath to keep them warm. After dinner we sat in her boudoir, on a sofa, which stood back to back with her desk, facing the fireplace. So as not to have too much heat in one's face screens stood in front of the fire, two tables in front of us with cards, and we both played patience, of which my aunt was very fond.

She only kept a tiny space for this on the table, as the rest was piled up with quantities of newspapers and illustrated reviews. She always read them holding a magnifying glass, as she said she saw better that way than with spectacles. She read everything and cut out either articles or pictures of interest, which were pasted in special albums. She possessed thousands of these, kept in various boxes or drawers. On a small table stood bottles of excellent orangeade and lemonade.

Aunt Alix received an incredible amount of letters, mostly begging ones, which she often read to me. She never hesitated sending these people sums of money. Once I suggested it would be a good thing to get information through the police concerning these people, as she could not possibly know if they really needed money. She got quite cross with me and answered, "How would you like to ask for help and not get it?"

I have rarely met anyone as generous as Queen Alexandra was. She felt everyone's sufferings, worries or anxieties acutely, just as if they were her own. No matter what people did, she always found some excuse for them. She never cherished a grudge against anyone. She had a wonderful childlike nature, and was up to any fun or mischief. I often teased her, and she never resented it. There was a special link between us from my earliest childhood, and I believe there was nothing we hid from each other; we could just sit and talk by the hour.

She was such a wonderful personality, and so beautiful physically: her complexion was quite out of the ordinary, even in her old age, and this made people believe that she was enamelled and painted up. As a matter of fact, neither of these suppositions had a word of truth in them. Her skin was as soft and fresh as a child's. At night she only smeared her face with cold cream, and after washing it off the next morning, she gently powdered it. She never put rouge on her lips.

It is curious that her hair never turned white; she only had a silvery thread here and there. The scent she used was delicious; I believe it was called "Daphne". Her hands were lovely with elongated fingers and almond nails growing downward; I loved watching them as she used them so gracefully. She was fairly tall, and her figure perfect and all her movements full of grace. She was wonderful in public; the way she bowed and smiled to everyone was quite unique. Each person in a crowd felt that he or she was being singled out. When she bowed she always gracefully waved her hands in a way which was very personal to her.

Her great drawback was her lifelong deafness; she was terribly sensitive about this and absolutely refused, even *en famille*, to use any kind of instrument. She only spoke about this defect in her later years, never even mentioning it before. It was a terrible torture to her, as she was so full of life and interest, and she always felt she was missing something. When anyone shouted at her, it gave her physical pain which she could hardly bear.

Her constant companion was her second daughter, Victoria, who was unmarried. We were great chums, she and I, from my earliest childhood. She was a general favourite amongst all the cousins, and played the role of a kind of confessor, as most of us took our troubles to her, being sure of her sympathy and help. I also often went to her eldest sister, Louise, the Princess Royal. She was always particularly kind and dear to me, and so loyal through all my troubles, during those terrible years. She was extremely shy and retiring, and did not like a worldly life. Her one terror was to be spoken about, or to have people know what she did or said. She was incredibly plucky and extremely generous, always thinking of giving pleasure. I never went to see her without her presenting me with a gift of some kind. She had lived in a big house in Portman Square since her marriage to the Duke of Fife. He had died a few years before the war of pneumonia, which he contracted in Egypt after they were shipwrecked and nearly drowned. They had two daughters: Alix, who married Prince Arthur of Connaught, and Maud, who married Lord Carnegie.

In autumn, Louise always went to Scotland to her place called Mar Lodge, which unfortunately I never saw. She had a passion for the theatre, and she often asked me to go with her. During the entre acts she would frequently send for the actors, as she knew them all, and was very popular with them.

During the war, I sometimes was asked privately to Buckingham Palace with my daughters for tea or luncheon. Their Majesties were both excessively occupied in those terrible years, and worked hard all day. The King went to France several times to see his troops and visit hospitals. In London, too, they both constantly went to see the wounded in the numerous hospitals.

In the summer of 1916, I made the acquaintance of my brother Christopher's future wife, Mrs. Nancy Leeds. She made a charming impression on me, and we became friends at once. She had a house in Grosvenor Square, not far from mine and so we met constantly. I can never be grateful enough to her for all she did for me, especially when the Russian catastrophe took place.[1] She immediately came to my assistance financially, without a moment's hesitation, and if it had not been for her, my children and myself would have been in a tight corner.

When the revolution came, I had to give up my house in Grosvenor Square and take a small one in Regent's Park. My gentleman-in-waiting, Baron de Stoeckl, and his wife and daughter, lived in another house on the same terrace. In the house next to us lived an extraordinary old German lady, married to an English art critic. This woman, without even knowing any of us, took a violent hatred to us, and never missed an opportunity of being rude or nasty when meeting us out of doors. As I was unable to keep a motorcar after 1917, we always went about in buses, and I remember this hateful old witch, she looked exactly like one, getting in with us and telling the people all round who we were and calling us Russian spies. Once the bus was very crammed, and my daughter Nina had to stand, and so this old woman said in a loud voice how pleased she was to see a Princess having to stand.

On one of these buses which stopped just at the back of our house, I remarked that the conductor wore the ribbon of the Russian St. George medal, the equivalent of the Victoria Cross. I immediately asked him how he got it, saying I was interested, being the wife of a Russian general. He said the Tsar had sent it to him after Mons, for having carried dispatches under fire. He also had some other military medals, and he complained that the ribbons were wearing out. I took his name and address and sent him new ribbons for all his medals, a pipe and tobacco, and signed my name on the accompanying card. Next day I received a touching thanks, the copy of the order for his Russian decoration, and his photo. Ever after he saluted me and my girls whenever we got into his bus, to the great rage of the German old lady.

Each time there was a moon we had terrible air raids in London. At first, when Zeppelins visited us, they came when it was dark, but the aeroplanes chose the moonlit nights. I was several times caught in them when dining out at Marlborough House, or with friends, and had to wait for hours before I could get home.

Queen Alexandra was not a bit frightened of them, and I remember once, when the bombardment was at its worst, her going to the window and opening the curtains to look out. She entirely ignored strict orders of keeping everything dark, and I had to rush all over the room to put the lights out. She even laughed at me for doing this. She had a box in which she had

---

1. Nancy Stewart Worthington Leeds, was a divorcee, and widow of William Bateman Leeds, from whom she had inherited an estate estimated at $120 million dollars. Before her marriage, in 1920 to Prince Christopher, she obtained the consent of both Kings Constantine and Alexander, and the marriage was not morganatic. Mrs. Leeds was declared to be, "A Greek Princess in her own right," by King Constantine, and thus achieved the highest royal ranking by any American.

collected all the bits of shrapnel and bombs found scattered about in her garden.

On my way home I could see all the people coming out of the underground stations where they had gone for safety. It was a pitiful sight. Crowds of women with children and tiny babies in prams with terror-stricken faces, pale and bedraggled. The three times the English airplanes got a Zeppelin down, I drove with friends to see the extraordinary sight. In one place I was shown the imprint of one of the German occupants, who had fallen or thrown himself out, deep in the earth clearly depicting his body with arms and legs extended. It was a gruesome spectacle.

When we were staying at Kenwood with Nancy Leeds, we had one of the worst raids. The household met on the ground floor, and all the lights were extinguished. We stood at the open door of the garden terrace to look on. It was a full moon and though gruesome, a magnificent spectacle. We could clearly distinguish all the German airplanes. The noise was deafening, especially from a huge 75mm gun not far off. Each time this gun fired one could see the explosions all over the sky like white powder puffs. Next morning my eldest daughter found a bit of shrapnel six inches long on the terrace, not far from where we had been standing.

During the last air raid three enemy bombs fell in Regent's Park, not far from our house. The crash was so tremendous that I though the whole house was coming down. All the window panes of the house on the terrace next to ours were smashed. A small lodge in the park was ruined, and a lamp post in front of it was cut off as if by a sharp blade. It was the only time I really got scared. With my children I went down to the dining room on the ground floor and we sat there until about two in the morning.

In 1918, I made the acquaintance of an American couple, Mr. and Mrs. Marsh, who had the lease of Warwick Castle, and they asked me to spend a few days with them there. I went with Mrs. Barton-Frenc, another American, and a very old friend of mine whom I knew since my childhood at Athens, where her father had been the United States Minister. There was quite a big house party and our visit proved very enjoyable. I was delighted to have such a good opportunity of seeing this lovely and historical old castle. I was much impressed by it, especially when entering the huge hall, from which one had a lovely view of the River Avon passing just below the castle walls. I was given a magnificent room on the first floor with this very view. This room had been re-arranged by Lord and Lady Warwick many years ago for Queen Victoria, who came there on a short visit.

In one room, next to the huge hall, there was a most remarkable collection of Canaletto pictures, which fascinated me by their beauty. I was told that this famous artist had stayed in his time at Warwick Castle, and had painted most of these pictures for his host. There were several of the castle itself, and also one very large one of the famous Venetian ceremony of the *Wedding of Venice to the Adriatic*.

A number of rooms of the castle were opened to the public. To approach this, the tourists had to pass through the Hall, and often, while we were having tea there, all these people passed by us. What struck me was their perfect manners, because not one of them even turned their head our way. Had this been in any other country, they would have certainly all stopped to stare at us.

My hostess also took me to Stratford-on-Avon, and showed me Shakespeare's house and his tomb, as well as Anne Hathaway's sweet little cottage.

After the Russian catastrophe I was obliged to have a meeting of my hospital committee to explain to them that, to my deepest regret, I would be obliged to resign as I had no more means to carry on. Since these hospitals had done a lot of good work, I thought it a pity to close them, and so I proposed that the Committee should keep them open or that they be given to the town. It was unanimously decided to keep them going, and I was begged to remain at the head, as before, while all expenses would be met until the end of the war. I was naturally overjoyed, and deeply touched by this proof of confidence, and so the hospitals continued their unceasing work until March 1919.

My last Christmas spent with the wounded was 1918, and everyone of them was able to be present at the Christmas feast we gave them. On March 27, 1919, I went back to Harrogate for the sad business of closing my beloved hospitals and taking leave of the Committee. The Committee came to say good-by to me, and presented me with a beautiful antique silver tray as a memento of our mutual work during five years. At the back was the inscription, "Presented to H.I.H. The Grand Duchess George of Russia, by the Committee of her three hospitals at Harrogate as a souvenir of good work in a good cause 1914-1919."

Thus ended a very precious chapter of my life.

GRAND DUKE GEORGE

GRAND DUCHESS MARIE

PRINCESS NINA
(from a de Laszlo painting)

PRINCESS XENIA
(from a de Laszlo painting)

GRAND DUCHESS MARIE (author)
and GRAND DUCHESS XENIA - 1904

Chapter XI

My husband often wrote me despairing details of the terrible disorder he found in all branches of the organization at the rear of the army. The Grand Duke was known for his kindness of heart and his sound judgement, and all those who really worked conscientiously for the good of their country always obtained his aid. On the other hand, those who were slack or dishonest, had a bad time. As I said, he always had to report personally to the Emperor about his work. My husband, realizing the seriousness of the situation, would not overlook the dishonesty of many military chiefs, and insisted they should be punished and even removed in some cases. He even wrote once that he would not be astonished if some of these men turned against him. His one thought was to do all in his power to help and ease the hard lot of the soldiers in the trenches and the wounded. He organized an admirable private hospital in our palace in St. Petersburg, to which he gave the greatest attention, notwithstanding his other work. My mother, who was then in Russia, often went to visit the hospital and wrote to me how wonderful it was, and how happy and contented the men were.

In 1915 my husband was sent on a mission to Japan by the Emperor. He wrote every day, and his descriptions were most interesting. He was splendidly received everywhere by the Japanese authorities. A battleship was sent to fetch him at a port in Korea. It seemed so strange to him, and even painful, to see all the Japanese generals and officers wearing the highest decorations of their country for having beaten the Russians in the last war. Of course, all that was forgotten, and they were all friends again and even allies. My husband was terribly upset when his ship passed Tsoutsima, the spot where the greatest disaster of the Russian fleet took place. The Japanese officers, with great tact, left him and his Russian staff alone during those moments, for which he was most grateful.

He was given an exhibition of wrestling by the sailors on board, which he wrote was interesting and rather weird, though very exciting. At Kobe he entrained for Tokyo. At the station of Tokyo he was met by the Emperor of Japan and all the princes and their numerous suites. My husband wrote that the Emperor's presence at the station was quite an extraordinary event, and something, in fact, never seen before, as His Majesty was not supposed to leave his palace.

My husband was conducted to an open golden carriage where he took place with Prince Kanin, the Emperor driving separately. They were escorted by a squadron of Lancers, and troops were aligned on each side of the street up to the Palace of Nassounigaseki, which was placed at the Grand Duke's disposal.

[Returning from Japan] at Vladivostok he received a telegram from the Emperor with orders to visit the German and Austrian prisoners of war and find out if they were well treated and content, and giving him the right to change anything which was not correct and well arranged. My husband wrote from all these prison camps, after having talked to the prisoners, and said he found very few complaints in those days, and that on the whole the organization was quite good. They complained of the lack of postal facilities, and my husband at once gave orders for this to be altered.

He was deeply impressed by the splendid aspect of the Russian troops all through Siberia. In those days—early in 1916—everybody was working feverishly and hard for the war, and Siberia, being so far from the centre, they had not yet been contaminated by the poisonous propaganda which had started in European Russia. He writes: "I wire every day to Nicky as I know how interested he is. I only tell him the truth and my good impressions of this far-away land, where everything is in good order. Our peasants are prosperous and rich and one sees no beggers or people in need."

Returning to Petersburg he was horrified by the state of affairs in political spheres and the bad spirit which was to be felt everywhere. Rasputin's murder in December seemed to have hurried on the approaching disaster.

Ever since 1914, I had tried every now and then to get back to Russia, as very naturally my husband wanted us to return. I was each time dissuaded by the Admiralty and others because of the danger of German submarines in the North Sea. Their argument was that the Germans were so well informed that there was danger of our being made prisoners, which might complicate matters. My husband even proposed we should return via Germany under the protection of the Red Cross, but all the Russian Ministers who had come on missions to London begged me not to risk this, as they were persuaded that the Germans would play us a dirty trick and keep us as prisoners.

When I heard that Lord Kitchener was leaving for Russia I was on the point of asking the King to give me permission to go with him, but as he left sooner than I expected I had no time to do so. When, on June 6, 1916, we heard of the terrible disaster that befell Lord Kitchener, I was grateful to have been spared. In May of the same year my husband sent his private secretary, Mr. Maichrowsky, to London to see us. He was in hopes we might return with him, but this plan did not mature.

By that time the news from Russia was daily getting worse. I had long talks with Mr. Maichrowsky, who was a personal friend of ours, about what was going on in Russia, and although he could not help seeing what was happening there, he never realized how serious it was. I remember that I was astonished at his illusions and tried my best to prove to him that it was bound to end in disaster. I begged him very seriously to take drastic measures to save our fortune and all our possessions. His only answer was that it was a passing cloud and that things were sure to right themselves, and that everything was much exaggerated abroad, as was always the case about Russian affairs. I was quite in despair over this obstinacy and blindness as to Russia's future. Russians are always full of illusions, but this man was the limit.

Early in 1917 my husband went to Kiev to see the Empress Marie who was living there, because her daughter Olga was working in a hospital in that town. My cousin Olga proved a wonderful nurse and so efficient that she was allowed to perform minor operations, when the great rush came. She was an extremely gifted person, and a great favourite with everyone. My husband's letters from Kiev were full of apprehension, and though he could not write openly, owing to the censor, I could read between the lines how upset he was and how well he foresaw what was looming ahead. His one terror was that the revolution might start before the end of the war, which, as he expressed it, would be a lasting shame on Russia and treachery towards the allies. From Kiev he was sent to visit the Russian army corps in Bessarabia and Roumania. There he went to see Queen Marie and Grand Duchess Kirill, who was on a visit to her sister. On his way back to Moguilev, the Tsar's headquarters, he passed through Pskov where he visited my niece, Grand Duchess Marie, who was working in her hospital there. In every letter his apprehension was growing as well as his anxiety. There were such a lot of rumours about that he could make neither head nor tail of them all.

On March 11, he arrived in Petersburg during the night. He was awakened early next morning by his valet who told him that firing had been going on in town for four days, that barricades had been erected and that the mob was disarming the soldiers and attacking all motorcars. The Grand Duke at once sent for the Colonel of the Gendarmes of the station, who verified these reports, so my husband decided to go to Gatchina and await developments. As the Grand Duke and I always spoke French together, I will translate parts of his letter written on that day:

> ". . . What I foresaw has happened; we are in the midst of a revolution and all the horrors that accompany it. At Pskov, I heard from the Generals and Marie that the last news from Petersburg was very bad and the mob is murdering, firing and sacking on all sides. I do not know any more whom to believe, the rumours are ghastly, as you may imagine. I went at once to see Micha[1], who is not here. Rodzianko, the president of the Duma, asked him to go to Petrograd and he is staying in town. The Emperor is expected back tomorrow morning from his headquarters.

---

1.   Grand Duke Michael Alexandrovitch, who was living at Gatchina with his morganatic wife, Natalia Brassov.

The Empress is at Tsarskoe-Selo and all their children are ill with measles. The soldiers of the reserve battalions are divided in two, one part firing on the other. All this was to be expected, and as I have often written to you, if things are allowed to go in this way, it will end in a formidable revolution. They have let out all the prisoners. My head goes round from all the horrible reports. . . ."

All the news from Russia which reached us in London was very confusing and mixed. My husband could not wire openly and his letters took quite three weeks to reach us. Through Queen Alexandra I heard more details which she had from the King, and although we expected the crash we did not realize it would come so soon and so suddenly. Everybody hoped that the Russians would finish the war before starting their debacle. On March 14th I was asked by some friends to a small supper at the Savoy Hotel in a private room. One of the secretaries of the Russian Embassy had also been invited, but as he did not turn up we sat down to eat. We had nearly finished when he arrived, saying that the most incomprehensible news was dribbling through from Russia. First, that a constitution had been given, then that the Tsar had abdicated, that there was a revolution and so forth. We all separated and went home feeling anxious and sick at heart. Next morning I sent my gentleman-in-waiting to the Russian Embassy to find out if there was any definite news of Russia. I will never forget his expression of horror when he returned to tell me that the revolution was in full swing, that the Tsar had abdicated in favour of his son and that the Grand Duke Michael was Regent, and that this decision had somewhat calmed the situation. We were all in despair and worried to death, and, as we knew more about Russia than others, we could easily read through the lines and realize that something terrible was taking place in that country.

I found Queen Alexandra at Marlborough House in a dreadful state of anxiety, especially over her sister's safety. Next afternoon I went to tea at Buckingham Palace and found Their Majesties very anxious and depressed. There I heard that the Grand Duke Michael had made his manifesto refusing the throne, until the country should have declared through the Constitutional Assembly the form of government desired by the people. Meanwhile, the Duchess of Connaught suddenly died and we all met at the Chapel Royal in St. James Palace, where her coffin was placed before taking it to Windsor for burial. It was all very sad and dismal.

It was here that I met the Empress Alexandra's eldest sister, the Marchioness of Milford Haven, who was in utter despair. One could think and talk of nothing else but the cataclysm in Russia and all the horrors of it. On March 19, we all went to Windsor for the funeral. On my return home I found a Russian colonel waiting for me who had just arrived from Russia bringing us letters from my husband. We talked for a long while.

I read in my diary: "Feel more and more upset, depressed and anxious. God alone knows what else awaits us."

In his next letter my husband says that no one can make out where the Emperor is, as he never arrived at Tsarksoe-Selo as was expected. The next rumour he heard was the abdication of the Emperor, that the little Tsarevich was to succeed him, with Grand Duke Michael acting as Regent, but later on he was told that the Emperor abdicated for his son also.

". . . On March 16, 1917, the Grand Duke Michael returned to Gatchina and described all he had lived through during his stay in Petrograd. For five consecutive days he had endless sittings with the members of the Duma, and at last proposed to write a manifesto asking the people to decide what kind of government they desired. Micha has made this manifesto, not accepting the throne before a legislative assembly can decide what is to be done. He fears that if he is proclaimed Emperor at once, without knowing the wish of the country, matters will never calm down. There are many in favour of a republic."

Again my husband writes:

"You see how we are advancing! We will therefore have no Tsar anymore. Russia once before went through this 300 years ago, before the first Romanov was called to the throne."

His letters, which are numerous, as he wrote his impressions daily, are full of pathos and deep misery as he was profoundly devoted to his sovereign and country. His despair not to have been able to do more than he did to save the Emperor from this humiliation is pathetic.

"It appears that a kind of apathy had settled on the Tsar, and many people said it was owing to unknown medicines which were sent him by Rasputin to calm his nerves. He seemed to take everything as a matter of course and not realize the dangers which were surrounding him on all sides."

My husband was one of the few honest people who begged the Emperor to sign a constitution and name responsible ministers. Alas, it was fatality and nothing could stop this terrible disaster which was like a tornado carrying everything and everybody with it, in its mad career. My husband wrote in another letter:

"Patrols walk through Gatchina all night to keep order. They have insisted upon placing a guard in the house and we have accepted. They are revolutionary troops but we will be safe from hooligans at least. This order seems to have been given by Rodzianko who reigns alone at this moment. This is what I have to see and survive. We have all decided to resign from the army, although it goes against my conscience to do so, as long as the war is still on. Micha's manifesto seems to have calmed the republicans but the others are angry with him and they might think of changing the dynasty, then I will be an ex-Grand Duke or something of the kind. I do not know what I am now, ex-Grand Duke, ex-general, ex-Museum Director, ex-faithful servant of my ex-sovereign, briefly all the possible and impossible ex's.

All the troops have revolted; they all wear red ribbons and rosettes, everything seems to have become red. I do not know any longer where I am or on which planet. The soldiers smoke, sit in the first class compartments of the trains next to their officers and generals and God knows what else. I cannot write more details about this new discipline, because being a soldier myself I am simply ashamed. It is enough to make one's hair stand on end. I would like to leave the country at once."

It was only on March 21, 1917 that he was able to discover that the Tsar had been sent back to Moguilev and was to be brought back, practically a prisoner, to Tsarskoe-Selo, where the Empress was already interned.

From my mother, who was living in her old home at Pavlovsk with her brothers, he heard that the revolutionary troops had entered the palace, saying they came to take away hidden arms. Much later my mother told me that these soldiers came at night and woke up her old Russian maid, who pluckily told them not to make so much noise because the Queen was asleep, worn out from working for the wounded in her hospital. Strange to say they retired in silence, and only stole a pair of diamond earrings belonging to Princess John.

My husband writes in another letter:

". . . .All letters addressed to any of us are confiscated, which explains why yours do not reach me. This is called liberty. Less blood would have been spilt if that blackguard Protopopov had not put maxim guns onto the roofs. That vile man was a traitor and played a double game all through. If the police had gained the upper hand, he would have turned out a hero in the eyes of that good-for-nothing ex-government: but now that the revolutionaries have won, he will say that he did all this to help the revolution. He can boast that he succeeded brilliantly. The blood of the innocents on both sides will be on his head."

Telephoning was simply dangerous because the lines were tapped by the revolutionaries in hope of hearing something compromising.

The following is an account of the meeting between Empress Marie and her son Emperor Nicholas II, as recounted by Grand Duchess Xenia:

". . . .When the Empress Marie heard that her son, the Emperor, had been taken back to Moguilev practically a prisoner, she immediately left Kiev to join him. She arrived just after he had signed his and his heir's abdication.

The Empress was accompanied by her son-in-law, Grand Duke Alexander. She spent five or six days with the Emperor living in their respective trains. The Empress was deeply impressed by the Emperor's wonderful courage and resignation. He only once gave way and sobbed, hiding his face in his hands. What had deeply hurt him was the hard and rude way in which General Russky had treated him at Pscov, shouting at him and thumping the table with his fist, saying: "Will you make up your mind to go?

To the Empress' question why he abdicated and if he thought there was a chance of his ever returning he said: 'What could I do when Nicolasha and General Alexeiev asked me to resign for the country's sake? No, I will never return.' The Empress was quite crushed by all she heard and saw. She took leave of her son, whom she was never to see again and then returned to Kiev where she was persuaded to leave for the Crimea."

Xenia was never allowed to see her brother any more, though she applied for permission over and over again. She was then staying in her house at Petersburg. She wrote him a letter begging those responsible to give it to him, but the Emperor only received it several months later when he was at Tobolsk.

When the Grand Duke Michael heard that his brother, the Emperor, was going to be sent away—no one knew where to—he asked permission to take leave of him. He managed to do this through Kerensky, who was himself present during this last meeting of the brothers, as well as the officer on duty. The interview only lasted a few minutes, but these poor brothers were so overcome that they could hardly talk. The Emperor proposed that Micha should also take leave of the Empress, but Kerensky refused, saying there was only a permission given for the brothers to meet, so they just embraced and said "Good-bye" forever.

The next news we heard was that the Duma had refused to accept the Grand Duke Nicholas as Commander-in-Chief of the army, which had been one of the Tsar's last orders. This obviously meant that it was the end of the glorious Russian army, and that everything was going to pieces. On the first Sunday I went to the Russian Church after hearing of all these disasters, I was painfully struck that the names of the Emperor and Imperial Family were not mentioned. It made me feel quite sick. Then came the news that the *appanages*, where the Imperial Family's fortunes came from, had been nationalized. This meant that we were all ruined. Our one hope was that our personal capital would be respected and left us, but that was all taken too, when the banks were attacked. Although I had begged and implored our secretary to take serious measures in time to save our money and belongings, nothing was done and so we lost everything we possessed in one blow. It was then that Nancy Leeds came to my help. The first thing we did was to look for a smaller house and cut down all expenses.

My husband's letters did not come any more by post, but he used to profit by officers coming to England and send them to me in this way. I used to receive about ten or twelve at a time, and his descriptions were steadily getting worse and more crushing. At the end of March he wrote that the new government was arresting all the ladies attached to the Empress and also the Emperor's aides-de-camp.

> ". . . . Our fate, that is, the fate of the Grand Dukes, has not yet been decided. They do not allow us to go to the front fearing that we might start a counterrevolution, which has not even crossed our minds. On the other hand they have not given us permission to leave for abroad. We can only wait and see what they will decide. The Emperor having been forced to abdicate we are all thrown into the arms of the revolutionaries. There are only three things to be done, i.e., first to try and escape, which none of us tried to do, secondly, to commit suicide, thirdly to recognize this provisional government, which we have done, instinctively, without even consulting each other, because there is no doubt that the old regime could not work any more. As to this, we all and immense Russia were of the same opinion. My only wish is to get out of this hell as soon as possible and rejoin you three, whom I have not seen for over two years."

On March 25, my husband wrote:

> ". . . . We feel a bit happier these last two days as affairs seem to be calming down. The government is trying to be as polite as possible with us Grand Dukes, I must own they have been quite correct towards us. Some of them we know personally, such as Terechenko and Rodzianko. Micha has made Kerensky's acquaintance. He is Minister of Justice and a terrible socialist. Up to now they have no intention of hanging us, but if the workmen get the upper hand then everything is possible, communism and even

182

anarchy. There is talk about sending Nicky to England, but the Radical-Socialists are against this, saying that the Emperor knows too many state secrets. We are quite unable to get news from Tsarskoe-Selo. More than half the rumours we hear prove to be lies. They say the Emperor's house is surrounded by a double file of revolutionary troops and not a soul is allowed near the place. The children are still very ill. I would be so happy to know that they are leaving for England."

In all his letters he is utterly revolted over the indescribable vulgarity of everything, the tone of the papers, the expressions used and the venom poured on everyone's head, which, he said, were perfectly nauseating.

He also names different members of the family who were being arrested for some unknown reason. The Empress' friend, Mme. [Anna] Vyrobova was arrested at Tsarskoe-Selo and taken to the fortress, and everyone rejoiced as she was generally detested owing to her well-known intrigues. One rather curious incident he described when he went to Petersburg for the day.

". . . . There are touching scenes to be witnessed at the stations. Today a soldier came running to the compartment in which Micha sat by the window, and taking off his military fur cap made a deep bow. We could not find a place on the train on our return and had to wait half an hour for the next one where they kept a few seats for us. We are not allowed to have special cars any more.

Today, at the station, I approached a group of soldiers who stood at attention in the old way and I talked and joked with them and they seemed delighted to talk to me. I think the public around was much astonished. I own that I saw one horrible face scowling at me among them. I could do anything with these soldiers who now want a republic with a Tsar! Little by little they are getting away from the clutches of the revolutionary workmen and will have nothing more to do with them. You cannot imagine how much I suffer seeing these masses of soldiers like misguided sheep, with frightened eyes like children who have done something very bad, and do not know how to make amends for it. It is a grave sin to have corrupted them to such a degree and I pity them from the depths of my heart.

Whilst seated in the train the conductor, an ex-soldier, got hold of my hand and kissed it over and over again without uttering a word. I hear that a lot of English officers went to visit the revolutionary soldiers in their barracks, and those who spoke Russian tried to explain to them what their duty to their country was and also the real sense of the word 'liberty'."

My husband wrote to Prince Lvov, then Prime Minister, to ask permission to leave for England, saying that he had resigned as he was not allowed to go to the front and consequently was free from any obligation. The answer was that though the Premier took my husband's position into consideration, he was deprived of the possibility of acceding to his wish to go to England, owing to the unanimous decision of the government to consider the absence out of Russia of any member of the Imperial Family undesirable at the present moment. This answer upset him terribly as his one and only wish was to get out of that hell and rejoin us in England. He went on to say that everybody had gone raving mad and to live in this atmosphere was enough to drive one insane. He wrote that although the government was doing its best to keep order, the Soviets of the Workmen, headed by Jews, were systematically ruining everything, and the obvious result was going to be the most terrific and hopeless anarchy.

One of the extraordinary things that happened on the second day of the revolution was that Goutchkov, the War Minister of the Provisional Government, signed the now famous "Order №I" by which military discipline was definitely eliminated. Another scandalous act of this government was to decorate the first soldier who murdered the first officer with the Cross of St. George. By these unpardonable acts one can easily judge how corrupted the whole army had become.

On April 19th he wrote:

". . . . The Americans at their Embassy here are perfectly right when they say that it is quite impossible to have a republic in Russia, and laugh about it, seeing how unripe this country is for that kind of government. Nevertheless, we are heading full speed for a republic; even a democratic republic is too little to satisfy them. They want to go further, to something between communism and anarchy. Lenin, who has just arrived, spoke yesterday from the balcony of a private house urging the mob to adopt communism. Lenin was sent from Germany by special car via Switzerland, the Germans knowing that he would prove an excellent ally for them through his capacity to cause anarchy throughout Russia."

As Prince Lvov, the Premier, refused to allow my husband to leave for abroad, he decided to ask leave to go to Finland, where he thought he would be closer to the frontier and also more in peace. Mme. Brassov, who, though the wife of the Grand Duke Michael, was so violent in all her judgement against the Emperor and the old regime, tried my husband's patience to the last degree, and being himself in a state of utter despair, he felt he could bear no more.

He only remained in that house because he was devoted to Micha and had the feeling that he might be of some use to him in those terrible days.

In another letter he wrote:

".... Micha and I went for a walk in the park of the castle and we visited the hothouses. It made me sadder than ever to see all these places so full of happy memories. Everything is being confiscated. Never could I have imagined that anyone could behave in this vulgar and brutal manner, before even knowing what the national assembly will decide for Russia's future. And to think that these brutes will probably govern the country. I am persuaded that in a very few years it will become a country of savages, because every decent person will leave. They are talking of a new project and that is to change the dynasty, but I cannot discover who their candidate is. Probably it is some Jew!

Micha and I have decided to leave our poor country, never to return. When later they have ruined everything, they will perhaps remember that once there were honest and decent people among the Romanovs. But I greatly doubt that any Romanov will ever return to reign after the horrors they have undergone. The culture here is so low, that it is idiotic to imagine that the country will enjoy prosperity in the twinkling of an eye for the sole reason that the Tsar has been removed.

Lenin is continually exciting the mob and encouraging them to pillage. A lot of young soldiers enter the palaces to see how much room there is to establish themselves there. They have also come to our palace, but Nicholas [George's brother] has given all the available space for the officers of the prisoners of war and so these soldiers left ... the staff of the Red Army established its headquarters in my private rooms.

.... Lenin is making a present of all private houses to the mob. The people have gone crazy and this disease will go all through Russia. We hear from the front that the propaganda for peace has already taken roots in the army and there are cases of fraternization with the enemy soldiers. Oh! what a horrible shame for Russia. I blush at the mere thought of it, and many officers and I tell ourselves that our allies will have the right to spit in our faces as one spits in the face of traitors."

One day my husband went to see my mother at Pavlovsk and on the return journey, now wearing mufti, he passed by Tsarskoe-Selo in front of the Alexander Palace where the Emperor and his family were kept as prisoners. Outside and inside the railings surrounding the garden revolutionary soldiers stood on guard. He could see no one of the Imperial Family about. He wrote that it looked as if they were keeping most dangerous homicidal maniacs in that palace, and the sight upset him terribly. He also heard that the Emperor and Empress were subjected to every possible humiliation and chicanery. For instance, he and his family were sent for by the second lieutenant on guard every evening and their names were called out, "Colonel Romanov," and the Tsar had to answer, "Present." Then, "Alexandra Feodorovna," and she had to answer, "Present." The same thing was done with all their children.

I believe few people are aware that the Emperor never became a general because, at his father's death, he was still a colonel, and he therefore never consented to promote himself to the grade of general, wishing to keep the last grade his father had given him.

My husband was getting more and more worried because our letters reached him so rarely, and he was unable to write by mail as the post office practically did not exist any more. All the personnel had been changed and the new staff never worried about letters, being too much occupied with politics.

The Grand Duke, therefore, went to call on the British Ambassador, Sir George Buchanan. Although I had written to my husband that in London the Foreign Office had refused to forward my letters to Russia, he thought that the British Embassy at Petersburg might take charge of his correspondence.

This is what he writes about his interview:

". . . .I was very sad and upset to hear from Sir George that he cannot send my letters through the Embassy's bag. He said rather shamefacedly that Lord Hardinge, Permanent Under Secretary of the Foreign Office, had given him orders not to accept any letters. I think this is disgusting of the British government, but there is nothing to be done. Then I spoke to him about my going to join you in England. Fancy! I was told that the British government had decided not to allow any Grand Duke to go to that country. He even said that at first he himself had wished the Tsar to be sent to England, but it had been refused and now the Grand Dukes were forbidden to go there. I must own that I was revolted by this want of noble feeling, and never expected such a decision. I told him that an exception might be made in my case as my wife and children were in England. Wanting to comfort me, he replied that perhaps later when the crisis was over things would change. I then said that I would address myself to the Norwegian Minister, and ask him to take charge of my letters to you three. Later, I called on the latter whose name is Prebensen. I told him all about my troubles, adding that I would also write a letter to his Queen and beg her to forward my correspondence through the Norwegian Legation in London. The dear old man consented at once and was more than kind about it all, and I left feeling happier. A couple of days later when I sent letters to the Norwegian Minister, they were returned with a note saying that since our conversation an order had been sent to each Embassy and Legation from the Russian government forbidding them to accept any letters or parcels from the Imperial Family."

This is what had taken place. It seem that Sir George Buchanan, having refused to take my husband's letters and hearing that the latter was going to call on the Norwegian Minister, he let Terestchenko, acting Foreign Minister, know of this fact, and by doing so caused the above mentioned order to be given.

My husband, quite exasperated at this heartlessness, wrote to me:

". . . .For many years England has been a refuge for all our nihilists and revolutionaries, never consenting to let them go. Now, that country refuses hospitality to the members of the fallen dynasty of the Romanovs. This is called liberty!"

He begs me to intercede for him in England and to try and persuade Lord Hardinge to allow him at least to rejoin us. This I did, and Lord Hardinge, as hard as nails, only answered that the Grand Duke was unnecessarily exciting himself as there was no danger whatever for him in Russia. This, when he knew and probably better than me, that the Imperial Family was exposed, not only to dangers but to a horrible death. The fact was, that Sir George Buchanan was entirely on the side of the Republican party. He had been to see the Emperor at Tsarskoe-Selo before the revolution and tried to induce him to give a constitution. The Tsar, thinking that it was not the business of a foreign ambassador to give him advice of this kind, received him coldly.

My husband wrote:

". . . .After this, Sir George went over to the other side. He even sanctioned political meetings in his Embassy and spoke to the mob at the start of the revolution both in Petrograd and Moscow, from a balcony. He was even seen driving in a motor with Tseretelli, one of the most fanatical socialist ministers."

Much later, when Sir George and his wife returned to England, I asked them both to come to tea as I wanted to hear all they knew. Lady Georgina came, but Sir George excused himself, feigning illness. I heard though that he had been well enough to play golf instead. Lady Georgina, even before I had time to open my mouth, started a flow of excuses for her husband's behaviour, which was surely a proof that she suspected my having heard many strange facts on that score.

One of the ideas that Sir George tried to live up to was that there was danger that Imperial Russia was going to sign a separate peace with Germany. This was the greatest calumny ever launched against the Tsar. Few people have realized how true the Tsar was to his allies. When he abdicated he wrote the most beautiful order to the troops, taking leave of them, and telling them to go on fighting for the salvation of their country and never to forget their sacred obligations to their allies. This order was never published by the Provisional Government, for obvious reasons. Sir George knew better than many others the Tsar's absolute loyalty to his allies.

GRAND DUKE MICHAEL
Eilers collection

GRAND DUCHESSES MARIE, TATIANA,
ANASTASIA and OLGA

Various staff to the left and behind; Grand Duchesses Tatiana, Anastasia, Emperor Nicholas II, Grand Duchess Marie Finland 1913

EMPEROR NICHOLAS II
Eilers collection

GRAND DUCHESS ELIZABETH (ELLA)

GRAND DUCHESSES ANASTASIA, MARIE, GRAND DUKE GEORGE,
GRAND DUCHESS TATIANA - 1916
(One of the last photographs taken of the Grand Duchesses)

Chapter XII

The great misunderstanding which arose in March 1915, concerning my brother King Constantine's attitude towards the Entente, was caused primarily by the then Greek Premier, Venizelos. Having heard of the Dardanelles expedition, and being entirely devoid of strategic capacity, Venizelos suddenly imagined that the fall of the Dardanelles was only a question of days, and would mark the end of Turkey, as well as that of the war. He therefore insisted that King Constantine should take part in this unfortunate expedition. My brother, being a very thorough soldier, and an extremely capable military leader, refused to accept this idea, foreseeing that the expedition could only end in disaster. My brother's opinion was strongly upheld by his General Staff.

The result was that Venizelos resigned. From that moment Venizelos started his intrigues and calumnies concerning King Constantine, attempting to ruin the latter's name and reputation before the whole world. He flattered the Entente, and made promises which he knew full well he could not keep. His great argument was that the King, being the Kaiser's brother-in-law, was entirely in the latter's hands. This was utterly untrue. King Constantine never was under the Kaiser's influence in any way. My brother always said: "I am not pro-German or pro-Entente, but pro-Greek," and stuck to his guns. Knowing my brother and his principles and ideas, it was terribly painful to me to hear all the unjust accusations against him, and to see the terrible articles in the Entente's press, which pictured him as a traitor to their cause.

In May of the same year, my brother fell desperately ill, and was saved by a miracle. The press, being continually poisoned by Venizelos' false reports, referred to his malady as a 'diplomatic illness'. My brother was attacked by the same dangerous disease as King George V was in 1929. An Austrian specialist was sent for to operate, but as the patient's state was so serious the surgeon, fearing he might die under the knife, unfortunately did not operate radically, which had consequences in the future. The population of Athens terrorized this doctor by letting him know that should the King die, he would be lynched!

There is an island in the Cyclades group called Tinos, where for centuries a miraculous ikon of the Virgin has been kept in a monastery. This ikon, venerated by the whole of Greece, had never before left the island. By the special desire of the whole country this sacred relic was brought by a man-of-war to the Phalerum, where the Archbishop of Athens received it and carried it to Athens. An enormous crowd followed his carriage on foot, many of the people walking barefoot the whole route of several miles, up to the King's palace where the Crown Prince took over the Holy Ikon and placed it in the sick room. Meanwhile, the entire crowd outside knelt on the pavement in earnest supplication. One curious fact of the procession was that a flock of unknown white birds flew overhead and disappeared when the ikon was taken into the Palace. The King was unconscious but soon after awoke and an improvement set in. From that moment he started getting better, though it took many weeks before he was convalescent.

During those long months of illness my brother was unable to occupy himself with state affairs, and his enemies profited by this fact to spread every kind of calumny. This unscrupulous campaign of slander and defamation was fomented all over Europe. He was dubbed a traitor and a murderer. I well remember reading in the streets of London on huge posters: "Tino the murderer," and so forth, besides the most offensive cartoons in many papers. My heart ached seeing all this exhibition of unjust hatred, the more so as I could do nothing to change people's opinion. Many persons who knew my brother personally were even carried away by these horrible lies, and doubted his sincerity. The one person who stuck to my brother and never wavered was our Aunt, Queen Alexandra. She never for a second doubted his honesty or straightforwardness, and suffered as much as I did over this painful situation. It is a proved fact that Venizelos spent millions, both in London and Paris, to ruin King Constantine's good name and reputation.

I, unfortunately, could not get much direct news from Athens owing to the severe censorship, but heard details from people coming from Greece. The worst complications took place in the spring of 1915, because it was just at that moment that the Entente tried to flatter the Bulgarians into fighting on their side, and promised the latter parts of Greece which had been won by my brother and his army during the Balkan wars. They treated Serbia the same way. King Constantine, as a matter of fact, had been aware since 1914 of the secret treaty which united both Turkey and Bulgaria to the Central Powers. The whole of Greece protested as one man at the revolting thought of giving away provinces of Greece, which they had won with their life's blood, to Bulgaria. The then Premier, Gounaris, in consultation with the King, after a minute examination of the international situation, came to the conclusion that if the Entente would guarantee Greece against any Bulgarian attack, it would be in Greece's interest to enter the war at once on the side of the Entente. On this basis, King Constantine more than once offered his services to the Entente, but unfortunately always struck against the incomprehensible Bulgarophilia of Great Britain and France. No guarantee was ever given to protect Greece from Bulgaria.

In August 1915, Venizelos returned to power and in accordance with the King decided to maintain an expectant neutrality. In September the Bulgarians mobilized, a fact which the King expected, and had even warned the Entente about. From that moment Venizelos wished to enter the war without taking into consideration the poor equipment of the Greek army, or anything else.

Greece then mobilized as a precaution, and Venizelos, behind the King's back, and in flagrant violation of the Constitution and international law, invited the Entente troops to land at Salonica, thereby forcing his country into the war through an act of treachery. Henceforward the relations between the King and Venizelos naturally became very strained, and the Premier, realizing the situation, decided to hurry his own fall, preparing for himself at the same time a martyr's crown.

On October 5, Venizelos made an unexpected and warlike speech in Parliament. After this, the King was obliged to insist upon the resignation of the Prime Minister, which was entirely within his constitutional rights. This created an uproar among the Entente who considered Venizelos as their personal and special pet, and the attacks on my brother surpassed every decent limit. The next Premier was Zaimis, who was soon followed by Skouloudis. The latter was very favourably disposed towards the Entente, but preferred neutrality to safeguard the interest of his own country. The most terrible campaign of intrigues was then started, inspired and guided by a certain French commander, de Roquefeuil, who was naval attaché in Athens. This man never hesitated to use the basest means to ruin King Constantine and Greece, in the opinion of the allies.

He had enormous sums of money at his disposal, and formed a vast spy system which he used for unbelievable purposes. This man was a personal friend of Admiral Lacase, then French Minister of Marine, who believed in him blindly, even against the opinion of the French Minister in Athens, and the commander-in-chief of the combined fleet, Dartige du Fournet. I will quote a phrase in Sir Basil Thompson's book, *The Allied Secret Service in Greece*, in which he writes: "Next day Admiral Dartige du Fournet received a visit from Roquefeuil fresh from dabbling in high politics with his friend Baron von Schenk. The two adventurers had been closeted together for some hours on the preceding night before they were able to come to an agreement that was to leave its mark on history."

Another man who played a very dishonest game was Mr. Compton Mackenzie, who did not hesitate to spread the most awful calumnies about King Constantine's personal character. Owing to the work of all these unscrupulous people and their incredible behaviour, the truth was completely concealed, and anything the King or any of his minsters said was considered by the Entente as inspired by Germanophilia. Although the Premier, Skouloudis, did all in his power to satisfy, in one way or another, the demands of the Entente, he was obliged to resign.

Early in July, my brother Andrew arrived in London, sent by King Constantine on a special mission to France and England. At the same time my brother Nicholas was sent for the same purpose to St. Petersburg. They were to put before the Tsar, King George and the French President, the impossible situation of Greece, and also because King Constantine was anxious that certain errors regarding himself and his views should be corrected.

A short time before my brother Andrew's arrival I received a wire from my brother Christopher, giving me the sad news that our beautiful and beloved Tatoi—our country estate near Athens—had been entirely devastated by fire. This was not an accident, but a deep laid plot by the agents of the Entente's secret service. The alleged reason was that these secret agents imagined that a carefully concealed wireless apparatus was used by the King for private communications to Germany[1]. It is useless to try and describe our horror and grief over this terrible disaster. Eighteen lives were lost and the King was saved as by miracle. One of our great friends, a military engineer officer, was burnt to such a degree that he could only be identified by his wedding ring. All the houses, including the one my brother and his family lived in, and the dear little chapel in the park, were reduced to ashes. Only the house belonging to my mother was spared. My sister-in-law, Queen Sophie, had to leave in a hurry with all her children. On the way she gathered up the doctor's family, who were running away from their villa, which was in flames. My brothers worked hard trying to save things. Christopher was lucky enough to rescue all the ikons from the church just before the whole structure collapsed. Two of my eldest brother's chauffeurs were burnt to death.

Troops and sailors were sent to fight the fire, which lasted over forty-eight hours. The whole of Athens was covered with ashes owing to the strong north wind blowing during those days.

Andrew did his utmost to clear up these terrible misunderstandings, but unfortunately prejudice had gone so deep that the Ministers would not take his word. Lord Hardinge, Permanent Undersecretary of the Foreign Office, even told him: "What can we expect when your Queen is the sister of the Kaiser?" to which my brother very rightly remarked that he did not think anybody had the right to ruin a country because of the relationship of its Queen[2]. In Paris he was told by Briand[3] that Greece's military cooperation was no longer needed. Nicholas, though better received in Petersburg, could also not come to a satisfactory conclusion. The fact was, the Entente had made a present of Constantinople to the Russians, who were not interested in Greece entering the war, or regaining favourable status with England and France.

As there was not much Andrew could do just then, I took him to Harrogate. We were only there a few days when we received an invitation from King George and Queen Mary to spend three days with them at Windsor. We were most cordially received by Their Majesties. I had never

---

1. No radio communications were ever monitored, and the fire was designed as an attempted assassination of the King.

2. The Kaiser, William II, it should be noted, was the grandson of Queen Victoria.

3. Briand was in-and-out of office as Prime Minister at various times, and when not Prime Minister, served in other ministerial capacities.

stayed there before, and only been to visit the castle as a tourist, so I had a splendid opportunity to visit it thoroughly.

One can never see that beautiful place without being deeply impressed. Queen Mary showed my brother and me all the priceless treasures kept there since centuries ago, and in which she takes the greatest pride and interest. Being a wonderful connoisseur in art, Queen Mary has worked more than any one rearranging everything in the castle in proper order, cataloguing and so forth. She also continues to collect works of art which she keeps there and at Buckingham Palace.

Windsor Castle is like a labyrinth and it is very difficult for newcomers to find their way about. My brother's Greek A.D.C. lost his way going to his room after dinner and spent most of the night looking for it. He did not dare knock on or open any door fearing he might enter the King or Queen's rooms. He was at last discovered by a night watchman who conducted him to his apartment. The King was highly amused by this story. Breakfast and lunch we had *en famille*, but dinner with all the court. After dinner all the gentlemen went with the King to smoke, and the ladies remained with the Queen. As I am an inveterate smoker this was real agony, since the ladies were not supposed to smoke. Later, the gentlemen joined us and, at about ten o'clock, we all retired to our rooms. During the war, as an example, no wines were served at court. Barley water, plain water or cider were served. My brother brought a bottle of whiskey with him from London, which he carefully concealed in his bedroom and had an occasional whiskey and soda on the sly!

A couple of days after our return to London, there was a terrific Zeppelin raid, and a bomb fell in Green Park. My brother was staying at the Hotel Berkerley, and his description of the panic that ensued that night in the hotel was extremely comical. On that day we also received news through the Greek Legation that Greece was going to abandon her neutrality, and that King Constantine was again very ill, an abscess having formed on the old wound. I was naturally terribly upset and anxious.

At the end of August, Venizelos organized, with the help of Entente propaganda, a national manifestation, which passed before his house, and from his balcony he made an inflamed speech against the King, accusing him of being a Germanophile and aiming at making himself an autocrat. It was after this that he decided to act openly against his King and country. About the same time the United Fleet, under the command of Admiral Dartige du Fournet, arrived at Salamis. On September 11, there was an attack on the French Legation by the mob, crying, "Long live the King, and down with the Allies" It was proved later that this attack had been organized by the secret agents of the Entente to compromise the King once more. The leaders were all saved by Roquefeuil, who sent them by a French ship to France, where they were interned in a fortress and forbidden to speak.

Admiral Dartige du Fournet was so exacting in his demands that the Premier, Zamis, had to resign. The King then called Calogeropoulos, a great friend of the Entente, to form a new cabinet. The new government did all in its power to come to an understanding with the Entente Powers, but it was all in vain as prejudice had ruined every hope of a satisfactory result. It was then that Venizelos, with the aid of certain foreign authorities[4], left Athens at night on September 24, 1916, for Crete and then Salonica, where he organized a provisional government [under the protection of French soldiers], which meant treason against his Sovereign and country. He was accompanied by General Danglis and Admiral Coundouriotis, who for years had been my father's and brother's aides-de-camp, and who assured the King of their loyalty a few hours before this departure. Eventually, Admiral Coundouriotis became first President of the Greek Republic.

Admiral Dartige sent an ultimatum to the Greek government insisting upon the delivery of the Greek fleet of destroyers and torpedo boats, with their entire equipment, and the complete disarmament of the bigger ships. These ships were later returned to their lawful owners in a disreputable state, even the linen and silver having been stolen. French sailors were seen selling silver spoons and things in the Piraeus to any one who wished to buy them.

The Entente forced Calogeropoulos to resign, and the King then formed a cabinet consisting of men outside the Parliament to try and satisfy the Entente. From this moment life became quite intolerable in Greece, because every day the French Admiral insisted upon some new exigencies infringing Greece's liberty. All this led to the painful incident in December when the clash occurred between the Entente and Greek troops.

It is interesting to note that after Venizelos' departure his house was searched by the Greek authorities, and 15 grenades, 66 fuses, 69 revolvers, thousands of cartridges and a quantity of dynamite were discovered. Most of these articles belonged to the French army.

After this event, which was entirely due to Admiral Dartige du Fournet and his counsellors' mismanagement, the former decided to bombard Athens[5]. A plan of the town had been made by his aviators, on which the buildings that were to be destroyed were marked in red. Among these was the King's palace, where a shell struck the wall outside his study at the moment the Allied Ministers were being received. The only one who kept calm was the King. This bombardment lasted over two hours, and Queen Sophie was obliged to take refuge in the cellars with her children. The French Admiral then proclaimed the blockade of Greece, on December 8, and this was his last official act, because a few days later he was deprived of his command and recalled to France. Admiral Gauchet succeeded him and imposed the so-called "pacific blockade," against Greece.

The people accepted this cruel act as one of their daily trials, and with calm resignation, although they were exasperated to see that France's sole idea was to give Greece over to the traitor Venizelos. The result of this

---

4.   Venizelos left aboard a British warship.

5.   It should be noted that throughout this period of time Greece was a formally declared "neutral" country, with full diplomatic relations with England and France.

blockade was hunger, and many of the poor died from want of food. Their one cry in all their misery was, "Long live the King!" and "We are pleased to starve for him!" I was told much later by ladies of Greek society, who worked among the poor, that Venizelos, with French help, sent flour from Salonica to be distributed among the population, hoping to win them over to his side. Instead of accepting, they threw the flour away, saying they preferred death from hunger than being traitors to their King. There were even cases of mothers snatching the bread from their children's hands, telling them they dare not eat while the King was hungry too.

The French admiral, not content with these terrible results, even took measures to prevent the fishermen from plying their trade along the coasts. Allied cruisers and torpedo boats arrested them and confiscated their tackle, saying: "If you want to fish in peace you have only to drive out your King."

The sympathy and care displayed by the King for his people during this distressing period brought him even closer to their hearts. The display of the people's feelings whenever he appeared was so vehement that he eventually avoided, as much as possible, showing himself in public. The people being aware that their King was still in a weak physical condition and strained to the utmost by the great moral sufferings of the last year, their love for him became an adoration, and their devotion boundless. Those who expected that by starving and ill treating the population, they would drive them to open rebellion, were greatly disillusioned and probably disappointed.

My brother Nicholas arrived in London in October 1916, from St. Petersburg, where he had been sent on a mission. My brother George also came over from Paris for a few days. Obviously, we could speak of nothing else but the Greek question, and we deplored the unjust means used by the Allies against a great and high-minded King and his country.

My brothers and I, of course, went constantly to our Aunt, Queen Alexandra, at Marlborough House. We had often to come back on foot after the theatre or dinner in town, as taxis had become so scarce. I remember one night coming home in the rain. It was very dark, too, owing to the raids, and we could hardly see where we were walking. Stepping off the sidewalk, we plunged into a deep pool of water and got drenched. My brother, Nicholas, left at the end of October.

Following the blockade, and up to April, 1917, there were too many complicated events for me to describe in detail. Suffice to say that the campaign of slander was at its height. Besides the Entente Powers, their diplomats and their secret service, Venizelos, backed up by Sarail, the French general in command of the Allied troops at Salonica, were all doing their hardest to ruin every hope of an understanding between King Constantine and the Allies. Sarail, fearing to attack the enemy, made an excuse that he feared King Constantine would attack him in the rear. And this, even when everyone knew as a fact that Greece had been totally disarmed.

I omitted to mention one curious fact which proved the intricate mentality of Venizelos and his blind hatred of his King. On November 8,

1916, the anniversary of the taking of Salonica by King Constantine and his troops in the Balkan War, Venizelos and his two satellites sent the following telegram to my mother, Queen Olga, who was then in Russia. I copy the exact text:

"On the fourth anniversary of the taking of Salonica, we are anxious to dedicate a wreath as a just tribute of pious gratitude to the revered memory of our lamented King George. By his great wisdom and untiring devotion during the fifty years of his constitutional reign, he crowned by the sublime sacrifice of his noble life, the prestige and glory of our Country, at the present moment in peril. Our thoughts naturally turn to the august companion of his life who set her people an example of orthodox piety, and we beg your Majesty graciously to join her prayers with ours for the salvation of the country, and we offer Her the respectful homage of our deep and unchanging devotion. Venizelos, Coundouriotis, Danglis."

My mother, not wishing to send an answer straight to these three traitors, addressed the following answer to the archbishop of Salonica:

"I beg your Holiness to inform Messrs Venizelos, Coundouriotis and Danglis, that I will gladly believe their sentiments expressed on the occasion of the anniversary of the glorious taking of Salonica by my son, when they remember their oath of allegiance to the successor of Him who sacrificed his life to a Greece made powerful by union and not torn asunder by anarchy caused by the forgetfulness of their duty to their King so disgracefully slandered. Olga B."

This telegram was only reproduced by the anti-Venizelist press in Greece. The foreign censor in Athens forbade its being telegraphed abroad. This act of Venizelos was obviously done to create a discord in our family. Another curious detail of those times was that later the Entente recognizing Venizelos' provisional government, and purposely ignoring the fact that he was a traitor to his King and Country, sent him their official representatives. Considering that the King was still on his throne, this act meant that the Allies were giving their support to a revolutionary gang.

A very characteristic proof of the hate and rage of the Greek people against Venizelos was that public opinion insisted and pressed the government to issue a warrant for his arrest for high treason. This step, which certainly was undeniably legal, aroused considerable indignation abroad. All the inhabitants of Athens, high and low, revived an ancient Byzantine custom which consisted in pronouncing "anathema and malediction" against the traitor to King and country. Each individual, and there were many, as old men, women and children each brought a stone to the Field of Mars and threw it in a spot prepared in advance. All the houses being built around were deprived of their stones which were used for this purpose. The next day, the sailors of the light fleet, which had been taken by the French, and were camping on the field of mars, collected all these stones and erected them into a high pyramid.

In March 1917, the United States entered the war. This event rendered Greece's position desperate. France had now an easy task to impose her favorite, Venizelos, on Greece, as there were no more fears of neutral criticism or of Russian displeasure. The only thing remaining to be done was to overcome British resistance. In March, on the anniversary of the Greek national feast, the demonstration of unbounded love and admiration by the people to their "Martyr King," surpassed any previous demonstration.

In May 1917, Zaimis, for the third time in two years, was made Premier by the King, as the only non-Venizelist politician who escaped the charge of being pro-German. As soon as he came to power Zaimis informed the Entente ministers of his resolve to cooperate with them, and also to do his best for a reconciliation between the King and Venizelos.

All Zamis' efforts to create a reconciliation were frustrated by Venizelos, who set to work to wreck Zaimis' plans. At the end of May, Mr. Ribot went to London to submit a proposal to the British government that they should send a High Commissioner to Athens with the mission of deposing King Constantine, depriving the Crown Prince of his right of succession, and of restoring the violated Greek constitution by raising Venizelos to dictatorial power. The execution of this violent action was entrusted to Mr. Jonnart, who was exclusively High commissioner of France. He received no mandate from England, and Russia protested, and energetically disavowed his action, which was taken with unauthorized use of her name.

The dethronement of King Constantine had been decided, not because it was legally or morally justified, but because France insisted upon it, and Britain had reasons for not wishing France to act alone. Mr. Jonnart then went to Salonica to confer with Venizelos who, of course, declared his approval of the French plan. All the required military measures were taken against Greece in order to crush her if she attempted to protest.

On June 9, 1917, Mr. Jonnart arrived in Salamis and lived on board the French battleship, *Justice*. What irony! Zamis went on board to confer with Mr. Jonnart. The latter, to win the confidence of Zaimis, spoke about the dynasty and the King with a certain deferential condescension, and saying that he was still awaiting instructions, he made an appointment with the Premier for the next day. On this occasion, Mr. Jonnart handed over to Zaimis without any preliminaries, and in the name of the three protecting Powers, an ultimatum demanding the abdication of King Constantine on the ground of "violation of the Constitution guaranteed by these Powers." In an "aide memoir," Jonnart added that the Crown Prince was excluded from the succession and indicated Prince Alexander—the King's second son—as successor, quite a young man, and devoid of any political training, thus well suited to Venizelos' plans.

A delay of twenty-four hours was granted for the acceptance of this ultimatum, and in case of refusal, Mr. Jonnart threatened to bombard the town and occupy the whole of Greece, which meant exiling the entire dynasty and proclaiming a republic. He further added that if after the war the Greek nation desired their King's return, the Powers would have no objection. Finally, Mr. Jonnart stated that the Powers intended to dissolve the Salonica government, and that they had no desire at all to bring Venizelos back to Athens. He could only return to power after fresh elections.

Mr. Jonnart, having decided to take no notice of the British protest in this affair, terrorized the feeble Zaimis with his monstrous demands. Had Zaimis had the presence of mind to ask Jonnart to give proof of his authority as "High commissioner of the protecting Powers," the latter would have been confounded and his whole action compromised.

Zaimis, after this conversation, went at once to the King, who, exhausted by years of moral and physical suffering, and tired of his long struggle against a concerted and insidious plan, at once declared his readiness to leave Greece for a time. Surely this was a proof of King Constantine's honesty and magnanimity. A crown council composed of all the former prime ministers was at once convoked at the Palace. The King, after asking the opinion of each member present, announced his decision, which he had already taken, to leave Greece with the Crown Prince in order to spare his country worse calamities. The King, however, refused to sign an abdication, and the Crown Prince took a similar decision.

Meanwhile, the foreign ministers, fearing the rage of the Greek people, hid on board their respective ships. As soon as the news of the King's decision spread in the city, the whole population rushed in crowds to the palace. There were cries of, "The King is being carried off! Vengeance!" In its exasperation, this crowd decided to resort to force to prevent their beloved King from leaving. Athens was plunged in deep mourning, and the church bells tolled as for a funeral knell. As the night advanced the atmosphere grew more and more charged with popular anger. Constant cries were heard of, "He shall not go!" By now the crowd had blocked all access to the Palace. Everyone's face was marked with grief.

My brothers, who were all with the King in the palace, were unable to return to their respective homes, as each time they tried to do so they were prevented by the crowd who feared that their King might slip out unnoticed. For more than twenty-four hours the Palace was literally besieged. The whole family spent the night roaming about the palace in an utter sense of desolation. Next morning the following proclamation by the King was published:

"Obeying necessity and accomplishing a duty towards Greece, I am departing from my beloved country with the Crown Prince, leaving my son Alexander on the throne. Even far from

Greece the Queen and I will ever retain the same affection towards the Greek people. I beg you all to accept my decision with serenity, trusting to God whose blessing I invoke on the nation. And that this sacrifice may not be in vain, I adjure all of you if you love God, if you love your country, if lastly you love me, not to cause any disturbance, but to remain submissive. The least disorder, even if prompted by a lofty sentiment, may today lead to the most terrible disaster. At the moment the greatest solace for the Queen and myself, lies in the affection and devotion which you have always shown to us, in the happy days as well as the unhappy ones. May God protect Greece. Constantine R."

When Jonnart was informed of these events, he began to grow uneasy and took immediate steps to put, as he expressed himself, a stop to the Greek people's exhibition of sentimentality. He had foreign troops landed that same day.

In order to give more emphasis to his act of renunciation, the King decided that his son, Alexander, was to take his oath of allegiance to the constitution in his new capacity. The poor boy was so deeply moved that he could scarcely restrain his tears. A statement was then published, inspired and approved by Jonnart, saying: "Today, after the administration of the oath to King Alexander, Mr. Jonnart announced to the Greek government that it could send at once representatives to Salonica, since the Provisional Government there is henceforth dissolved. It is equally well-known that Venizelos shall not, by any means, come to Athens and that the powers have no ulterior design of establishing him in power. Greece is nowise bound to pursue the policy of the *Triumvirate*, but is free to adhere to her neutrality."

When the people began to realize that resistance was hopeless their frenzy gave way to blank despair and their indignation to passive resignation. They had no illusions as to Mr. Jonnart's promises, being clear-sighted enough to understand that all this would be followed by a forcible return to power of Venizelos. Meanwhile, Mr. Jonnart, who was growing more uneasy and nervous, notified Zaimis that he insisted upon the King and Queen's immediate departure from Athens, as the King's presence might cause serious danger, and he, Jonnart, would be obliged to use his troops which were already on their way. All the attempts made by the Royal Family to leave the palace were frustrated by the dense crowds surrounding it, and they were only successful owing to a ruse. With the greatest trouble they managed to get away. Their Majesties, with their children, got to their waiting motors and drove away, avoiding all central streets and reaching Tatoi late in the afternoon. The Royal Family spent that night at Tatoi, as well as the next day, when swarms of people belonging to all classes came up to Tatoi to take leave of their King.

On June 14, 1917, the King and his family drove to Oropos, a small village by the sea on the Gulf of Euboea, to embark on an old ship, the *Sphacteria*, used many years ago as a yacht by my father, and left for Italy.

The road leading to Oropos, as well as this village itself, were literally packed with people. The small pier was strewn with flowers. All the Athenian society, ministers, officers and every class of people, were densely crowded around, and the King and Queen, followed by all the members of the Family, had the greatest trouble in making their way. There was no longer any distinction of social class, and the people's one thought was to shake hands with their beloved King, and bid him God speed. When, after much trouble, they reached their boat, lots of men jumped into the sea, hanging onto the King's boat in a last desperate attempt to prevent him from leaving. From that moment Greece ceased to be a free country.

Mr. Jonnart, to advertise his triumph, published a new proclamation in which he said that henceforth began a free and prosperous life for Greece, and assured the people that no disturbance of public order would be tolerated. To complete these promises, Jonnart drew up two lists of names of those against whom reprisals were to be carried out. Among other prominent persons he named the King's brothers, who were to be exiled. After this, all Jonnart's promises were broken, and he imposed Venizelos, by force of foreign bayonets, on the Greek people.

On June 21, Venizelos arrived at the Piraeus from Salonica on a French warship. A couple of days after, an entire French division occupied Athens, and all its salient points. On June 26, Venizelos formed his new government on board the French ship. Before the appointed hour of Venizelos' entry, French troops occupied the route by which he was to proceed to Athens, where machine-guns were placed at every crossroad and the precincts of the palace were guarded by Cretan gendarmes. Venizelos and his cabinet, in several motor cars, then drove at full speed through the empty thoroughfares to the palace to King Alexander to take their oath. On the termination of this, they all drove to the Hotel Grand Bretagne, where Venizelos appeared on the balcony and made a fiery speech to the people, which was most insulting to King Constantine, and at the same time, lauding the Entente Powers. After all these events, and Venizelos having been imposed on the Greek people by the Entente, his reign of tyranny, which knew no bounds, began.

Mr. Jonnart left Athens soon after, making many excuses, but in reality he had been recalled by the French government. Once Jonnart had gone the passions of Venizelos had free play. His reprisals against all classes were innumerable. He even removed the Archbishop of Athens, who, by the constitution, was irremovable. Politicians, officers of every grade, were imprisoned in common prisons. Even ladies of the Court and Athenian society had to undergo every kind of persecution.

During the three years of dictatorship by Venizelos, eighty three persons were sentenced to death and shot after a mock trial. In the islands, even women were shot by Venizelist agents.

Могилевъ 1916

EMPEROR NICHOLAS II and TSAREVICH ALEXIS

1916

GRAND DUCHESS MARIE - 1916

GRAND DUKE DIMITRI, GRAND DUKE MICHAEL,
GRAND DUKE GEORGE, an Aide - 1915

PRINCE CHRISTOPHER OF GREECE
(Brother of Author)

PRINCESS ANASTASIA
Wife of Prince Christopher
(Formerly Nancy Stewart Leeds)

PRINCESS ANASTASIA
Wife of Prince Christopher

Chapter XIII

In June, 1917, my husband at last managed to get permission to go to Finland. He rented a villa at a small out-of-the-way place called Retiervi, near a lake. He chose Finland because he hoped to be able to get to Sweden or Norway more quickly and easily when he got leave to go abroad. From there he continued to write daily. At first he was happier there, away from Petersburg, which, he wrote, was in a state of absolute lunacy. He went on describing all the terrible events taking place and forecasting the utter hopelessness of the future situation. He describes Russia as being governed by three parties: the so-called provisional government, the soviets of workmen and soldiers, and the Bolsheviks. All these parties were at loggerheads, one trying to oust the other. The provisional government was losing ground daily, and was terrorised by the other two, giving in to them in order to be able to keep its place.

My husband, seeing that the provisional government was scared and not able to take any serious decisions, made up his mind to get into communication with the soviets, and to appeal to them to give him permission to go abroad. Through a friend, he made the acquaintance of a radical-socialist, a friend of Kerensky, and went to see him. This man received him most politely, and seemed greatly astonished that a Grand Duke had the courage to come to him alone. He told my husband that although he was a radical republican, he was against anarchy. He promised to do his best.

A few months later this same man arrived in London and came to see me. I was quietly sitting in my room when my butler came to say that there was a Russian gentleman below who wished to see me. My gentleman-in-waiting was out, so I decided to go and see for myself who this man was.

I entered the sitting room and saw a short, fat man with fair hair and a short beard, standing there, his hands behind his back. I offered him my hand and asked to what I owed the pleasure of his presence. He told me he had been sent by the provisional government to inspect all the Russian Embassies in Europe. He belonged to the police, he said. I asked him if he had come to arrest me, to which he replied, "God forbid," and I said, "Yes, for I do not suppose you could do such a thing in this civilized country." I did not ask him to be seated. He then started by telling me that my husband had been to see him, and that he had reminded him very much of the Emperor

Alexander II. Also, that my husband had asked him to visit me and bring me many messages. I then asked him to tell me what was happening in Russia, and how it would all end. His answer was, "We will have anarchy, bloodshed and probably chaos, but we hope that in time everything will settle itself."

I asked him what posts he had held, and where he had served during the Tsarist regime. His answer was that he had been a political exile in Siberia, to which I couldn't help replying, "A great pity you ever came back." Then I pitched into him over the horrible way in which the Tsar and his family had been treated. He said it was of course a sad necessity, but unavoidable, seeing that Nicholas Romanov had been a tyrant. This made me see red, and I retorted that I begged him to remember that Nicholas Romanov was His Majesty the Emperor, in my house, to which he made a bow and called the Tsar by his proper title until he left me.

I said I wished to know exactly why he thought the Tsar was a tyrant, and had he ever seen or talked to him. His reply was he had done neither, but came to this conclusion after having read the Emperor's remarks on official papers written in his own hand. I remarked that that surely was not the way to judge a man, and that I, who knew the Emperor intimately, could assure him that this was not at all the case. He was so interested to hear that I knew the Tsar intimately that he said, "Oh, this is most interesting, and will you tell me all about him and the Tsarina." Thereupon he asked endless questions, such as: Did the Empress speak Russian, and how did they live privately, and did the Tsar really love his country as he professed to.

When I had answered all his questions he suddenly asked me, "Will you kindly tell me who you are?" to which I answered, "I am the daughter of a Russian Grand Duchess, Olga Constantinovna, who married King George I of the Hellenes.

To my utter astonishment, he immediately stepped down from his pedestal and said, "The daughter of King George? So then you must be King Constantine's sister?" "Yes, and proud of it too!" I answered. He went on to say, "It was a terrible injustice committed by the Allies to send your brother away against the will of his people, who were so devoted to him. Russia did not take part in this, and our minister in Greece was told not to recognize the new government there." This was quite an unexpected thing to hear from a revolutionary! After discussing that subject, he said he felt obliged to tell me that the Soviets of Workmen and Soldiers in London, the Russian ones, who were on missions in England and also wounded, had complained to him that I and my daughters stood in a too prominent place in the Russian church, and that I was to know that Imperial blood did not count any more. I again saw red, and retorted, "Please tell those people whom I despise most profoundly, that everybody has always been equal in church, and long before liberty was invented in Russia." At this, he knocked his heels together and made a deep bow! When I took leave, he actually kissed my hand. He then followed me to the entrance where he probably thought he would meet some servants and, to impress our equality upon them, he waved his hand to me saying, "Au revoir." I rushed up the stairs for him not to see I was in fits of laughter.

My husband wrote in July:

"Russians have understood the word 'liberty' in quite different ways to any other nationality. To them liberty means dirt. They have already ruined everything, the streets are filthy, the soldiers' barracks, which used to be spick and span, have been turned into real pigsties. It is the reign of dirt, disorder and *sans façon* in all classes and the vulgarity surpasses anything imaginable. One is ashamed to think that a country could go to pieces like it has, in four short months. They have now made that mad Kerensky president of the Council of Ministers. It is true that he seems more capable than the rest of his colleagues, and has realized to a certain degree that his silly and tactless speeches to the crowds only increases the general anarchy. He is 'possessed' to my mind, but then it is quite out of the question for a normal brain to cope with the present situation. It must either be an unbalanced man like Kerensky, or a genius. But, alas, I see no genius anywhere and Russia, since March, is going fast downhill, and over the precipice into the abyss.

It is thanks to this mad Kerensky that the army is entirely and absolutely ruined. The word *discipline* is replaced by 'liberty', and 'freedom', etc. The troops at the front, instead of fighting the enemy, have meetings to decide if they will obey the orders of their chiefs!"

I also received a letter from my Russian lady-in-waiting, who had been allowed to remain in our palace, but not in her former comfortable suite of rooms. She had been given a small servant's room. One day she was ordered out of the house and told not to take anything of her private belongings, as these now belonged to the "people." In her despair, she decided to complain to the chief of soviets, living in our apartments. She was told to present herself in a room which happened to be my private sitting room. When she entered and saw what it looked like, and remembered all the happy days spent there, she burst into tears. The commissary, thinking she was crying over her plight, patted her on the back and said she might take her clothes with her, and a few other belongings. She then left the palace and lived for some time with her maid, who later behaved shamefully to her. Since then I have never been able to trace her, although I heard she had taken places such as governess, nurse or companion to earn her living.

In the winter of 1917, my husband left Retiervi because the house was too cold, and went to live at Helsingfors in a small hotel where some of his friends and acquaintances resided. There were also a few British naval officers from the Embassy staying at the same hotel, and my husband liked them and made some friends, and they were very kind and sympathetic. General Pool, also on a mission to Russia, came to Helsingfors, as well as Sir Francis Lindley, councilor of the British Embassy. The latter was supposed to have inspired Sir George Buchanan to be so hard towards members of the Imperial Family, and though the Grand Duke did not know him, he heartily disliked him. General Pool persuaded my husband to make Lindley's acquaintance, hoping they might get reconciliated. General Pool took my husband's sad plight very much to heart, and even took measures to try and get the Grand Duke out of Finland by taking him away when the mission was to leave. My husband writes that he was very hopeful, and nearly sure this plan was going to succeed, when Sir Francis Lindley frustrated all the arrangements, and General Pool left without him. After that the Grand Duke very naturally, had no kind word for Lindley, who behaved in a most heartless manner. Being afraid of the censor, my husband could not write all details openly, but hoped to give me them when we met again.

He continued writing every day all the rumours he heard and his own impressions. In Helsingfors there were quantities of sailors, as most of the ships of the former Imperial navy were then stationed in the Finnish ports. They all went about looking like wild men. Their hair was uncut, and they were unshaven and dirty, with bits of red rags in their caps.

In January 1918, my husband wrote very sadly about the news he had just received, that the Tsar and his family had been exiled to Tobolsk in Siberia. Among other things he wrote were:

> "We have become semi-beggars and prisoners of the mob who as yet have not begun to massacre us; but we are still living under a note of interrogation. Our lot has not yet been decided. Are we all to be massacred or sent to the devil, that is exiled? To my mind there are only these two alternatives. The post has stopped working even here, and we have no papers or letters and no news whatever from the outer world."

There was fighting in the streets at Helsingfors, and my husband wrote he could hear the bullets hit the walls and the roof of his hotel, even breaking a window here and there.

Once, at four o'clock in the morning, he was suddenly awakened by violent knocking at the door which was quite close to the head of his bed. He unlocked the door and was confronted by three awful looking sailors, armed with rifles. One of them stuck his revolver in the Grand Duke's face, saying, "Give up your arms."

My husband told them he had none, but nevertheless they looked everywhere, even under his pillows and mattress. Finding nothing, they left and did this to all the inmates of the hotel, even to the ladies who were naturally terrified. About a month later, a few of these brigands, because they were nothing else, in fantastic uniforms, calling themselves soldiers or sailors, again came to the hotel to examine everybody. My husband and a friend of his were playing bridge with Countess Witte and her daughter, who were also staying there. These intruders asked everyone to produce their passports and identity cards. My husband was questioned by a student, who looked at him with great curiosity and interest after reading his name in the passport. The Grand Duke then asked him if he would give him some kind of new passport to enable him to leave the country. The man said he would report to the central committee and he would telephone the answer. Eventually, the Grand Duke was told to go and present himself at the central committee. He writes that never in his life did he see such a collection of awful looking scoundrels. As the place was so filthy he did not even take his hat or coat off. The rest of those horrible looking types were sitting about in coats and hats as well. The president, who seemed to be a Jew, again looked through my husband's papers and said they were not enough, and that he was to come back and get others. This man also said he could give no permissions for abroad because that depended on the Petersburg government. My husband writes:

> ". . . . I think all this comedy was enacted simply to force a Grand Duke to come to a vile hole of that kind and to see what he looked like. They probably expected to see an arrogant person and were astonished to see a simple human being."

Unfortunately, my husband, who was so desperately anxious to get out and rejoin us in London after four years of separation, made a terrible mistake in asking those people to help him to get away. As long as he kept quiet in his hotel with the rest of the inmates with whom he had become quite friendly, the anarchists did not bother him, except once or twice to assure themselves he was hiding no arms. Countess Witte and his other friends begged and implored him to have nothing to do with these soviets, assuring him that in time Finland would separate from Russia, and then he would automatically be abroad.

My husband, alas, had the erroneous idea that these people had still a vestige of heart left, and that by explaining to them his sad position and plight, they would take pity on him and let him cross the frontier. From the moment he addressed himself to them they kept worrying him and they evidently communicated with Petersburg, because on April 3, he was suddenly arrested at the hotel and taken to Petersburg under an escort of Red Guards, just as if he were a criminal. A letter or two are missing, because he wrote from Petersburg saying that he had been thrown into prison at Helsingfors for a few days, and he never knew why.

In Petersburg, the Grand Duke went to live in our secretary's house, where a room had been prepared for him in a hurry, our palace being occupied by the staff of the Red Army and various soviets, who lived in our

217

apartment. On the following day he had to go and present himself to the notorious Commissary Ouritsky. Ouritsky was a pure Jew, and the man who was specially occupied wreaking vengeance on the whole of the Romanov Family.

This is what the Grand Duke wrote:

"Today is the great day for me when the question of my exile is to be decided. I went today to Ouritsky, the great master of our destiny. I had been told that he would be nasty and rude to any of us, but as some of my revolutionary friends had told him about me, and how unjustly I had been thrown into prison at Helsingfors, he was quite polite and I have no reason to complain. He kept me for an hour and a half. He suggested three towns from which I was to choose my exile: Wologda, Wiatka or Perm. I chose Wologda to which he at once consented. Then he wrote a paper which I had to sign, in which I was ordered to leave in a week. I am afraid of writing details, but my conversation with this Jewish chief of the "Commune" was interesting and original to a certain degree.

The strange part is that this man was very interested in a theft committed at our palace where our footman, whom I had left as caretaker of our apartments, had stolen a lot of our belongings and taken them to his house. This footman was put into prison and Ouritsky wished me to appear as witness at the trial. This I refused to do, and said I would send my secretary. All the objects stolen from our rooms by this footman were taken from him, and when I asked to have back an old ikon I had had since my early childhood, the answer was, 'Certainly not, all these things now belong to the people. We only wished to have you as a witness to point out which things had been in your possession'.

Considering that the footman was a member of the 'people', why should he have been imprisoned for taking them? This is certainly a proof of their strange mentality to say the least of it.

. . . . Then he went on to say that the Tsar would be judged by the people and we all would be set free. He also said that he sends us into exile because of the advance of the Germans, who might think of putting one of us on the throne. Of course, I do not believe half of what he said. After this visit I went to see your mother, who is living in the Marble Palace with Elizabeth [her brother Constantine's widow] whose three sons have already been exiled to Wiatka with Serge [the Grand Duke's brother].

Petersburg is not recognizable. Everywhere ex-officers and clerks and bourgeois can be seen removing the snow from the streets, the only way for them to earn their living. All the soldiers and workmen occupy the well-paid places.

As it is the 'Commune' you can imagine anything you like as to what is happening here, and even then you will be far from the reality."

The Grand Duke Michael had also been arrested, but no one knew where he had been taken to. My eldest brother-in-law, Nicholas, and my mother's youngest brother, Dimitri, were already at Wologda. This famous commissary, Ouritsky—he was murdered later by a young Jew—invented an excuse for exiling them all, and this was that the Grand Dukes were mixed-up in a counterrevolution, which was totally untrue. My husband was much upset because he had no idea what kind of conditions he would find at Wologda, as no abode could be found for him there, and his week of grace was quickly coming to an end. Two days before his departure he had again to go and see Ouritsky. He went there with his secretary. This is what he wrote:

". . . .This morning I went again to Ouritsky as I was ordered. I had to wait below in an ante-chamber. It is terribly difficult to get to him, one would think he was a sovereign. At last an old woman appeared and yelled out, "Romanoff". I went up and passed all the machine guns placed at every window. Ouritsky received me at once. I did not remove my coat or galoshes, and sat down in an armchair by his desk. He was reading papers on which he wrote various resolutions. He loudly abused some young Jews working next door in his chancellery. After twenty minutes he made me sign a paper in which was written: 'George Mikhailovitch Romanoff is sent away from Petrograd and its environs, to Wologda, and on arrival there will have to report to the 'soviet' of the soldiers, workmen and peasants, who will hand him a permit to live freely at Wologda.' The thought of leaving for this place makes me miserable because it is still further away from you three, but I thank God you are not here as I would have gone off my head with anxiety. I have to bear it all in silence because it is God's holy will, and as he knows and sees all that happens to me and allows it, it means it must be so. Thank God you are not in this country which was once called Russia and now does not exist any more."

He went to take leave of my mother on the day of his departure and persuaded her to get out of Russia as soon as she possibly could. Thanks to the Danish minister, Mr. Skavenius, who showed the greatest courage during all this terrible time, my mother was able, later, to get safely out of Russia. During the week my husband stayed at Petersburg a great number of friends and acquaintances came to see him, and a lot of officers were so enraged at his being exiled that they wished to revenge themselves. The Grand Duke had the greatest trouble to calm and pacify them, knowing that they would only get themselves into trouble, because just then hundreds of officers were being massacred and tortured all over the country.

When my husband arrived at Wologda, he was met at the station by a commercial agent in whose house he was to live. This man took him at once to the "soviets" to get a *permis de séjour*. The president was a Caucasian, who seems to have been quite polite, and gave the Grand Duke new documents to replace those he had received from Ouritsky. The house he was to live in was tiny, and he felt very much in the way of his host, hostess and four children, and decided to try and find other quarters. He went to see his brother, Nicholas, who was in good spirits, but 'deeply offended', as he wrote, to have been sent away from his beloved Petersburg.

My husband then found another house that belonged to a rich merchant. The house was a wooden one of two stories, quite new and clean. The owners seemed delighted to have my husband there, as they were terrified that some obnoxious Bolshevik would be forced upon them. The Grand Duke had to get permission, though, from the soviets to change houses. He went to visit the Japanese Mission, which was living at Wologda. He knew some of them, and wrote that they were particularly kind to him, and offered to take charge of his letters and send them to us, which makes him remark: "Pagans seem kinder than Christians."

Letters or telegrams from us seemed to reach him but rarely, which made his life still sadder and his loneliness made him suffer terribly. He knew no one at Wologda except his brother and my Uncle Dimitri. They had very little to eat and their clothes were wearing into tatters, as they had all been sent away in a hurry. Most of my husband's clothes had remained in Finland, as he had been hurried off in less than an hour, and was given no time to collect his belongings. To buy new things was out of the question, because of the exorbitant prices. My husband had taken his camp bed from Petersburg, but the chiefs of the Red Army, occupying our rooms, had stolen the mattress, so it was hard and uncomfortable. Notwithstanding all these privations and discomforts, he always wrote that he had no right to complain, as his lot was better than that of many others. He wrote:

". . . .I do not wish to complain, but I am utterly crushed by all that is happening here. As you know, Russia does not exist any more, she has been sold to Germany by the Jews with the help of Russian traitors. The Russians have nothing but vodka in their brains, which they have been absorbing for generations, and so have become atrophied. If some day the Americans come here, I will not be astonished if they sell the inhabitants as they used to sell negroes. The Zulus are more civilized than the Russians."

Meanwhile, he was getting very anxious and alarmed owing to the incredible rumours which reached him from the Dowager Empress, who was living in the Crimea—practically like prisoners—with her daughter Xenia, her husband and children. As a matter of fact, the Provisional Government, by order of Kerensky, early in 1918, had ordered a 'requisition' of the members of the Imperial Family residing in the Crimea. The Chiefs insisted on everyone being examined, asking them their names, residences, etc. They were prevented from going to the Empress' room, and so she was ordered to appear on the balcony. When she had answered all their questions she calmly pointed to her dog and said, "You have forgotten to ask his name and details about him."

They were all living together at Ai-Todor, but in different villas, and had a guard of sailors. One fine day at five o'clock in the morning, sailors came from Sevastopol, and marched into everybodys' rooms and woke them up. The Empress was forced to get out of bed, and was told that if she wished to get dressed they had brought a woman to help her. She refused this proposal, seeing what kind of woman they had brought. She had no time even to put on her dressing gown, and as she was only in her nightgown, she stood for hours behind a screen, where she caught a chill which brought on pneumonia, while these brigands ransacked her room. They pretended they had come to find compromising papers and looked for them even in her mattress. They opened all her chests-of-drawers, took away her little New Testament, a Danish one she had always used since her childhood, and various other objects. At the same time, these horrible people went to Xenia and woke her up. Her husband they removed to some other place, holding pistols to his head. One sailor remained with Xenia and forced her to keep her hands outside the coverlet. A horrible looking female came and rummaged about in Xenia's things, stole a few of her jewels from the dressing table, and retired.

The sailor then told her she could get up and dress. She told him exactly what she thought of him, and also asked him if he were a Christian, as he did not take off his cap when he saw the ikon, as every Russian always does. He shamefacedly took it off. When he told her to get up, she said she had no stockings, and sent him for them to the next room. She then made him turn his face to the wall and dressed in a hurry. She was in a great state of anxiety, not knowing what was going on in the rest of her house, and in her mother's villa. At last she discovered that they were all safe, but each one was arrested in his or her room. Later, she and her six sons met in the dining room, where all these brigands were sitting together.

Her third son, Nikita, had been a cadet in the naval school, and when he appeared, she cooly said to these sailors: "You see this son of mine was to become a sailor, because we all loved the navy, but we took him away for him not to become a scoundrel like you." They accepted this verdict in dead silence, and hung their heads. She told me later that these sailors looked like nothing on earth. Dirty, unshaven with long hair and altogether revolting. After some time they left.

It appears that these hordes had been given strict orders not to carry anything away with them under threat of being severely punished. Nevertheless, things did disappear with them, but a few days later the gardener found under a tree a big parcel containing golden forks, knives, spoons, etc., which they had evidently thought better of, and thrown away when leaving the place.

A few months after this unpleasant experience, the family were all arrested and sent to the Grand Duke Peter's villa, Dulber, close by. There the Empress with Xenia, her husband and children, were interned. As the Grand Duke Peter was himself living there with his wife and three children, as was his brother, Grand Duke Nicholas, with his wife, there was not much room. The boys lived three and four in the same room. There they were all kept in strict isolation for three months.

Besides all this discomfort, they had hardly enough to eat. The petty officer of the sailors who guarded them turned out to be their saviour.

While they were shut up at Dulber, the Bolsheviks of Sevastopol and Yalta decided to kill them. Meanwhile, the head guard argued with these soviets to refrain from murdering at least the doctor, who could be useful, and also Xenia's youngest boy, who was only a child.

As luck would have it, these murderers had finished off so many people on one day they were sick of it, and put off the massacre of the family to another date. The petty officer gave strict orders to his guards at Dulber that they were not to allow anyone, under any circumstances, to enter the place during his absence, telling them he had orders to leave. He then wired to the German troops at Simferopol to come at once to save the Empress and the Imperial Family. The Germans made a forced march over the mountains and arrived at Dulber in time to save them.

At their approach, the Bolsheviks disappeared. Then it was that the Imperial Family realized and discovered who had saved them. They asked this wonderful man why he had always been so gruff and had not even given them an inkling of his good-will towards them. He answered that it was only by keeping his thoughts entirely to himself that he was able to help them, as the slightest suspicion of one of his men would have led to their undoing. They gave him every recompense they possibly could get together, and treated him as a friend. Later, he had to leave and no one was able to discover for sure what became of him, but rumours said he had been murdered. The Germans allowed all the members of the Imperial Family to return to their own villas. The Empress did not go back to Ai-Todor, but chose our house at Harax, where she lived with her suite until the day she left for England in 1919.

The Empress Marie was so courageous and fearless that she freely and jokingly discussed with her gentlemen and ladies-in-waiting the possibility of being murdered at any moment. To one of her ladies, who was rather nervous and apprehensive, she used to say: "When this moment comes, I hope you will die with dignity." This poor soul would leave the room in a state of panic and shut herself up in her own room.

Of course, all these details never reached my husband, as the post at that time was practically non-existent, so he lived in daily terror of hearing that they had all been murdered.

My husband made the acquaintance of the British Consul at Wologda. He was quite a young man, and spoke Russian fluently, as he was born in the country. The Grand Duke took a great fancy to this Consul, who was particularly nice, sympathetic and kind to him. They used to have endless talks together. Years later this Consul came to see me in London, and told me he did everything he possibly could to save my husband, and had even concocted a whole plan to smuggle him out of Russia. The Grand Duke, though, would not hear of this, saying that if he were saved, his brothers and cousin would probably have to pay for it with their lives. The Consul told me he would have saved the other two Grand Dukes as well, but considering all three were well over six foot in stature, he feared it would be out of the question to try to hide them.

Meanwhile, my mother was still living at Petersburg, staying with her sister-in-law, the Grand Duchess Constantine, at the Marble Palace. They had hardly anything to eat, and were very badly off financially. There was a big organ in the palace, which my grandfather used to play on in his youth, and the Grand Duchess decided to sell it to the German Protestant Church. The moment the Bolsheviks heard that the pipes were being removed they confiscated them, saying she had no right to sell things which had been bought with the money belonging to the people! To be able to live and buy some food, the Grand Duchess was obliged to steal her own things and smuggle them out and sell them. This was terribly risky, but she was never found out.

At last the Danish Minister came to my mother and told her that she was to leave the country, that as she was a Princess of Denmark, he considered himself responsible for her safety. He had trouble getting her a visa because when the authorities read on her passport, Queen of the Hellenes, they said they did not recognize titles. At last they compromised by writing "Mme. Olga Hellenes!"

The minister arranged that she should leave on the same train in which a batch of German prisoners were returning to their country, but in a private car accompanied by her lady-in-waiting, and a secretary of the Danish Legation. My mother consented to go, though she was terribly upset over the thought of leaving the country of her birth, which she so deeply loved, and grieved over leaving all her family at the mercy of those inhuman Bolsheviks. As I said before, her brother Dimitri was exiled with my husband at Wologda, and she somehow felt she would never see them again.

After her departure, the train was stopped during the night, and some local soviet, hearing there was a foreign queen in a special car, tried to unhook it from the rest of the train. The Danish secretary, luckily, woke up in time to see what was happening, dressed, got out and started arguing with these people, telling them a few home truths. After much trouble he succeeded in making them hook the private car in between the others, and so they continued travelling to the frontier with no other mishap. My mother changed at Berlin and went on to Switzerland to join my eldest brother, Constantine, who was in exile there with his family, and two more of my brothers.

My husband wrote that he breathed a sigh of relief when he heard that my mother had left. Knowing her devotion for Russia, he always feared she would refuse to leave, and he kept on urging her to get out of the country as soon as possible. He was beginning to feel heartily sick of Wologda, the more so because he had been told that this exile would only last a month at the utmost. He had already been nearly three months there, and hated the place as the climate was detestable, very cold at first, and then a terrible damp heat that came on in June and exhausted him. He used to see his eldest brother, Nicholas, and his cousin Dimitri, daily. All the trouble he gave himself to try and get a permit to join us in England came to nothing, which exasperated him, and tried his wonderful patience more than all the privations inflicted upon him.

In June he began to hear rumours of the Tsar's assassination, and wrote that he refused to believe them, but added he was much afraid that these rumours were spread about the country to see what effect it would have on the population. This turned out to be the case, and as the Bolshevik government saw that no real protest was being made, they murdered the whole family at the end of July.

GRAND DUKE GEORGE

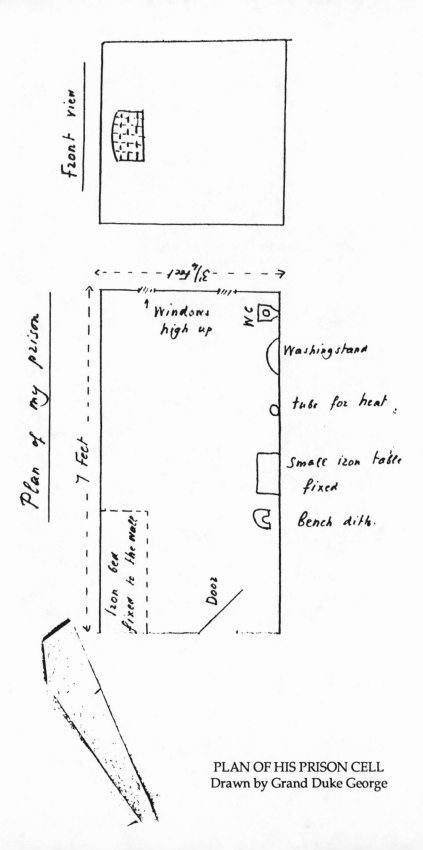

Front view

Plan of my prison

7 Feet

3½ feet

Windows
high up

WC

Washingstand

tube for heat.

Small iron table
fixed

Bench dith.

Iron bed
fixed to the wall

Door

PLAN OF HIS PRISON CELL
Drawn by Grand Duke George

Chapter XIV

On July 1, 1918, my husband was arrested in Wologda, together with Nicholas and Dimitri, and interned in the local prison. His next letter is from prison, dated July 11, in which he described their arrest:

"On Monday I lunched as usual with Nicholas, after which we sat talking and smoking, when suddenly I saw from the window a motor stopping at the door with a man in civilian clothes accompanied by two unarmed soldiers. I immediately felt it was to arrest us, and I was right, because three minutes later a young man of twenty entered the room and showed us a wire from Ouritsky saying he was to arrest at once the three Romanovs of Wologda. We had nothing to say but to put on our hats and follow him. As a matter of fact, he deceived us, because I forgot to say that he first said we were wanted by the Soviet, and in the motor he told us he was taking us to prison. I asked to be taken to my house to get my coat. We then went to get Dimitri, who was not at home, and so continued to the prison where we have been lodged eleven days now.

We were each given a cell and later on were joined by Dimitri. I saw him arriving through the iron bars of my window, and was struck by his sad expression. The first twenty-four hours were very hard, but after that they luckily allowed us to have our camp beds and also our clothes. There is no one in the prison but we three, and the guard, which is changed every day. These men are from the Lettish regiments, which distinguished themselves particularly during the war. I had met these splendid regiments in several places during my inspections at the front. Nicky, the Tsar, who had a special liking for them, asked me to recompense them as much as possible. We have made friends with them and they are charming to us, and some day I will tell you how touching they are. They treat us like comrades, and have not locked our cells after the second day, while they allow us to walk in the small garden in the courtyard. Our food is brought from outside. I have been feeling seedy, but am better now. If you should come into my cell, number 14, you would have laughed at the ridiculous idea of shutting up three old men of 59, 55 and 52 years old, in three big convict cells. We are luckily allowed to meet and talk. We have not yet been told the reason of our arrest.

You cannot imagine the rage of the inhabitants of Wologda against the Bolsheviks. During the first five days the ex-aides-de-camps of Nicholas and Dimitri were allowed to visit us, but this has now been forbidden. The man who arrested us is called Condé; what a high-sounding name, and not a Jew. He comes to visit us often. Today he told us he hoped we would be released in a few days. Till now I was afraid to write as they poke about in all our things, but I hope to give this to my valet who comes daily. If you wish to know why we are in prison, and what they intend doing with us, I have no answer to give you. Mr Condé says he will tell us all about it later, when we are free, and intimates that he is saving us from something.

Anyhow, I feel ashamed to be in prison at my age! Perhaps after this they will allow me to leave the country to join you. I will stand anything at their hands as long as it can help me to get away.

I told this to an inspector who came from Moscow to see us, and he said he could not understand why I am not allowed to leave.

I am perfectly calm and nothing troubles me any more except being parted from you three. It is the second time I have been imprisoned, the first time being in Finland. I even sleep well."

A few days later he wrote that the two aides-de-camp and his valet were allowed to see them, but that they had to talk in the presence of a soldier of their guard. The guard seemed to become more and more friendly with them, and appeared to be sorry for them, seeing that they were imprisoned without any reason.

"We have been shut up for a fortnight already, and it is awful that no one gives us any reason for this. All that the American, English and French missions here have done to help us has come to nothing. As the weather is fine we pass most of the day in the courtyard sitting on benches. Our guards lie about in the grass or sit on the bench with us, and we all talk in a very friendly manner. Many of them remembered me from the front. Their ideas are rather mixed as a consequence of all the socialistic propaganda they have been fed. They are just like a lot of misled children

Yesterday, Sunday, we went to church and were placed behind iron bars like animals.

After three long weeks in prison the same Condé came to us and told us that by order of Ouritsky we were to be taken next day to Petersburg. We suppose that we are being removed from here so as not to fall into the hands of the Allies, but on the other hand, after the terrible news of the Colonel's—the Tsar—assassination with all his family, I cannot be sure they will not do the same to us. I am sure they will put us into prison there, and maybe we will be tried. I am not afraid of this, as my conscience is clear and with God's help I will die calmly."

On July 21, 1918, they arrived in Petersburg under guard and were imprisoned with a number of other people as innocent as themselves. They were six in a tiny cell. In other small cells there were forty to fifty people huddled in together. After a week they were transferred to a huge prison called *Shpalernaia,* where criminals were kept. They each had their cell, seven feet long by three feet wide, an iron bed and very hard, which he wrote he had become accustomed to, and slept well. Twice a day they were taken out for a walk in the courtyard, but separately, for half an hour or forty-five minutes. In the middle of this court was a big cage in which the counterrevolutionaries were made to walk, with the usual criminals. Everybody was very severely treated, but the warders, all ex-soldiers, were kind and polite. One Grand Duke's secretary was actually able to smuggle in some letters of mine and my children. This was a great joy to my husband, who had not heard from us for three months. A few days after their arrival in prison, the Grand Duke Paul was interned there with them, having been arrested at Tsarskoe-Selo. The four of them had cells in the same corridor, on the fifth floor.

A Red soldier told my husband—in the first prison—that the Romanovs were put into prison because the Soviets feared that the counterrevolutionaries would get hold of them. They were not allowed to communicate, but managed, when passing by each other's cells, to speak a few words through a tiny observation window in the door. Princess Paley, the morganatic wife of the Grand Duke Paul, came to pay her husband a visit, and the interview, which lasted fifteen minutes, was in the presence of a commissary. She was told beforehand what she could talk to him about and what subjects were prohibited. After this she was allowed to visit her husband two or three times a week up to the end.

With the soldiers that guarded them my husband became friends in a day and spoke to them as to comrades, and they were always very kind and obliging. He wrote:

"None of us can see any issue to our sad situation, as

there is no reason to release us just as there was no earthly reason to imprison us. It would have been much cleverer on their part to send us out of the country. None of us was mixed up in politics, but they judge by themselves, and are trying to find something which might compromise us. Yesterday it was my 55th birthday and strangely enough my 55th day in prison. Imagine my joy when the dear kind nurse of this prison brought me a whole packet of letters from you and the children. It has warmed my heart and given me new courage in my miserable plight and loneliness. Alas, they will again be taken away from me as it is dangerous if they discover that I get letters. This prison is crammed with officers and even ladies. At night some of them get removed, usually to be shot. It is a horrible sensation not even hearing what has become of them. This night 85 new prisoners were brought in, and they made an awful noise locking them up in their cages."

A few days later he wrote that the four of them were at last allowed to meet and to walk together in the courtyard twice a day. He wrote:

"One morning about nine o'clock we were honoured by the visit of the famous Ouritsky accompanied by two Jews. All our cells were unlocked. One of them asked me if I had any complaints to which I answered curtly and drily, I had none. I had no wish to talk with such people.

Dimitri asked Ouritsky why we were imprisoned, and his answer was that it was to save us as the people had intended shooting us at Wologda. This, of course, is an absolute lie. He also said that when the German government would release Liebknecht and Adler, two socialist leaders, then we too would be liberated, adding that for Liebknecht the four of us would go free. This means that we are hostages. Have you ever heard such monstrosity and idiocy! I do not know any longer where I am or in what century I am living."

I have never been able to discover how he smuggled out his letters to us, and how he got ours, but it was done through the great kindness of members of the Danish Legation. These people did more to help the members of the Imperial Family than anybody else. They were courageous and humane and we owe them a great debt of gratitude.

Meanwhile, my children and myself had no idea what was really happening in Russia, as wires never reached us. On August 5, I suddenly got the following telegram from the Grand Duchess Kirill who was in Finland, which had been sent from Stockholm. "Are anxious for life of your husband. Have now discovered him to be in a dreadful prison in Petersburg with some other relations, barely fed. Unless immediate help very little hope for them. Situation for whole family desperate."

Terrified and horror stricken I rushed to Queen Mary at Buckingham Palace to show her this message, and to implore her to do her utmost to help. The King was in France just then, inspecting his troops. She promised to do all in her power. I also wired at once to the King of Spain and King of Denmark, who both set to work. I also went to Cardinal Bourne to beg him to ask for the Pope's help. I met Dr. E. J. Dillon, whom I implored to interview members of the government, and impress on them all the horror of my husband's desperate plight, and the others'. Alas, the government never moved a finger to save those four unfortunate and perfectly innocent Grand Dukes.

Mr. Lloyd George, having recognized the revolution after the Tsar's abdication, could not or would not compromise himself by saving the Imperial Family. At the end of September Cardinal Bourne advised us that the Pope had wired him to say that the Germans were trying to persuade the Bolsheviks to send the four Grand Dukes to the Crimea. This unfortunately was never done. Later, when President Woodrow Wilson arrived in London, I tried to see him to appeal to him, too, but was told he was too busy to see me. I then wrote to him a detailed letter, describing the terrible and dangerous situation of my husband and his relatives, imploring his help to save them from being murdered.

This letter I gave to Queen Mary, who personally handed it to him, as he was staying at Buckingham Palace. He never answered, not even to acknowledge it. So much for the man who tried to pass himself off as the Messiah! A devoted and kind friend of mine actually went to Finkelstein, alias Litvinov, and now Soviet Foreign Minister, to try and impress on him what a lasting shame it would be if these innocent men were slaughtered without any reason. He answered he would do his best, and even wrote out a telegram, which, he said, he would send to Moscow. Whether he kept his promise or not I do not know, but the result was nil. But then he was a Bolshevik and a Jew.

In one of his letters the Grand Duke wrote and asked me to try and work for his release through the Jews in London. I happened to know Sir. Adolphus Tuck, the well-known publisher, and I asked him to whom I could address myself among the elders of his sect. He named a certain Mr. Wolf, who later was financial counselor at the Peace Conference. I sent my Chamberlain, Baron de Stoeckl, to lay the whole affair before him. Mr. Wolf said that he feared he could do very little, because they—the Jews in England—considered the Bolsheviks, Trotsky and company, as renegades, and since they had attacked their religion, they were no more in communication with them, but he promised to do his best. Needless to say that this attempt too proved of no avail.

Food was brought to my husband from outside, at first twice a week, and later, three times, but it was always cold, which in the long run was very trying. What astonished him was his absolute calm and resignation to his sad lot. He wrote:

> "If it were not for you three who are everything to me in life, it would, I believe, be indifferent to me if I were shot. You see everything has become so miserable in my country and everything is lost for me, and having my Emperor no more, I am of no use here.
>
> After all these nightmares one has gone through, there usually comes a nervous reaction, but this has not happened to me and I am more than calm and nothing alarms me any more. God has helped me to have courage and my heart has behaved all right after the one bad scare I had in January at Helsingfors, when on turning the electric light on, I saw a revolver aimed close to my head and a bayonet at my chest. When such tricks are played on you, and God has helped you to keep your nerve nothing impresses you any more. It accustoms one to expect death at every second and this is even good because it strengthens your faith in God and prepares you to look death in the face. I have already decided that if I am to be shot, I will refuse to have my eyes bandaged as I wish to look at the rifles which will shoot me. I assure you there is nothing frightful about it. Because if this should happen, it will be by God's Holy Will and how, then, not die in confidence? The brigand on the Cross said to Our Saviour 'Remember me Lord when thou comest into Thy Kingdom', and the Saviour answered, 'Verily, I say to thee, today thou shalt be with me in Paradise.' I have always thought that this brigand was the happiest human being in the world."

There was a library in the prison and they were allowed to read as much as they wished. The Grand Duke wrote that he had never in all his life read so much as during these long months in prison, practically in solitary confinement. He read Dostoyevsky's books all over again and many historical ones which refreshed his memory.

> "To give you an idea of the aquarium or menagerie we represent in our prison, I enclose a small list of the arrested people I know personally or by sight out of the 700 prisoners:
>
> 3 ex-army corps chiefs; 2 admirals; 1 ex-minister, 1 ex-senator; all the family of Ouritsky, one of which an old woman of 90, all Jews. At least 2 or 3 hundred officers and privates of every army; 1 banker; many ladies and common women: my secretary of the Museum Alexander III, two

officers formerly attached to Grand Duke Dimitri, several priests, and numbers of small merchants, peasants and lots of real hooligans."

On August 30, 1918, he wrote that the Director of the Prison, a charming and clever old gentleman, came to tell my husband that Ouritsky, Commissar for Counterrevolution, had been murdered that same afternoon by a young Jew dressed in student uniform (the students of the Universities in Russia had a special uniform). The assassin tried to get away on a bicycle, but was caught in the street. It seemed to be a revenge as Ouritsky had had many people executed, both innocent and guilty. All the prisons were chock-full of harmless people. Next day, the revolutionary press wrote that there ought to be reprisals for Ouritsky's murder, and the victims were to be one hundred Bourgeois, a few generals, senators and all the Grand Dukes!

One day the Danish Minister, Mr. Skavenius, came to see them. My husband and the others were taken down to the office to meet the Minister who had been sent there by the Queen of Denmark, who was my husband's niece. They all told him they had no complaints, but begged him to intervene for them to get a permit to leave the country. Mr. Skavenius did his best to help them in this, but unfortunately his repeated appeals were of no avail.

In each letter, my husband mentioned the great kindness shown them by the old governor of the prison, the nurse and their guards, all ex-soldiers. The latter, he wrote, were more than touching, and took the greatest part in their sad plight and expressed their sympathy in every way.

There was one young man, 20-years old, who looked after my husband with special care and affection. He got so little to eat that the Grand Duke always gave him the little he could spare from his own provisions. It often happened that imprisoned officers passing by his cell asked him for food, as they were simply starving. He never refused giving them what he could, although he was very hungry himself. He was beginning to feel weak and ill for want of proper nourishment and fresh air. They were only allowed out for two hours during the day, and the rest of the time they spent in solitary confinement. He heard through his guards and the director various details of what was going on in town, which made him perfectly ill, and he kept on writing that he had the impression of being in China or among wild tribes of the jungle. The so-called 'Bourgeois' were continually arrested without the slightest reason and lots of them were forced to clean the streets or dig graves for cholera victims, and were usually jeered at by the population. When these people were at work the Bolsheviks pillaged their houses or apartments and stole everything they could lay hands on. They were allowed to read the 'Red' papers, and my husband wrote that never in his life had he thought it possible to write such appalling articles and horrors.

All the prisons and the soldiers' barracks, which were turned into detention camps, were chock-full of innocent people. In my husband's prison the inmates were constantly changed as nearly every night a lot of the prisoners, mostly officers, were taken out and shot, and no one ever heard about them any more. He wrote that they shot anybody who was not of their opinion, and especially people with known names, and this gave them quite a special pleasure.

He constantly mentions the nurse of the prison whom he calls a saint. He wrote that she spent all day comforting and helping all the unfortunate prisoners. Seeing that the Grand Duke suffered so much from constantly eating cold food, she brought him a small spirit lamp to warm things up, for which he blessed her. He had to sweep and clean his cell himself, which he did every evening and all he collected was taken away next morning by the warder. He was very proud of the cleanliness of his cell. The electric light was turned on at seven o'clock, but as it was already September it began to get dark very early and for several hours he lay on his bed in darkness as he could not see to write or read. This was terribly trying to him.

Princess Paley did all she could to get Lenin to liberate the four Grand Dukes. She addressed herself to Maxim Gorky, who, although a kind of Bolshevik all his life, suddenly decided to do his best to save the Grand Dukes. The famous singer, Chaliapin, a friend of Gorky's, also worked hard to save them, but my husband wrote that he did not put much faith in their intrigues. My husband was fully persuaded that the Imperial Family was imprisoned by the Germans, because he maintained that the Bolsheviks never did anything without asking German advice. Someone once advised him to ask the help of the German Consul to have his release and so be able to join us, but this he flatly refused, saying he would never abase himself to ask a favour from a Hun. Meanwhile, King Christian of Denmark, let them know that he would be happy to receive them in his country whenever they were free to get away.

About September of that year Kerensky turned up in London. As luck would have it he came to live with a Doctor friend of his, who had a house in Regent's Park on the next terrace to ours. Consequently, we often met him when going out for a walk, which made me and my girls perfectly ill. The thought that the Grand Duke was in prison under terrible circumstances, no knowing what would happen to him at any moment, and to see that man walking about freely and in safety in London, after all the misery he had inflicted on the Tsar and Russia, made us feel desperate. He was a short and common-looking man with a yellow face and nasty eyes.

On the next terrace to him lived my brother-in-law, the Grand Duke Michael, so Kerensky had chosen good company.

When Lenin got the upper hand, Kerensky—like the coward he was—absconded, dressing up as a nurse. Mr. Sheldon Whitehouse, secretary of the American Embassy, lent him his motor to run away in. He got to Archangel and escaped on a British man-of-war.

A lot of Russian officers got out of their country in some way or other, and most of them came to see me, and some brought letters from the

Grand Duke. It made one's heart ache to see them as they all were in a pitiful state of misery. They all came over with the intention of enlisting in the British army to be able to continue the fight against the common enemy. They felt so humiliated and abased by the despicable separate peace signed by the Bolsheviks, that they hoped to make good. Alas, their application was refused, except in the one case of Colonel Paul Rodzianko, who became a private in a British regiment. Later he went to Siberia with General Knox.

In October the authorities began being disagreeable to the Grand Dukes in many small ways. They tried to remove the nurse who was such a comfort to them, but somehow, the dear old director of their prison was able to keep her on a bit longer. Ouritsky had been replaced by another Jew, who in his turn was removed, and a woman, Yacovleva, took his place. She had the reputation of being a very cruel woman which fact they were soon made to feel. One day an old woman in spectacles came to the prison and came into each cell giving a form to each prisoner to fill in. It consisted of twelve questions:

1. Name
2. Family name
3. Citizen of what country
4. Age
5. When were you arrested
6. Where were you arrested
7. By whose order
8. Have you been questioned
9. Of what are you accused
10. What was your occupation in the last two years before your arrest? Where did you serve and what was your grade, your business and on what money did you live?
11. Your address, and whereabouts in detail during these two years?
12. Are you a member of any special party, if so which?

Next day these lists were collected by a young man. My husband offered to shake hands with him when he came into his cell, but the man put his hand up to his shoulder to show he did not wish to shake hands. The Grand Duke wrote:

"I know that many people just now are afraid of shaking hands because of the cholera; anyhow, I was delighted not to give my hand to one of those disgusting assassins."

His valet, the only one who had stuck to him through thick and thin, managed to smuggle in a note to the Grand Duke, which was hidden in the

235

basket containing food he brought three times a week. He wrote to give him the pleasant news that all our belongings had been pillaged at the palace, which made him remark that the only consolation was to know that everyone was in the same boat.

These unfortunate prisoners, the four Grand Dukes, were constantly speculating as to when and how they would be released. Various rumours came to their ears that people were at work to save them. They were told that their liberation might come on the day my husband called "Lenin's ascension to the throne," the anniversary of the Bolshevik coup d'état. Then they were told it was a question of money, and that they might buy their liberty. Considering they had no money, this was a difficult proposition.

The various rumours that reached them concerning the events abroad were quite incredible. One of them was that as the Bolsheviks refused to recognize their war debts to the Allies, the latter would occupy Russia and control everything in this country, so as to get their money back. My husband wrote that this idea seemed quite logical and feasible, and would probably be the only way of preventing further bloodshed among the inhabitants.

Anarchy was daily augmenting and the food supply dwindling alarmingly. He only dreamed and thought of the blessed moment when he could get out of his native country, which he loved so dearly, and which now had been turned into a kind of hell. A terrible blow to them too was that the old director of their prison had been removed and the kind nurse likewise. The authorities found he was kind to them. My husband missed his daily visits, his kindnesses and comforting words.

On the anniversary of the Bolshevik coup d'état, their new director was dead drunk, being a Bolshy himself. During the three days this anniversary was feted the prisoners were not allowed to have their usual airing in the courtyard. On the third day they read a telegram published in a communist newspaper that all the prisoners who were kept as hostages, except a few, would be released, and my husband wrote:

> "Who are these few? It is possible it means us four, because it is written that these 'few' will be kept as long as the white troops keep a few 'reds'. These people are not human and it is a horrible feeling to be used as puppets in the bloodstained hands of these murderers. There was a rumour that we might be released one of these days, and though I have no reason to believe it, I am feeling a bit excited. I have already gathered my few belongings so as to be ready to leave at any moment."

As time went on the want of foodstuffs was becoming alarming owing to the disorder in transportation. In the towns certain kinds of food could not be bought any more for love or money. My husband wrote that as there was difficulty in feeding the prisoners, the authorities decided to find out which of them got their supply from outside, and have it all divided among all the prisoners. This made him rather anxious, because he was underfed as it was, and had become so thin that he had to tie his rings together with a string so as not to lose them. The prison diet consisted of dirty hot water with a few fish bones floating in it, which upset him each time he tried to eat. White bread was, of course, quite a thing of the past and only black bread could be found and bad at that. Milk and butter also could not possibly be had. Another privation worried him and that was the complete lack of matches, and in consequence he could not light his spirit lamp to warm up his food. Petrol and spirits of wine were also a great luxury, which he could not afford any more. The restrictions were becoming more and more marked.

In one of his letters in November, he writes:

"Paul has had a consultation today with his doctor, and our commisary of the prison, to try and arrange that the question of our release should be examined by a commission. But the awful part is that at the head of this commission is that dreadful Jewish woman called Yacovleva, who is well-known for her bad and immoral reputation. I imagine that she always assists at the executions of these innocent people and looks on with excited joy. After that you may think what it means that 700 of us prisoners are at her mercy. This woman was officially nominated to her post by Lenin, Trotsky & Co. That is what we have come to in the twentieth century. Bolsheviks are not socialists or communists, but a band of tyrants who kill, pillage and take everything away that belongs to other people, for themselves. They have tortured thousands of officers who stuck heroically to their oath. It is diabolical. Paul's wife is in despair because she did everything to have him transferred to a hospital as he is really ill, and even Gorki, who has done his best to help, refuses to have anything to do with this Commission as he is suspected of being a counter-revolutionary, having saved Gabriel, a cousin of mine. This is the limit because it is difficult to find some one more 'red' or revolutionary than Gorki, but he at least is a cultured man whilst the others are simply hooligans.

By this you can see that there are people trying to help us, but they fall against entirely barbaric obstacles. But God will help us when and as He wishes, and against this they will not be able to do anything much, as they love their 'Devil'!"

During one of his walks in the courtyard he saw quite a simple young peasant woman carrying a baby which was born in another prison.

237

As she had no milk some society sent her a bottle and a half of milk for the child, but she had nothing to eat except that horrible prison soup, so the Grand Duke told her he would send her some of his own food whenever he could, which he often did. She and her husband were both in prison because someone living in the same house as themselves sold clandestine spirits of wine unknown to them. Besides this woman, he sent food to his cousin Dimitri, whose supply from town was insufficient, and also one of the guards who brought him hot water, the result being that my husband had hardly enough to live on himself. He was always thinking of those who he thought were more miserable then himself.

I was able once to send him some warm clothes, such as socks, gloves, sweaters, etc., through the Danish Legation, which actually reached him. He wrote that he was sent for one day to go to the office and these things were handed over to him, but not before they had turned each garment inside out, to be sure there was no kind of written messages inside them. Other things I sent before through a British mission never reached him and were sent back to me.

His last letter is dated November 27, 1918. In it he said that it was getting more and more difficult and dangerous to smuggle out his correspondence for us. It is evident that he went on writing, as he told us it was his only consolation being able to open his heart to someone. He even asked me to keep his letters which had become a kind of diary, for him to be able later to make use of to write his memoirs.

On December 10, 1918, the Danish Minister in London, Mr. Castenskiold, asked to see me to advise me that he had had news from Copenhagen saying that Mr. Skavenius, the Danish Minister in Petersburg, had wired to his government to propose that the four imprisoned Grand Dukes should be bought out for five hundred thousand roubles—£50,000! Mr. Castenskiold asked me whether I could possibly manage to get this sum of money at once, because Mr. Skavenius was to leave Russia on December 16th. To gather such an enormous sum of money in a few hours was out of the question. I was in a desperate state of anxiety, not knowing what to do. Not long after the Minister left he rang me up from his Legation to say that he knew of a Danish banker who happened to be passing through London, to whom he had explained the situation, and who was ready to lend me this sum if I would give him my jewels as a guarantee. They immediately came to my house where we talked it all over. I gave him the few jewels I had brought with me from Russia in 1914, when I came to London. He was to wire at once to Mr. Skavenius and put this sum at his disposal. This was a great relief and somehow it made me feel easier. Next morning the Danish Minister telephoned that he would return my jewels as my cousin, King Christian, had already sent the necessary sum of money. A few days later came the news that Mr. Skavenius had left Petersburg without the Grand Dukes. It was just then that my nephew Dimitri turned up in London. He had come from Persia via India and Egypt, with Lady Marling, the wife of the British Minister at Teheran. My nephew had been exiled to Persia after

Rasputin's death, and it is thanks to this exile that he is still alive.

He looked desperately ill and weak because he had caught typhoid fever in India on his way, and very nearly died. It was only owing to Lady Marling's untiring care that he was saved. He came all the time to my house, which was a great consolation and comfort to me. He, too, was terribly anxious and worried over his father, the Grand Duke Paul, who was in prison with my husband.

Although we did all we could through the Danish Legation to have news of our dear ones, it became more and more difficult as time went on. We read several times in the paper that they had all been murdered, but as there was no real proof we did not believe it. Up to the last day we were persuaded that something unforeseen would happen and that they would be allowed to leave Russia. This terrible and indescribable suspense went on till February 4, 1919, when the crash came. We again read in the papers that the four Grand Dukes had been shot. On the following day, Baron de Stoeckl received a wire from Terioki in Finland signed: "Maichrowsky," secretary to my husband, saying that the four Grand Dukes had been executed in the Fortress of St. Peter and Paul. It is useless to try to describe the agony I went through having to tell this news to my poor girls and my nephew Dimitri.

Still not able to believe that this ghastly news could really be true, I at once wired to General Mannerheim, who was then Governor General of Finland, begging him to find out the truth. A few days later came his answer confirming the fact.

It appears that Maxim Gorki went to Lenin and told him to release the four Grand Dukes as there was no sense keeping them in prison and to allow them to go abroad. Lenin consented, but that inhuman monster in Moscow, Peters, hearing of this decision, immediately wired to the Commissariat in Petersburg to have the Grand Dukes shot. They were taken out of their prison and told that they would be allowed to leave the country, instead of which they were driven in a lorry crammed with other prisoners to the Fortress of St. Peter and St. Paul and shot early at dawn.

QUEEN OLGA

QUEEN SOPHIE OF GREECE

KING CONSTANTINE

Chapter XV

King Constantine and his family, after leaving Greece, went to Switzerland via Italy. His expulsion was soon followed by that of his brothers. Whilst in Switzerland the English nurses of my brother's children were sent for one day by the British Consulate. They were cross-examined about their employers and told that as British subjects they were liable to be exposed to the severest consequences if they continued to serve "traitors to England." They were even threatened that if they did not give notice at once they would be deprived of their passports. They were terribly upset and had to leave for England.

My brother Constantine was one of the first victims of that terrible Spanish influenza which at that time was raging over Europe. He was then staying in a villa at Zurich. As he was still far from strong after his last serious illness, and exhausted by all his sufferings, his state soon became alarming. The doctors practically gave up all hope of his recovery, and my brothers were sent for. During Easter night, when they were at the midnight mass at the Hotel Dolder close by, in one of the rooms which had been turned into an Orthodox Chapel, they were told that the King had taken a turn for the better. Though he improved from that night onwards, his convalescence lasted a long time, and his health was never normal again. It was during this convalescence that our mother arrived from Russia.

A short time after our mother's arrival in Switzerland, my brother Christopher's marriage to Nancy—Mrs. Leeds—was celebrated in the Russian church at Vevey[1]. I asked the British authorities in London to allow me to go to Switzerland for this wedding, and to visit my family. The answer was that if I went to see them I would not be allowed to return to England, and so I gave up my intentions.

In the early part of May, 1920, I was in Paris staying with my brother George: there I met our nephew, King Alexander, who had just arrived with his morganatic wife, Aspasia Manos. I had not seen my nephew since 1914, and was struck by his good looks. He told us quite a lot of Venizelos and his intrigues, and about his own very difficult position, because he was treated as a figurehead, and how he was surrounded by Venizelos' spies. King Constantine's court had all been replaced by Venizelists. Queen Sophie, his mother, tried to communicate with Alexander by telephone, but Romanos,

---

1.   February 1, 1920.

the Greek Minister in Paris, as well as his suite, successfully prevented this. He was not even allowed to correspond with his parents. On his way back to Greece Queen Sophie tried her best to meet him at some station he passed by, but this too was not allowed. As a matter of fact, this unfortunate boy never saw his parents again, as he died soon after.

In April my brother George, who had resided in Paris some years, let me know that our mother was going to Cap Ferrat, near Nice, coming from Switzerland, and wished us to join her there. I left London for Paris, and with my brother, his wife and children[2] travelled to the Riviera. It was a great joy to see my mother again after a separation of six long years. So many sad events had taken place during that space of time that it seemed more like centuries. My mother was staying with her niece, Princess John of Russia. Her husband, my first cousin, was murdered by the Bolsheviks in Siberia at the same time as his two brothers, the Grand Duchess Serge, and my youngest brother-in-law.

We all lived at a small hotel not very far from her villa, and were thus able to spend the whole day with our mother, only returning at night. We remained there a fortnight, my mother returning to Switzerland and we to Paris. I stayed at St. Cloud with my brother and his family. After a week I returned to London to join my daughters.

In August, my two brothers, Andrew and Christopher, were allowed to go to Italy with their families. They chose Venice, and Christopher and Nancy wired to me to join them at the Lido with my girls. As we were leaving the Gare de Lyon we met young William Leeds, who was also on his way to join his mother at the Lido. Passing through Montreux my brother Nicholas came to see me with his two eldest daughters. They travelled with us to the next station. It was most interesting hearing all the news from my brother concerning the Greek situation. In Venice we were received by my two other brothers and their wives. They took us by motorboat to the Lido and we all stayed at the Excelsior Hotel. It was such a great pleasure to meet again, and especially to see Christopher happily married to that charming wife of his, that I sat up till one o'clock in the morning with my brothers who had so many interesting though painful events to relate.

Though I had often been to Venice before, we constantly went sightseeing. We bathed twice a day, but I had every reason to regret this later, as it brought on the most painful attack of arthritis in all my joints and for three weeks I suffered agonies.

The Duchess Hélène of Aosta[3] came several times to see us, and once brought her sister, the Duchess of Guise[4] and her to daughters to tea. One of them was to become Christopher's second wife many years later. There were

---

2.   Princees Marie Bonaparte, Prince Peter and Princess Eugenie.
3.   Born Princess Héléne of Orléans, married Prince Emanuele Filiberto of Savoy, Duke of Aosta.
4.   Princess Isabelle of Orléans, married her first cousin, Prince Jean of Orléans, Duke of Guise, who was head of the Royal House of France.

quite a lot of acquaintances staying at the same hotel. Some were extremely nice and kind to us. Others called us, "The Greek traitors," and turned their backs on us. We had often to go through humiliating and painful moments. One American lady, an old friend of Nancy's, even hid under her umbrella when our motorboats passed each other leaving the Lido, which made us laugh considerably. I am sorry to say, it was only the English and American acquaintances who behaved in this undignified manner. The Italians were all perfectly charming and went out of their way to be polite and kind with us all. Countess Morosini, a well-known figure of Venice, asked us to a ball in her lovely old palazzo, where we again met the Duchess of Aosta and the Duchess de Guise.

After three weeks at the Lido it was decided that we should leave for Rome. On the day before our departure my daughter Xenia fell and hurt her knee very badly. She had to be transported to the station on a stretcher suffering agonies. Andrew's wife had also hurt her knee, and my daughter Nina had crushed her fingernail, so we were a rather dilapidated party at the moment of our departure.

My girls and I stayed at the Grand Hotel with Christopher and Nancy, Andrew and his family going to the Hotel Royal, which did not prevent us from constantly meeting and sightseeing together. I made the acquaintance of an Italian colonel who had been attached to the Tsar during the war, and he brought a lot of very interesting photos to show me and my daughters. One day I called on King Victor Emmanuel at the Villa Savoia, Queen Elena being still in the country. I went alone because the difficult position of my brothers prevented them from seeing His Majesty. Another time we all went to pay our respects to Pope Benedict, who received us most graciously, and asked about the situation in Greece and spoke about Venizelos with very little admiration.

Rome, just then, was in the throes of communism, and several times a week we saw processions of men passing the hotel, holding red banners and wearing red rosettes and singing revolutionary songs. It was then that Benito Mussolini's name began to be heard and it was known that he was creating a new party creed called "Fascism". The Italian papers were full of his wonderful work and extraordinary energetic way of doing things. We were warned to keep out of the way of any demonstration or assembly in the streets, because the mob was aggressive and disagreeable. We were having constant news from Greece, and many royalists passing through Rome came to see us.

In August on the day following the signing of the Treaty of Sèvres, an attempt was made in Paris against Venizelos' life by two young Greek officers, with the hope of freeing their country from the tyrant. Venizelos escaped with a slight wound. I was told later by a friend of mine attached to one of the foreign embassies in London, that he had happened to be in the Gare de Lyon when this attempt took place. He saw Venizelos arriving officially at the station, surrounded by all his satellites and escorted by a large number of French police. Suddenly a terrific crash was heard, caused by the first shot. My friend saw Venizelos lifting up his coat collar and rushing madly to a place of safety, his satellites immediately abandoning him. This great tyrant who showed such courage in Greece when aided in his work of destruction by foreign bayonets, displayed at that moment his want of courage and proved himself to be a real coward.

In Athens, this attempt was followed by the most savage reprisals against the populace, by the police and the partisans of Venizelos. Shops were pillaged and the few politicians and officers who were still free were thrown into prison. A deputy of Parliament, an old playmate of our young days, was cruelly murdered by Venizelos' bodyguard. The house of ex-Premier Skouloudis was ransacked and his precious collections of Tanagra figures and Sèvres china were reduced to powder.

Early in October we received the sad news of our nephew Alexander's accident. He had been bitten by a monkey at Tatoi belonging to the wife of one of the employees. Blood poisoning immediately set in and though everything was done to save him, his case became hopeless and he died on October 28, 1920. His unfortunate mother was beside herself with anxiety, and applied at once for permission to go to her son. Venizelos cruelly refused. In her utter despair she telegraphed to my mother at Lausanne, imploring her to go to the sickbed of her boy. My mother agreed without a moment's hesitation. She left almost at once for Brindisi, accompanied by her lady-in-waiting, where my brothers, my girls and myself went to meet her. The Greek government sent a small private yacht to take my mother to Greece and she encountered the most terrific storm all the way, owing to which she arrived too late. It is to be remarked that Venizelos and his family always travelled on board a battleship when going abroad, but King George's widow was only allowed this small private yacht, and was not even given the right of hoisting the Royal Standard. My mother arrived, as I said, too late, her grandson having died a few hours before she got there.

After King Alexander's death Venizelos offered the throne to King Constantine's third son, Paul, who was in Switzerland with his parents. Paul refused this honour, remarking very rightly that it was only the Greek people who were entitled to choose their King. Venizelos, very much offended by this rebuff, proceeded with new elections, being persuaded that he would win them and put the question to the nation, "Myself or Constantine!" On November 14, 1920, the nation, expressing a wish for liberty and peace, replied by a huge majority, "Constantine." Venizelos, without waiting to complete the formalities usual on the occasion of a change of government, secretly fled the country like a criminal.

Meanwhile, all of us in Rome were getting more and more excited over the rapid progress of events in Greece. We constantly received news from Athens and things seemed most promising and hopeful. On November 14, as I have mentioned, the elections took place. Our feelings during all that day of expectancy can never be described. Next morning early, Doctor Stucker, my brother's old Swiss tutor, knocked energetically at my door, saying, "*Grande victoire du Roi*". It is quite useless to say what I felt. In my enthusiasm I kissed the old gentleman. After hearing this news, my brother Christopher rushed into my room, hugged me, and rushed out again and tore over to Andrew's hotel. The latter was on his way to us and the brothers met in the street and publicly embraced. I read in my diary: "Excitement continues unabated. Venizelos not even elected deputy. He has fled on a ship. The Powers are aghast, because they had been assured of Venizelos' victory. Mad joy in Athens."

Further, on the same page I read: "The Bolsheviks have got to the Crimea. General Wrangel beaten. This means the end of our Harax. Too sad and crushing. Torn between two feelings, my old home's happiness and destruction of my children's home."

We at once wired our congratulations to my brother, who answered, "Heartfelt thanks to you all. Long live the Greek people."

On November 18, came the following telegram from my mother from Tatoi:

> "Ralli forms new government. I as Regent take oath
> tomorrow. You may return home when you want. Joy.
> Thank God. Olga B."

That evening Prince and Princess Youssoupoff, refugees in Rome, asked my girls and me to dinner. They had adorned the dinner table with the Greek national colours, blue and white, and placed a small Greek flag over my napkin. Their unselfishness and genuine part they took in my joy touched me deeply. I was ashamed to feel so elated, knowing what their, as well as my girls', feelings were.

Telegrams of congratulations were pouring in from everywhere and many Italian friends sent most beautiful flowers till our apartments looked like a garden. After receiving our mother's telegram, Andrew, Christopher and I decided to start at once for Athens, our families following later. On November 20, we three left with a lot of Greek friends and acquaintances for Brindisi, all in high spirits. Next night we embarked on board the Lloyd steamer *Leopolis*. The captain very politely gave me his cabin. On November 22, we reached Corfu at three p.m. The whole population, hearing of our arrival, came out in every kind of boat to meet us. Thousands of people came on board and there was such a crowd that we could hardly move. We at last managed to get into a waiting boat and landed at the jetty. We were asked to step on shore but this was easier said than done. The amount of people was such that there was literally no place to put one's foot. At last, with great trouble, we managed to scramble out. The Archbishop was there surrounded by all his clergy. We got into a motor and could only advance with difficulty, as the people were hanging on on all sides. Flowers in quantities were showered upon us from every window. At last we had to get out and walk as it was quite out of the question to advance in a motor. My brothers held me one on each side, and we forced our way through to the church where the relics of St. Spiridon are kept, and where prayers of thanksgiving were read.

From there we went on to our palace, always followed by the population. Reaching the palace we had to rush in and have the doors closed behind us. We then went up onto the balcony from where Andrew thanked the people in warm terms for their touching demonstration. When the crowd dispersed we motored to Mon Repos, which belonged to Andrew since my father's death. There we had tea and rested awhile. As we were going to leave, we saw crowds of people who had come there on foot, standing by the house. They kept on cheering and crying out, "Bring back our King." We got back to the ship towards seven o'clock and sailed at once.

The demonstration shown to us in Corfu was to be surpassed in Athens. Next morning early, passing by Patras, we were awakened by a salute of 21-guns fired by the destroyer *Ierax*, which was sent by my mother to meet us. It was commanded by Captain Ioannidis, one of Venizelos' victims, and who had spent three years in prison for having remained true to his oath to his King. The captain wirelessed to the *Leopolis* welcoming us and placing his destroyer at our disposal. At Corinth the *Leopolis* anchored, and Captain Ioannidis came on board to tell us that the Regent, Queen Olga, had sent him to take us to the Piraeus. We embarked on the *Ierax* and went full speed through the Corinth Canal to the Piraeus. Our reception on board the destroyer was more than touching. The officers and crew, with tears in their eyes, welcomed us as long lost friends. The ship was decked with olive branches, this being the emblem of the royalists. Passing through the canal, we found the peasants of the surrounding villages had collected on either side. Shouting and gesticulating, they threw flowers into the ship, as well as picture postcards of King Constantine.

We arrived at the Piraeus, and never, as long as I live, will I forget that sight. All the ships in the harbor were decked with flags and crammed with people. Even the foreign ships were decorated, except one French man-of-war, which was conspicuous in its complete absence of bunting. Except for the bluejacket on duty on the deck, not a living soul was visible. I will now copy a letter I wrote to Queen Alexandra three days after our arrival.

"In one second the whole sea was covered with boats. The noise was terrific, people cheering and yelling, sirens blowing, and church bells pealing. It was a real popular frenzy. Then we saw our mother, now Regent, in her steam launch. She kept near us till we anchored and then came on board. We were all in tears by that time from emotion and happiness. When at last we landed the pandemonium began. Andrew and Christopher supported my mother, one on each side, and I hung on to Christopher. We had a circle of officers and friends around us, trying to get us through the frenzied crowd. We managed to get into the motor after much trouble. The crowd blessed my mother saying she was their Good Angel, and by her return had brought back liberty and peace to them. They were continually asking 'When is our King coming back?' Our motor broke down under the weight of the people because they were sitting on the bonnet and mud-guards. We changed into another and gradually were able to get out of the crowd. As we approached Athens most of the inhabitants came out to meet us. To oblige us to stop they deliberately threw themselves on the ground, and so we were blocked again. They wished to carry my mother to town but she declined this honour. In a twinkling they got my two brothers out and actually carried them on their shoulders all the way up to town and the palace. My mother and I drove on and arrived at the palace an hour before my brothers.

Our poor old palace was in a terrible state of dilapidation, owing to Venizelos, who had turned parts of it into a hospital. This, by the way, had been quite unnecessary as there was ample room in the hospitals about the town. We were received by a vast number of people in the great hall, known and unknown. Everyone of them stood there with tears of joy streaming from their eyes.

When my brothers arrived, still borne by the crowd, we all went up onto the balcony, headed by my mother. The people below were crying out wildly calling for my mother to talk to them, so she asked Andrew to say a few words of thanks in her name, and tell the throng how proud we were to belong to such people.

We learnt that there was not a calumny which Venizelos had not circulated against all the dynasty. He had done his utmost to stamp out every kind of feeling of love and loyalty to the King. All the King's photos and pictures found in any private house, let alone public buildings, were confiscated and destroyed. People wearing medals with the King's effigy were put into prison. And yet, on the day the martial law was abolished, thousands of pictures of the King appeared everywhere. People had hidden them in the linings of their clothes, in their mattresses or nailed them under tables, and so on. We could not help thinking that if we had such a reception what would it be like when Constantine arrived? We are quite anxious over it. We have seen lots of friends and all the suffering they underwent is simply terrible. Most of them had been in prisons for two to three and a half years, thanks to their loyalty. How many known and unknown people have been killed, ill-treated and ruined! It is too revolting. They all say that they can now breathe again and talk freely. Venizelos disappeared two days after the elections surrounded by his Cretan bodyguards armed to the teeth. No one thought of touching him."

Our dear old palace was in such a state that we could not live in it. My mother was therefore obliged to live at Tatoi, where it was cold and lonely. Later, when my brother George arrived, she stayed in his house. That same evening, after this incredible reception, we all drove out to Tatoi, where we lived till my eldest brother's return. My brothers and I used often to drive down to town to visit friends. People stopped us continually in the streets to have a little talk and tell us all they had suffered, just like children.

Each week brought another member of the family whom we went to meet. The people's enthusiasm continued unabated and, I can even say, grew warmer. It would reach its acme on the 19th of December when King Constantine, Queen Sophie and their children would arrive. As the Powers were against my brother's return, and were making trouble, it was decided to have a plebiscite so as to avoid any doubt about the Greek people's wish to have their King back. My brother also insisted that the opinion of the whole country should be consulted before deciding on his return. I will here translate the proclamation my brother sent to the Greek people from Lucerne after the elections:

"Hellenes!

Three years have gone by since submitting to necessity I left Greece to live on foreign soil. Three years in which I had the misfortune to see my country suffer while I was far away, and rejoice in her victories without me. You may be assured that her troubles and joys have always touched me very deeply. Living far from you I have taken part in your happiness, trials and sorrows. Your call now dims all the bitter remembrances, which the recent past left with me. Warm and enthusiastic your call brings me back to you, dispels the clouds which parted us and insolubly forges a solid link between you and the Hellenic Dynasty. Grateful for this call I will soon return among you and work for the future. To this end I will use all my strength and power, for which we will lift our united prayers to the Almighty."

Constantine B.

Lucerne, 28 November 1920"

The plebiscite took place throughout the country on December 5, 1920, the results being brilliant[5]. It was decided that the King should return immediately. The battleship *Averoff*, escorted by the *Ierax*, was sent to Venice

---

5.   The vote was 1,100,000 to 10,000.

to bring back the King and Queen, their family and my brother George. My brother Constantine was officially received by the Italians in Venice, and was saluted by guns. They embarked on the *Averoff*, sailing next morning for Greece. They had the most awful crossing and were all very ill. Owing to the terrible storm they had to go to Corinth instead of round the Peloponessus to Phalerum Bay. This meant that the King would be obliged to change onto the destroyer *Ierax* and go through the canal. This occasioned great dissatisfaction and disappointment among the crew of the *Averoff*, who insisted upon having the honour of bring back their King. The King, not wishing to hurt their feelings, decided to go to Athens by train from Corinth. On December 19, old style December 6th, and St. Nicholas day, the King arrived. Headed by our mother, we all went to the station. It was so arranged that the train should stop just outside the station in the street. The crowd was innumerable and the excitement at its height. We then saw the huge engine emerge into sight all covered by olive branches and flags. The train slowed down and stopped right in front of us and we entered it at once. I cannot describe what we all felt at that moment. We were all reduced to tears. Poor Queen Sophie, whose heart was aching for her son Alexander who was no more there to welcome her home, bravely smiled through her misery.

The space which had been cleared for them to walk to the awaiting carriage was quickly filled by the frenzied crowds and Queen Sophie, supported by the King and my brother George, got to the carriages with the greatest difficulty. People were fighting to get near them and kissed their clothes. They drove off in an open carriage drawn by six horses and had to go at a foot pace all the way to the cathedral owing to the dense crowds everywhere. It was a never-to-be-forgotten sight. We all drove to the cathedral in motors and taking side roads arrived there three quarters of an hour before the others.

The King and Royal Family were received at the entrance of the cathedral by the Archbishop of Athens and all the clergy, whom we followed into church for a short service of thanksgiving. After the ceremonial we all drove to the old palace where Their Majesties then went onto the balcony and were acclaimed by a few hundred thousand people. The enthusiasm when they appeared was quite indescribable. The crowd waved small flags and pictures of the King. Only after quite a long time was the King able to make his speech, which was listened to by all these masses in reverential silence. He thanked them in the warmest terms for their loyalty and marvellous reception, praising them for their wonderful patience and forbearance during those three years of tyranny, and also for their touching sympathy on the death of his son. Although my brother tried his best to be calm, he could not help faltering at times, choked by his great emotions. At the end of his speech the Premier handed him a memorandum on a slip of paper to add some political clause. I heard later from friends standing in the crowd that an old man, seeing this, said in a loud angry voices, "Why does this man tell the King what to say? Our King knows all right what to tell us."

During that first night a great part of the crowd remained all night around the King's palace to "See if he was safe" as they expressed it. The rejoicings went on for days and the King could not show himself in public without becoming the object of frenzied demonstrations of devotion.

Shortly after the King's return he sent for the Archbishop of Athens, who had been sent away by Venizelos and exiled to some monastery in the country. The Archbishop was officially received at Athens on his return and reinstated. The King sent his brother Andrew to receive him in his name at the station. My mother and I went to call on him later. The poor old man, he was over seventy, was overjoyed to return and see us all again. He told us all about the terrible ordeals he had been through. To start with, he had been thrown into prison and kept in solitary confinement for three weeks. Wooden planks had been nailed across his windows so that he was in the dark practically all day. At last some ladies of the Athenian society discovered his whereabouts and brought him food. He only complained about the rats that kept running over him. What impressed me most was when he said that he was proud that God had found him worthy enough to send him all this suffering. When King George, my nephew, was exiled from Greece, this same archbishop was again removed to some monastery where he eventually died after becoming blind.

The Powers, unfortunately, refused to recognize Constantine's restoration, owing to France, although Jonnart had clearly stated that if the Greek people desired to have their King back, he would be free to return. As the honour of France was so closely implicated in this question, strong pressure was brought to bear on the British government, which finally compromised and sent two notes to Greece. The first one said: "The restoration by the Greek people of King Constantine whose disloyal stand during the war caused embarrassment and losses to the Allies, will be considered as a ratification by the Greek people of the hostile acts of the King." In the second, that, "Greece would be deprived of war credits from the Allies." As to the question of Asia Minor, the hazardous adventure was conceived by Mr. Lloyd George, inspired by Venizelos. The King, even before his return, had expressed himself against this very risky expedition, and therefore, it was most unfair to accuse him and his government of being responsible for the subsequent disaster.

Because our old palace was in such a state of dilapidation, I was offered hospitality by some old friends in their private house, where I stayed with my daughters for nearly five months. During my brother's stay in Switzerland, both his eldest son George, and his eldest daughter Helen, had become engaged to be married to the eldest son, Carol, and eldest daughter, Elizabeth, of the King and Queen of Roumania. George's wedding took place at Bucharest in February. Early in March the newly married couple arrived in Athens with the Queen of Roumania and her other daughters to·be present at her son Carol's marriage to my niece, Helen. There was a grand reception for them on their arrival at the Piraeus, and we all went to meet them. The people's excitement was great to see the young Crown Prince, who was extremely handsome. The next morning we all met at my brother's palace to be present at the civil marriage which was followed by the religious ceremony in the cathedral.

In the midst of all these festivities my poor sister-in-law, Nancy, fell desperately ill and had to undergo a very serious internal operation. As soon as it was possible she was taken to Paris where she continued to be under doctor's care. Her son, William, hearing of his mother's illness hurried to Athens, and a week later he and my second daughter, Xenia, were engaged to be married. My brother Christopher decided to leave Greece May 4th, with his sick wife. My children and myself accompanied them. We travelled to Brindisi on the very same small yacht which had taken my mother to Greece the previous autumn. We had a rough passage and were extremely ill, except Nancy, who stood the voyage wonderfully well.

We left again in the afternoon for Paris, arriving there the next evening. My brother and his wife went to the Ritz and I with my daughters to St. Cloud where we stayed with my brother George, who had left Athens a short time before us. We remained there about a month, returning later to London. My first visit was to Queen Alexandra, who wanted to hear every detail of all the happy events in Greece, and all about Constantine, whom she dearly loved and never doubted.

At the end of September I went to Paris with my girls for Xenia's marriage to William Leeds, which was to take place in October. We again stayed at St. Cloud. Nancy was on her feet again, after a second operation. On the 8th of October my daughter's civil marriage took place at the Mairie du Louvre. The mayor made a most touching speech to my daughter, telling her never to forget her country or her childhood spent there and to always keep a warm corner in her heart for Russia, in spite of the terrible and sad changes which had taken place there.

Next day in the afternoon, with my little daughter looking sweet in her bridal attire, we all proceeded to the American Church where the Protestant rite took place. She was given away by her Uncle, the Grand Duke Alexander. At the end of this ceremony we drove to the Rue Darue to the Russian church for the Greek Orthodox marriage. All the Russian refugees were present and consequently the church was crammed. Later on there was a reception at the Ritz and the bridal couple left for their honeymoon in the evening.

I returned to London with my mother, who went to stay with Queen Alexandra at Sandringham. In November I went to Harrogate to unveil a memorial cross I had put up on the "Stray," in memory of those that died in my hospitals and for those who went back and died at the front. All of my old hospital committee was present and several of the wounded who had found work at Harrogate. It was a very touching little ceremony.

On the last day of that year my eldest daughter, Nina, became engaged to Prince Paul Chavchavadze, a member of a prominent Georgian family. His grandfather, a well-known general, had been the right-hand man of Nina's grandfather when Viceroy in the Caucasus. On the 3rd of

September, 1922, their marriage took place in the Russian church in London. It was with terrible difficulty that we succeeded in obtaining a permit from the Foreign Office allowing my mother, my brother Christopher and Nancy to come over from Paris to be present. They were only allowed ten days in London, such was still the prejudice against the Greek Royal Family.

At three o'clock I drove with Nina to church. She was looking her best in her bridal dress and veil and people cheered her loudly, both when we left our house and on arriving at the church. Queen Alexandra was present too. I took my child to the altar where her bridegroom was waiting. The church was crammed with people. After the ceremony, which impressed everyone by its beauty, we all went for the reception to my sister-in-law, the Grand Duchess Xenia. She kindly lent us her house because mine was too small. The bridal couple left directly after for Warwick Castle, which my friend Mrs. Marsh had put at their disposal.

I returned home to my empty house feeling very lonely and was touched to tears when Queen Alexandra appeared, knowing what my feelings were. My children returned to my house after their honeymoon for a few days before going over to their own. As I could not bear remaining completely alone after their departure, I closed my house and went to stay with Baron de Stoeckl, my former gentleman-in-waiting, and his wife.

For some time the news from Greece had been unpleasant, and I was feeling very worried. Early in September came the crash. I do not intend going into details, but I am bound to say that one of the chief causes of the "Greek Debacle" was the fact that France and Italy had denied Greece the right of searching their ships, most of which were carrying contraband of war to Kemal Pasha. Another important reason was the war-weariness of badly provisioned troops, who had been under arms for ten years, and the perfidious Venizelist propaganda.

On the morrow of the defeat a group of officers, intimates of Venizelos, who had refused to fight the enemy, turned the confusion and popular alarm to their profit and marched on Athens, lead by General Plastiras. This group of traitors called upon the King to abdicate in favour of his eldest son, George, under the protest that Constantine's restoration to the throne stood in the way of Greece's return to the good graces of the Powers.

The King, fearing that this conspiracy would lead to bloodshed and civil war, decided to make his greatest and last sacrifice to the country he loved so well, and decided to abdicate. He addressed a proclamation to his people saying that yielding to the universal wish expressed by the Hellenes in December 1920, he returned to the throne. But lately, painful events having placed his country in a critical situation, he was ready to abdicate. He ended up by writing:

"As to me I am happy once more to sacrifice myself
for our Greece. I hope to see the people so dear to me in
perfect union with their new King."

Constantine was exhausted and could not bear the thought that he might be the cause of Greek blood being shed.

The Crown Prince then took his oath and was proclaimed King George II. Constantine and his family at once left for Italy and landed at Palermo. The only member of my family who was allowed to remain in Greece was my brother Andrew with his family at Corfu.

At once after King Constantine's departure, the members of the former cabinet, headed by Premier Gounaris, were thrown into prison. By that time I could bear my loneliness and anguish no more and left for Paris to join my mother and brother Christopher and Nancy. My mother had just arrived from Denmark where she had been on a visit to the Empress Dowager of Russia. A few days later we received the alarming news that my brother Andrew had been arrested and brought to Athens. My mother applied to the Greek Revolutionary Government to return to Athens, but this request was refused.

On the 28th of November we heard that all five ex-ministers and the ex-commander-in-chief had been condemned to death and executed a few hours later. Our poor mother, knowing her son Andrew was in mortal danger of also being condemned to death, decided to go to the President of the French Republic, M. Milleran, and personally appeal to him to intercede for his life. It was only owing to the intervention of the Kings of England and Spain that Andrew's life was spared.

From Palermo, King Constantine followed the Greek events very closely, and these last blows were too much for his bad state of health and mental agony. He died of a broken heart about three months after leaving Greece.

PRINCE GEORGE OF GREECE

Chapter XVI

After hearing that my brother Andrew was safe and had left Greece with his family on board an English cruiser, I left for Germany with Baroness de Stoeckl. Ten days later I was married with my family's blessings to Captain Pericles Ioannides, who met me at Wiesbaden, coming direct from Athens.

Wiesbaden was then still under French occupation, and it was strange seeing French troops everywhere. The prices then in Germany were quite ridiculous as they dwindled to nothing if changed into francs or pounds. I remember paying one million marks for a leather coat which really meant £4.

At Wiesbaden I met again my old French governess, Mlle. Hinal, who had been established there for some years. She was then very old and nearly had a fit when she so unexpectedly saw me again. She was, of course, present at my marriage. We left later for Frankfort where we spent a couple of weeks, going on to Munich for Christmas.

On January 11, 1923, we received the crushing news of my dear brother Constantine's sudden death at Palermo. We could hardly realize it and were heartbroken. Queen Sophie wired to me saying she was taking the coffin to Naples where it would be deposited in the Greek church. The Italian government took an official part by sending troops to escort the coffin. Eventually, Queen Sophie went to Florence, and my brother's coffin was placed in a small chapel of the Russian church there. At King Constantine's death, his son King George II, was not allowed by the Venizelists to fly his standard at half-mast on the palace. But the Greek people mourned in secret the loss of their King and leader that they loved so dearly.

We arrived in London on the 16th February, being met at the station by my eldest daughter, Nina, and her husband, and crowds of friends. We then drove home to my old house in Regent's Park. The next day we went to Marlborough House where I presented my husband to Queen Alexandra and the Empress Marie. They both welcomed him in the sweetest way, and even kissed him. My mother was staying at Spencer House, then leased by Christopher and Nancy, who were still abroad. The latter, at first, seemed quite well and was able to go about, but later she fell ill again and in August grew steadily worse. To our great sorrow she passed away on the 29th of August. It was a great grief as Nancy had endeared herself to all of us, and

257

had always taken part in our joys and sorrows. After her death Spencer House was given up, and my mother came to stay with me.

In December came more sad news for us, namely, that my nephew, King George II, had been turned out of Greece by the same gang. He left at once with his wife, Queen Elizabeth, for Roumania. The Republic was proclaimed and Venizelos returned to Athens. One of the first deeds of the Revolutionary Government was to confiscate everything belonging to the Royal Family, even depriving us of our nationality.

On the 20th of May I had the great joy of welcoming my first grandchild, Nina's son David. It was a great consolation after all the sad events of the previous years. Towards the end of May the Italian sovereigns came to London on an official visit, and we were asked to Buckingham Palace for the state ball. I was very pleased to meet Queen Elena again, whom I had not seen for very many years. Both she and the King have always been particularly kind to me.

Just then the exhibition at Wembley was in full swing and we went there often. I was delighted to be able to see a real rodeo by the cowboys which I enjoyed thoroughly. In September we went for a cure to Harrogate and then straight to Sandringham. My mother was there visiting Queen Alexandra. My cousin, Victoria, who had been very ill with pneumonia, was ordered to spend the winter abroad in a mild climate and she left for Italy. It was then that King George asked me to spend the winter at Sandringham to look after his mother, during Victoria's absence. I was only too happy to do so, and to be able to give back a little of all I owed to her since my childhood. We therefore settled down at Sandringham and remained there until the next May.

In the morning I used to sit with Aunt Alix while she had her breakfast in her dressing room. She never ate much, a cup of coffee, sometimes an egg and usually fruit. She liked grapes particularly. At about ten o'clock I either went for a walk or drove about with my husband in our motor. At one thirty, lunch with the suite, which consisted of Miss Charlotte Knollys and Colonel Streadfield. At about three o'clock every day a motor drive with my aunt, often accompanied by the faithful Miss Knollys. On Sundays, church at 11:30 in the lovely chapel just beyond the garden. After our drive everyone took tea together in the hall, after which the Queen put together jigsaw puzzles, her one amusement. We all sat round a table and helped her. During this time my husband played an old fashioned pianola, which caused King George to call him 'organ-grinder'.

Dinner was at nine, usually with the suite, but was taken upstairs in a private room. The Queen always appeared in a black velvet tea gown, wearing her lovely pearls and jewels and a bunch of flowers, always looking smart and dainty.

The King, during the shooting season, came often to visit his mother. Queen Maud of Norway came in the autumn and stayed at her lovely cottage nearby, Appleton. It was a beautiful winter, and we had sunshine nearly all the time. It was only in early spring that it snowed. Christmas Eve was quite a grand affair, as the King, Queen and their children, Queen Maud and the Princess Royal were all present. After ten we all went to the ballroom where a huge Christmas tree stood, and there were tables all around, covered with lovely presents for everyone.

On Christmas Day, we all went to church and the Royal Family received Holy Communion. Then came a huge lunch. My aunt personally gave all her servants charming presents. As long as King George and his family resided at Sandringham they came every afternoon for tea.

On the last day of the year there was again a Christmas party in the ballroom, this time for all the people and workmen of the estate.

Their Majesties left for London in February, and we were once more alone and settled down to the usual routine. Although Queen Alexandra was pretty well, she was beginning to lose her wonderful energy and had moments of great lassitude. Every day, no matter what the weather, she insisted upon going out straight after lunch to throw bread crumbs to the numerous pheasants strutting about on the lawn in front of the house. I usually ran after her with a cape, being terrified she might catch cold, but the moment I put it on her shoulders she flung it off; we sometimes had regular fights!

Every Sunday afternoon she went to feed her various animals. She had a real passion for animals, and treated them like human beings. She always had a small Peke with her, which she addressed as "Tootsie dog". During meals she threw all the food she did not eat to this beast, which I regret to say we all hated.

In February 1925 a cable came from New York announcing the birth of little Nancy, my daughter Xenia's baby. I was very moved now to have two grandchildren. In May Xenia arrived in London with the precious baby and I went to see them. Soon after Xenia came to Sandringham for a few days. Queen Alexandra was delighted to see her, as she was always happy to see our children.

When my cousin Victoria returned from Italy, I took the opportunity to go to Rome to see my mother who was staying there with my brother Christopher in his lovely new Villa Anastasia, where he put us up. My brother arranged the villa charmingly, as well as the garden in which it stood. My mother's room contained most of her personal furniture from her private apartments both in Athens and Tatoi, which gave them a home-like look. There were so many dear remembrances of our old homes which brought back our happy childhood.

While we were there, Queen Margarita [of Italy] came to call on my mother; as I had not seen her since the year 1900 when I was in Rome after my first marriage, I found a great change in her. She had become white-haired and thin, but mentally was just as fresh, charming and amusing as formerly.

We remained in Rome about a month and my brother showed us a lot of interesting places, one of which was Assisi, which I particularly appreciated. In August we left for Vichy for a cure, returning to

Sandringham on the first of September.

I was extremely pained to see a great change in Queen Alexandra. She had become very thin and somehow had lost her interest in everything and continually fell asleep. Nevertheless, she instinctively would not give in and continued her usual life. She always lunched downstairs with the suite and daily took her motor drive for an hour or more when I always accompanied her. Her deafness had considerably increased, and we had to write down anything we wished to tell her.

Returning from our drive she usually lay down on a sofa in a darkened room and slept till tea time, when I came to wake her up. It was the saddest thing seeing her getting weaker every day. My cousin Xenia came for a week, which gave our aunt great pleasure. On the 19th of November Victoria and I went to the Queen, still in bed, before our usual morning walk. She seemed alright and inquired where we were going, and said we were to return very soon. Just as we were going downstairs, the nurse came running to say that the Queen had had a heart attack and the doctor was told to come at once. We of course rushed up to the bedroom. The Queen was quite conscious and even smiled to see us back so soon. My cousin and I stood at either side of her bed and she gave a hand to each and kept looking at us pathetically.

The King and Queen, and Queen Maud were immediately sent for. The former was out shooting, and the latter riding, but were luckily found at once and came to their mother. They were only allowed to remain a few minutes as the doctor said she was to be as quiet and calm as possible. She was so happy to see the King, and even tried to talk to him.

Sir Thomas Horder, the famous heart specialist, was telephoned for and arrived from London at three o'clock in the afternoon. After examining the Queen he could give us no hope, and said it was only a question of hours. We were all crushed, and the thought of losing her made us quite miserable. Victoria and I were in and out of her room all the time, and she always stretched out her dear hands to us, which we held for hours.

That night I did not go to bed but slept on a sofa in my dressing gown, ready to be called at any moment. At five in the morning I went in to see the Queen, who was sleeping peacefully, but was losing strength rapidly. I got back to my rooms, had a bath and breakfast, and went again to my aunt where I found Victoria. The rest of the family came and went. The Princess Royal arrived from London during the afternoon and immediately went up to her mother who still seemed to recognize her.

After that the beloved Queen lost consciousness and passed peacefully away at 6 o'clock. Princess Royal, Victoria, Nurse Fletcher and I stood by her to the last. Such a calm and peaceful death.

A short time after, all her wonderful beauty returned, and she lay on her death bed with a happy smile, the picture of peace and so beautiful.

Next morning the clergyman came and there was a short service by her bed in the presence of all the family. All that day the servants and all who had served her so faithfully filed past to see their beloved Queen for the last time. In the evening she was put in her coffin, and on the 22nd of November at nine in the morning her coffin was taken to the church, accompanied by Victoria, myself, my husband and the suite. The coffin stood facing the altar covered with her Royal Standard.

People came from far and wide to visit the church, which was one mass of floral offerings. The most pathetic figure was poor Miss Knollys, who had been the Queen's faithful and constant companion for fifty years. She died five years later.

On the 26th of November, the Queen's coffin was taken to London. Eight non-commissioned officers of the Life Guards carried the coffin out of church and placed it on a gun-carriage. The men all followed on foot and the ladies in carriages. At the station the coffin was placed in a specially prepared coach. In London the coffin was driven in a motor hearse to the Royal Chapel where it remained during the night. Next morning at eleven the Queen's body was taken to Westminster Abbey. The streets were lined with troops and millions of people crowded everywhere, most of them in tears, as Queen Alexandra was sincerely mourned by her subjects who had devotedly loved her during all the long years she had spent in their midst.

The King and all the male members of the family, as well as the representatives of foreign countries, walked behind the gun-carriage. Queen Mary and all the ladies drove direct to Westminster Abbey. It was a terribly cold day and the procession took place in a blizzard. Arriving at the Abbey we all were ushered to our places where we waited a considerable time in dead silence. At last we heard the bands playing Chopin's funeral march in the distance. A few minutes later the coffin, borne on the shoulders of eight splendid-looking Life Guards, was seen entering the Abbey. At that moment, a ray of sunshine appeared which made the scene still more imposing as it touched the coffin.

The latter was then placed on a very high catafalque surrounded by tall candles in gilded candelabra and the funeral service began. The whole scene was impressive in its grand simplicity. One could feel that every single person in the church was sincerely praying for the repose of the soul of a beloved Queen, who had spent all her life doing kind deeds to everyone.

On the following day the interment took place at Windsor. The blank left by her death was indescribable and for me personally, England has never been the same without her.

Early in January 1926, we left England for Rome via Paris where we spent a few days. We then decided to make our home in Rome to be close to my mother. We set out to look for an apartment, living meanwhile in an hotel. After five months we found one with much trouble, after having looked at every possible Palazzo and house. We took a flat in quite a new and modern house where we lived quite comfortably for seven years.

Three weeks later, after a short illness, my beloved mother passed peacefully away[1]. This was a terrible blow to us all, and meant the end of

---

1.   Queen Olga died June 18, 1926.

our family circle. Being in exile and scattered all over Europe, my mother's presence in Rome was always a reason to meet there. My mother, up to the end, always hoped to go back to Greece and die there, to be buried by my father's side at Tatoi.

Her coffin was placed next to my brother Constantine's in Florence. A third coffin has been added since, that of Queen Sophie[2], who died in a nursing home in Frankfort.

Please God, some day we hope to be able to take those three precious coffins back to our old home[3], that they may rest in peace in the soil of Greece which they loved so much, and to which they sacrificed all their lives.

---

2.   Queen Sophie died in 1932.

3.   The Royal Hellenic Dynasty was restored in 1936 in the person of King George II, after this book was written. King George brought back to Greece the bodies of his parents, King Constantine and Queen Sophie, and his grandmother, Queen Olga. They were given a hero's welcome by hundreds of thousands of grieving Greeks. The bodies were then buried at Tatoi. Thus, Princess Marie of Greece and Denmark, Grand Duchess of Russia, had the satisfaction of making this last, sad, journey home, and to once again feel the warmth and love of the Greek People for herself and her family.

EPILOGUE

When Xenia, my mother, died in 1965 at age 62, I inherited a small leather suitcase crammed with letters that my grandmother, Marie, had written to her through the 1930s. As this book was being readied I felt I had better read them. Each was on airmail paper and eight to ten pages long. It was a revelation, and brought my beloved grandmother close to me again.

The letters were written from Rome where she lived. They were about whom she saw, mostly relatives, the diplomatic corps and Roman aristoracy, and their daily life; however, under it all ran a current of the unrest and uneasiness Italy faced. Amama hated Hitler and Carol of Roumania, and railed against both. She foresaw a nasty war and wondered how they would all fare.

There were a few visits to England (Marina's wedding), Germany (to take the cure) and Greece. Greece's visit was most moving. She described the family's trip back with the coffins of her mother, Queen Olga, her brother, King Constantine, and his wife, Queen Sophie. The description of the crossing of the Adriatic, the ceremonies and rites, and the love the populace showed them on this sad occasion was minutely gone into and fascinating to read. The beauty of the Orthodox Church's rituals and the consolation it gave those left behind was comforting to her.

Her last two letters were heart-rending. One from Rome from a hotel prior to her enforced departure, clearly showed her strength failing, and the exertion of having to pack up her beloved belongings and leave her home almost killed her. She finally left with the Greek diplomatic group as relations between the two countries had ruptured. The final letter from Greece tells of her joy to be back in her homeland, her exhaustion and indecision of where they will settle to live. She hoped her belongings would make it over to Greece, but, in reality, they did not, and were stored in the Vatican, arranged by Queen Mother Helen of Roumania through the Pope's kindness.

She bewails the distance separating her from her immediate family and wonders whether they will ever meet again and how we all are.

Having started her life in such a dramatic milieu, and having led such a difficult one after the revolution in Russia, I am most grateful that her final years were reasonably quiet. Her last few months were distressing, thanks to Mussolini, but her life did end on a proper note: she returned to the country she loved so much; her nephew, King George II, was back on the throne, and she died in her nephew, Crown Prince Paul's house, surrounded by her next-to-immediate family before the hated Axis powers occupied Greece. Last of all, she was spared having to flee again, which the Royal Family did as soon as she was buried.

Nancy Leeds Wynkoop

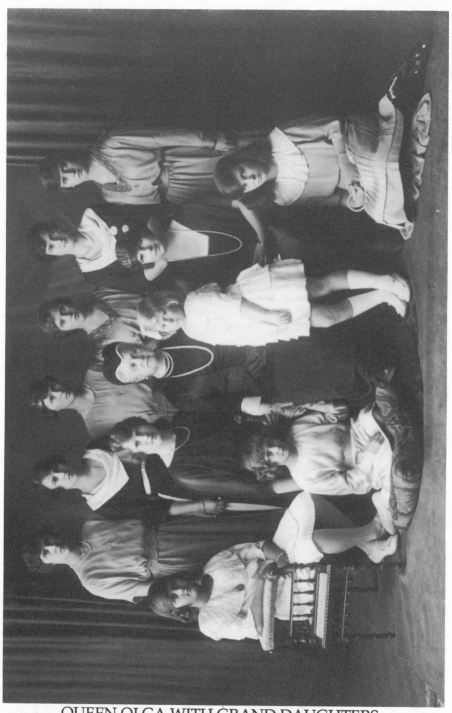

QUEEN OLGA WITH GRAND DAUGHTERS
Top: Elizabeth, Xenia, Olga, Theodora, Nina, Margarita
Center: Cecilie, Irene, Queen Olga, Sophie, Helen
On floor: Katherine, Marina

NANCY LEEDS and DAVID CHAVCHAVADZE

NANCY WYNKOOP

Metropolitan Opera Ball

PRINCESS NINA

PRINCESS CATHERINE CHAVCHAVADZE

PRINCESS MARIA CHAVCHAVADZE

PRINCE MICHAEL CHAVCHAVADZE

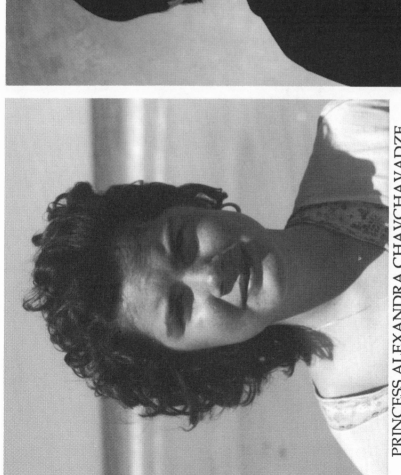

PRINCESS ALEXANDRA CHAVCHAVADZE

PRINCESS XENIA - 1946

NANCY and ALEXANDRA WYNKOOP

Princess Xenia, Nancy Wynkoop,
Alexandra Wynkoop
ALEXANDRA and NANCY WYNKOOP

NANCY and EDWARD WYNKOOP

PRINCESS EUGENIE CHAVCHAVADZE

PRINCE DAVID CHAVCHAVADZE

INDEX